# Popeye

# Popeye

## A Memoir of a Cultural Barbarian

*Thomas J. Hickey*

Popeye: A Memoir of a Cultural Barbarian © 2019 Thomas J. Hickey. All rights reserved. No part of this publication may be reproduced, distributed, or transmitted in any form or by any means, including photocopying, recording, or other electronic or mechanical methods, without the prior written permission of the publisher, except in the case of brief quotations embodied in critical reviews and certain other noncommercial uses permitted by copyright law. For permission requests, write to the publisher, addressed "Attention: Permissions Coordinator," at the address below.

Author Photograph by Thomas J. Hickey

Forty Press, LLC
427 Van Buren Street
Anoka, MN 55303
www.fortypress.com

ISBN: 978-1-938-473-31-9

### Dedication:

**Halina** - Partner and Rock of Gibraltar

**Luke** - "That's my boy!", hope, and friend

**Gina** - Forever my little girl, light and joy

Without you three, I am not


Mr. John Clayton "Mississippi" Caden

Without you, this book is not

*"I exist as I am,
that is enough"*
— Walt Whitman

# Foreword

Welcome Aboard!

I will empty out my bag of memories: the good; the bad; and the red face ones. Cumulatively amassed they have shaped me into who I am today. This voyage starts in 1965 and ends in 2019 with ports of call across this country and the globe: Minnesota, Chicago, Washington D.C., Ireland, Honduras, Germany, Jackson Hole, France, South Africa, East and West Berlin, Communist Poland, Auschwitz, Italy and many additional harbors. We shall backpack through Europe, witness the fall of Eastern European communism, explore and settle in the American West, weather the hurricane of the Great Recession of 2008, and the typhoon of mental illness, 2011 to date. From toddler to middle aged male, you shall hear of the ups, downs, exploits, embarrassments and joys of an adventurous soul who was stubborn enough to not compromise well. Some events I am not proud of, some are the greatest memories of my life. Each day was attacked with zeal, wonder and an insatiable desire to learn, to grow, to experiment, to reach conclusions that work for me. I have been fortunate to love much, laugh often, and shed many a tear.

To not be who I am, would have been my greatest mistake.

A few quick notes: This is my recollection of events and is solely based on my memory. One hundred percent of everything in this text occurred and none of it is fictitious. Some names have been changed in the interest of maintaining the privacy of friends and individuals. Using only my recollection is intentional on my part. I want anyone who struggles with similar challenges to know that they are not alone, I sure felt that way.

*Popeye – A Memoir of a Cultural Barbarian* is written using the oral tradition, it should feel as if I am on a bar stool next to you, trading yarns. Each section is a stand-alone snippet, yet woven together they offer an honest, reflective, and panoramic view of my colorful life to date with an eager eye and much hope for what adventures lie ahead

So, rearrange your deck chair, get comfortable, enjoy the string quartet and off we sail on a half century adventure.

– Tom H<br>
aka Popeye the Sailor Man<br>
"I Yam what I Yam"

### Pappy - William Anthony Hickey (May 21, 1927)

On the day Charles Lindberg landed in Paris, my dad was born on the west side of Chicago in a neighborhood of fellow Micks. Grandpa Hickey drove a bread-bakery truck after his police career quickly came to a halt due to graft. Yes, as hard as it was to do, Grandpa got booted from the boys in blue for shaking down men having trysts in Grant Park. Grandma Jeanette was a devoted Irish Mother who busied herself taking care of Dad and my Uncle Ed. Their home was a small, two bedroom apartment on Jackson Avenue with Dad sleeping on the couch in the living room during winters and on the porch during the summer months. Dad attended Resurrection Elementary School, St. Ignatius High School, and Marquette University, the Jesuit college up the road in Milwaukee. Bill was a star quarterback, all-city Chicago. He was able to attend college only because he was offered a full-ride to play football. Without the scholarship, it would not have been possible for him to attend college. Pappy was the first Hickey ever to graduate from college, a point of great pride to Grandma Jeannette.

Dad was a devout Catholic of the Jesuit tradition. Social justice for those in need and a firm believer in hard work. His moral fiber, honesty, integrity and honor were impeccable, way beyond that of his youngest son. As an example, Rosemary Deegan, one of Dad's cousins had polio as a child and was relegated to crutches, a walker or on bad days, a wheel chair. Not once had Rosemary been on a date, dance or anything remotely social. To remedy that situation, Rosemary asks Dad to escort her to the dance. Thus, the star starting quarterback who could have had any number of dates for the Senior Prom, agrees to be Rosemary's date, never once hinting that he would be anything less than thrilled to have the honor. For Rosemary, a new dress, hair done up fancy, and a date for the prom. Dad arrives in his best suit, flowers in hand, and off they went. Together they had a blast and for the rest of her life, Rosemary would light up and you could see the twinkle in her eye when that night was mentioned.

One year into his college football career, a promising one headed straight towards Pro football, a letter arrived from the United States Army. Dad had been drafted. Off to the Pacific Rim he went where he was a military police officer in Tokyo for two years after WWII ended. Douglas MacArthur found out that Dad was a collegiate quarterback and ta-da, Bill was the starting QB on MacArthur's football team. After his service, back to school went Big Bill. During his senior season, Bill blew out his right knee (OUCH!). Not really knowing how to fix knees back then, Dad's career prospects in the NFL were in grave doubt. With a bride in his near future and the hopes of starting a family, Pappy was offered $5000 to play Pro Ball for the Chicago Bears or $5400 to start a career with Sears-Roebuck and Company. Stability won out as it so often did with Dad and into corporate life he went, always pondering in the back of his mind what might have been on the gridiron.

## Me Ma - LouAnn Marie Rabun Hickey
## (November 1, 1933)

The youngest child of Louis and Anna Rabun, Mom was born in Miles City, Montana. Grandpa Rabun, the most interesting and wonderful man I ever knew, was a brilliant train engine mechanic who could take an entire locomotive engine apart, rebuild it, then go home to a glass or two of bourbon, Wild Turkey being the preferred brand. Mom had two older brothers, Tom and Jim Rabun. Yes, they are the Rabun's of Rabun County Georgia. Grandma Anna was a compassionate, literate woman who was instrumental in creating a home-life, as they relocated every year or two throughout the West and the Midwest. The Rabun's were a very happy clan. Extroverts who could fit in wherever the railroad tracks led.

Mom attended Rosary College in Lake Forest, Illinois, today known as Benedictine University. Following along with Grandma's love of reading, LouAnn majored in English Literature and was headed towards a career in teaching, an ideal match for her interests, passion and intellectual curiosity. I remember my whole life, Mom would go to the library and get ten to fifteen books at a pop, she could knock back a good detective novel in a night, a serious piece of literature in a few days. Mom's Achilles heel was Lucky Strike cigarettes which she chain smoked throughout the day. Damn I hated those things, especially on long car trips. Like her Father, Mom enjoyed a Whiskey 7 or two each evening, joining my dad in the living-room to discuss the day's events before another of Mom's incredible dinners. She could cook anything: homemade lasagna, pot-roast, grilled cheese, and on and on. It didn't matter, whatever she cooked it was incredible.

Together, Bill and LouAnn made a formidable team and in 1955 they would wed in Chicago, Pappy a promising young executive, LouAnn a highly sought after educator and public speaker. Together they would go far, do much to positively affect others and raise three knuckle-headed boys who mercilessly beat the crap out of each other, played sports, broke stuff and ate like a brigade of hungry marine recruits.

### Enter Thomas John Hickey (January 6, 1965)

I nearly killed my mom coming into the world. Mom had terrible problems delivering children, having had four miscarriages, three of which went full-term and then surviving Bill, Bob and then me. After I arrived she was so weak and lost so much blood during my delivery that she wouldn't be able to hold me for the first ten days. The doctor told her outright,

"If you get pregnant again it will kill you!" And thus, Mom underwent a full hysterectomy and the eighty percent male Hickey Irish Mafia was complete. Mom would have to defend the female gender alone which she was more than capable of.

# ACT I

## Early Memories (1965-1975)

### "Penny Days" and Morning Mass

Each morning, after sending my brothers Bill and Bob off to school, Mom would load me up and off we would venture to 7:30 a.m. morning mass at St. Therese Church in Deephaven, Minnesota. At the time, the new church wasn't built yet so mass was celebrated in the basement of the school which constituted dark pews, ebony and old, creaky kneelers. Many women attended daily and still do to this day. Since I was just a little ankle-biter, I wasn't expected to pay attention or even sit still. I was free to roam, driving my Matchbox cars all over the place, crawling under pews and generally entertaining myself. After the forty minute mass, off to Aqua Bowl we headed where the ladies drank coffee and smoked like industrial smokestacks. I would open my metal Band-Aid tin (they were still steel back then) and solicit pennies from the ladies. I made sure to practice good manners (better shot at a penny or two more) and then go to the corner to drink my cocoa and count my vast wealth.

### Outside Events

Our life on Patricia Lane was idyllic with kids everywhere. Dad's career rising tied closely with Sears. The Hickey boys played any and every kind of sport. On the outside though things were getting weird: some guy named Martin Luther

King Junior got shot; then another Kennedy - Bobby got shot. Both of those events upset my mom quite visibly. Dad was also concerned, but he didn't talk about those things in front of us. Then there was a war going on in which our soldiers were fighting in Vietnam. I had lots of army men too. They were made of green plastic and our wars were played with a Size D battery in the basement. Last soldier untouched wins, no blood, etc. Every night my parents watched a guy named Walter Cronkite on the Columbia Broadcasting Service, CBS, tell us the news. Increasingly, the news wasn't good and at 5:30 sharp, the TV went off as supper was prepared.

### Protected Status (Late 60's - Early 70's)

I am a child. Across the street lives a man, Mr. Solomon: mid-fifties, not fat, not thin. Mr. Solomon is protected by my father, actually by every father on the street. As you can imagine with boys, or any kid for that matter, the quickest distance between two points was a straight line no matter what lawn, bush, fence, garden or whatever was in the way. However, my older brothers Bill and Bob are always most respectful to Mr. Solomon when their ball rolls into his yard. I am just an ankle biter at the time, just barely aware of the special man in our midst.

Mrs. Solomon takes care of him. At lunchtime she brings out white bread sandwiches, Fritos and fruit punch. They sit on the stairs and eat, talking quietly. Mrs. Solomon always looks a bit tired. She is nice to us, always waves at us and occasionally brings us cookies or brownies to eat if we are playing in the Swanson yard, next to their house. The Solomon house is simple, austere, and quiet. Nothing fancy, all functional. Never problems or issues but there is something about their place. It has some sadness, sullen, some kind of history enshrouds it.

As mentioned, Mr. Solomon had a friend in my father. Mr. Solomon had friends in every father on the block. He was to be left alone, we were not to play in their yard, not to ask questions, to be respectful at all times, no yelling near their home. Failure to comply with these unwritten strictures would result in the full force of retribution from my father, the fathers, to me, my brothers, to any kid in the neighborhood. It was the one and only time that I felt my father wasn't on my side, he was on Mr. Solomon's. Why did Mr. Solomon garner such unique status?

Mr. Solomon had served in the Pacific during World War II. He was captured by the Japanese and held as a prisoner of war. In time, he was forced to go on a march, known as the Bataan Death March, a scary name to us kids for sure. Many soldiers who went on the march died. The rest, like Mr. Solomon came home different, never to be the same. Years later I would learn the full extent of the Bataan Death March through my studies of history. What I learned from books has always paled in comparison to what I learned as a little boy in my neighborhood: honor and respect Mr. Solomon and leave the man in peace, he has earned it.

### To the Moon (July 20, 1969)

Here is what I remember of that day. Mom was ironing clothes in the living room, smoking Luckys, and I was playing in my room, and Bob and Bill were away at school. Mom hollered for me, "Tommy, come here, hurry up." Down the hall I sped. "You need to watch this, you will remember it all your life," she added emphatically. There was the Walter Cronkite guy again, on our black and white TV that got four channels which you changed by going to the TV and cranking the dial. Anyway, this guy in a white suit with a bubble-head climbs down a short ladder and he jumps onto this white, dusty ground. Something about steps and leaping for mankind. That guy sure is moving slow, that's weird! "Thanks Mom, can I ride my bike over to Shep's house?" I ask. "Sure," Mom replies adding, "just be home for lunch."

## An Engineering Feat of Homeric Proportions Winter (1969)

Dad had a black, Volkswagen Beetle, the classic beetle, rounded roof, motor in the back, etc. For Christmas that year, our family gift was a toboggan, ten to twelve feet long, curved front, made of wood with a long pad for passengers to sit or kneel on. It was time to christen the vessel but first, somehow it would need to be attached to the roof of the beetle. Dad would spend close to an hour trying different configurations of ropes and anchors to secure the toboggan for safe travel; hard breathing, curses, grunts and grimaces aplenty throughout the process.

Once in place, the bundled up boys; snow boots, snowmobile suits, gloves, hats and whatever else was required by Mom, (who wisely would be sitting this adventure out) in we all piled into the VW. Tom age four, Bob six, Bill nine and our captain, Dad at the wheel. We drove to Meadowbrook Golf Course, about a ten to fifteen minute drive from home. There were good hills to be had at Meadowbrook and it was an ideal locale to test out the maiden voyage of the toboggan.

The sled was freed from its mooring, and we began the long trudge across the golf course and then up the test hill. By the time team Hickey crested the top of the hill, we were all broiling in our layers of clothing and had to rest to catch our breath. Once our heart rates were down and our body temperatures dropped below magma, we were ready for the inaugural run of the rocket.

Our racing order was as follows: Tommy in the front by the curled hood, Bob behind me, Bill and then Dad. It was exciting and yet daunting as we had no idea what to expect. 1-2-3 GO and we were off and gravity was quickly pulling us down the hill. Houston - we have a problem; nobody had a clue how to steer the damn thing. Our projectile was now veering severely right and directly before us loomed a large elm tree. At the moment contact was made, I bailed out to the left-side of the toboggan, sadly so did everybody else. Bob landed on the back of my head, compressing my face into the permafrost. Bill landed on Bob. Dad landed on Bill. And as to be expected, chaos ensued. Once I resurfaced and cleared the snow from my nose and mouth, I began wailing, cries that certainly were audible at nearby Methodist Hospital.

With that, our expedition was over. Team Hickey limped back to the car, Dad reverse engineered the toboggan onto the roof with the requisite huffing, grimaces, and occasional curse and we were homeward bound after just one run, pride running low for all members of the team. Such is the reality of family life.

### Kendall, Hippies and the White Album (1970)

Even though Mom was out of the teaching game for now to be able to raise us boys, she wasn't out of the literary game. She frequently gave book reports, talks, and led discussion groups across the metro area. These were important events where a rugrat like me just couldn't roam about, thus I was taken up the street to the Harding's house. Louise Harding was one of my mom's best friends, and I would hang there for the morning or afternoon, whatever it took. Now the Hardings had two boys, Kendall and Bill, who were much older than the Hickey boys. Bill really loved these new sandwiches everyone was going crazy for, the Big Mac. Bill could eat three of them at a time! I could barely eat a cheeseburger. Kendall often was home when I stayed there, and I would go into his room and listen to music while I played with cars or whatever. Kendall was really different though. He had long brown hair like Jesus had, also a beard and he wore strange dyed T-shirts and these rubber tire sandals. Kendall was determined to not go to this Viet Nam place; instead he might go to Canada. There I was, making motor noises with my mouth for my cars as they raced around and Kendall listening to this one

"White Album" over and over while these smoke sticks filled the room with a weird smell. When I was bored with Kendall, I'd go outside and chase squirrels or something until Mom showed up.

## Knock, Knock (Summer 1970)

A dear friend of my mom, an elderly nun from Illinois, was coming to visit. I was home. My brothers were off somewhere, playing ball probably, somewhere where I wasn't big enough to bike to yet. It was a beautiful morning and Sister Celeste was due in for coffee about ten. My Mom had baked some incredible pastries, cookies, etc. This was an important visit for my mom, and I had been instructed to be polite and then disappear shortly thereafter.

Sister Celeste arrived right on time, and I am excited to meet this important person. As she walks from the door to the kitchen, she limps badly in her habit and ankle length nun dress. Once seated in the kitchen, I am allowed a few minutes to talk with her. She asks me a few questions. I respond as politely as any five-year-old can.

Sensing I am about to be dismissed, I ask her, "Sister, what is wrong with your leg? Did you hurt it somehow?"

With the smile of an angel, Sister looks at me and replies, "I got sick, something they call cancer, and they removed my right leg, now I have a prosthetic leg, a fake leg. Would you like to see it?" Fearing I had gone too far, I sheepishly look at my mom and Sister interjected, "It's okay, come here and I will show you Tommy."

With that, Sister lifted the hem of her dress to just below her knee. She had a dark brown wooden leg that looked like a baseball bat upside down. Permanently affixed at the bottom was a black shoe that matched her shoe on her left foot. I even got to knock on her fake leg before being shooed away by Mom. I headed across the street to play with Bret Swanson, a neighbor about my age. I told him all about the miraculous old nun, with a baseball bat leg and how she let me knock on it.

Five minutes later, the doorbell at our house rings and my Mother answers the door. "Mom, can Bret knock on Sister Celeste's leg too?" Saint that she was, Sister Celeste obliged and gave me a great big hug for being a curious, brave young boy. With that, Bret and I were off and I left my mom and Sister Celeste in peace.

### Growing up Non-Racist (Early 1970's)

My brothers and I were loaded into the green Buick LeSabre, headed with my mom to Chattanooga, Tennessee to visit my great Aunt Ruth and her second husband, Andy Maddox. It was one heck of a drive, fourteen plus hours with three young boys, and a carton of Lucky Strikes for Mom. We made the trek twice that I recall, my dad staying home to work, glad to sit this one out, being a Chicago guy, the South made Dad somewhat uneasy. Bill, Bob and I played every car game imaginable to pass the time: car Bingo, 20 questions, the A-Z game with signs, slug-bug, my car–your car, etc. I was still small enough that I could curl up in one of the foot wells on the floor in the backseat, thus we squirreled away hours in slumber while Mom drove, smoked, stopped to pee and tried to get as comfortable as her bad back would let her. As we got into the South, things changed, there were white neighborhoods, there were black neighborhoods, there were no mixed neighborhoods for the most part. In some little town we stopped for a break, the bathrooms in the city park were still clearly marked "Whites Only" and "Coloreds Only" the one and only time I ever saw that remnant of hate law.

As we neared Chattanooga, my Mother wanted to have a talk with us, a talk that sticks with me to this day. Aunt Ruth's second husband was a successful chef, restaurateur, and a racist pig.

"Now boys, we will be guests in Aunt Ruth and Uncle

Andy's house and Uncle Andy will be making comments, using words and stating opinions that I disagree with regarding people of color, blacks, and other non-white races. I want you to know that I completely disagree with his opinions and I appall his use of such language, however that being said, we will be 'guests' in their home and we will not engage our elderly host, Uncle Andy. When we leave here in a week we can talk about this again, and I will answer any questions you may have."

End of discussion, that's how it will be, the 'Great and Powerful Mom' has spoken.

Forgive me, but I will give you some examples of Uncle Andy's ignorance, fear and hatred. He would eat mixed nuts which included Brazil nuts, a big brown nut that looked like a toe. And yes, he called them "nigger toes" as he gleefully chomped away. Uncle Andy saw a black man in their neighborhood once, they promptly listed the house for sale and moved. You know, "property values, crime and all." To her credit, Aunt Ruth never joined Uncle Andy in his antipathy. She was a genteel Southern woman and wouldn't engage in such demeaning conversation, she had been raised better. A week later we would leave Chattanooga, and we really didn't have to have a follow-up conversation. We had seen and heard it all first-hand, and we found it repulsive and frankly, sad.

Back in the Twin Cities, Bill was in seventh grade and playing on the Catholic youth basketball team when a new family moved in a few blocks from us, a super nice, kind black family. Black was the term then, Afro-American wasn't far off. Well, it didn't matter to us what color your skin was, did you play sports, any sport? The Nelson boys sure did, one of them, Kevin was Bill's age, they quickly became good friends and Kevin signed up to play on Bill's hoops team. Silently, behind the scenes, several Catholic families lobbied to keep Kevin off the team, being silently racist was somehow still okay I guess. Well, LouAnn, my mom heard about it and about blew a gasket. She explained to the Parish Council that if Kevin wasn't allowed to play, Bill wasn't allowed to play, perhaps we should have a sermon on Sunday about why Jesus wouldn't want Kevin on the team, etc. You get the picture, LouAnn shut that one down in a nanosecond - good to have an equal opportunity Mom.

The last thing I will share with you on race was a talk I attended in college. Ms. Rosa Parks came and told us the story of her bus ride, her protest and the life that ensued. Rosa was extremely frail, not much left on them bones but her conviction and spirit rang out, she was stronger than hatred. On that fateful day, December 1st, 1955 she wouldn't move to the back of the bus, she wouldn't give up her seat, "People always say that I didn't give up my seat because I was tired, but that isn't true. No, the only tired I was, was tired of giving in."

My sincere gratitude to my mom, Rosa Parks, Nelson Mandela and President Barack Obama & his family. Against a cultural milieu in the late 60's, 70's and on to today, I didn't grow up hating someone based on the color of their skin, I have tried to judge them based on their character, words and deeds. (Yes, I have failed many times myself using those same measurements).

### Shopping in my Mind (1971)

I am six and in Southdale Mall in Edina, MN. Southdale opened in 1956 and is the oldest fully enclosed, climate-controlled shopping mall in the United States. However, I am not in awe of this shopping marvel because I am lost. Strangely though, I am calm. Somewhere my mom is out there, looking for me, panicked. And in the end, this will all work out okay. Weird I know that, yet I do. So, I think. I entertain myself. I enjoy the place, six years old and I intuitively knew all this stuff.

After an hour or so, I am located by concerned people. Not my mom but the strangers will be the link to me seeing my mom again soon. This whole process continues to be comfortable for me, no anxiety. I was just passing time. Within ten minutes, a very harried, flushed Mom comes trotting down the vast corridor, relief on her face and the pressing desire to touch me. I am whole, safe and hers.

Into the Buick LeSabre we pile and begin the ride home. My anxious Mother wants to know where I was, what I was doing, etc. Thus, I tell her the truth.

"I knew I was lost but I knew I was okay - I was thinking" was my response.

"What were you thinking?" was her follow-up question?

"I was thinking that what if you weren't my family? What if it all is pretend, that I had no real family, that I was just simply on my own, that everything was just what I think."

That was enough to send Mom over the top. She was hot! What I had said meant to her that I questioned that I was her son, that I doubted all the love, the effort, hard work and dreams, ergo, I shut up quick.

What was I really trying to say? "*Cogito ergo sum*" ("I think, therefore I am") *a la* Rene Descartes. I knew she was my mom. I knew I had a "real" family. Yet at a basic level I knew that my reality lay in my brain, and that everything needed "me" to think about for it to be real, nothing more. Somehow, someway I had connected at age six to the notion that everything was subject to validation and interpretation in my coconut. I wasn't being mean to my mother, I had told her the truth as I understood it. Since she didn't like what I said, I shut my mouth. I knew who was cooking dinner that night, and I was going to be hungry by 6 p.m. So, if I wanted supper I had best just shut my gob.

### A Truth Revealed Early On (Summer 1972)

Even at the age of seven, the following was an arrow to my core though I am the only one to recall it. My oldest brother Bill and I were in our new family room addition to the house with its orange themed deep shag carpet, avocado greens, and hardwood furniture that my mother so loved for its solidity and a Brady Bunch meets overstuffed furniture feel.

I can't remember what the heck Bill and I were talking about but per usual, I was adamant that I wanted what I wanted and I wanted it now! Typical in many ways for a seven-year-old but with me there was a fierce determination to get it "now" to hell with waiting, to hell to anybody who stood in my way. After having listened to my fire for long enough, Bill looked me straight in the eye and blurted out "Don't you have any self-control?!"

---Silence---

---Silence---

The conversation veers off, probably onto pro-wrestling or something and we went back to beating each other up like usual. I knew then as I know now, that an unspoken truth had been uttered about me and the answer would have consequences for the rest of my life:

---No, I have no self-control---

## Lima Beans, Liver and other such delectables

In the name of God, what made parents of that generation wage the war of the food intake? My son Luke ate grilled cheese sandwiches three times a day for several years. I didn't care, just eat boy, but I digress. Roughly twice a year, something would show up on our plates that we were expected to eat. The worst of which for me was Lima beans. What is a Lima bean? I always envisioned mushed worm guts squished into a casing of boogers. If there is anybody who likes Lima beans, please seek professional help.

The rules at our table were sacrosanct: eat what's on your plate, clean your plate, and if you have seconds then you had to finish those before having dessert. I think they were chiseled in stone though I never saw them. Meatloaf, mashed potatoes, gravy and Lima beans. I wolf down the first three and the war of attrition is on. Two hours later I am sent to my room, cold lima beans on my plate, Tommy - 1 Mom/Dad - 0. Same thing every-time. I was so damn stubborn I rarely caved.

One time Mom served liver, a huge hit with us boys. (Come on Mom and Dad - you guys are just asking for it!) So, down we sit, bloody red meat bleeding on our plates and it's time for the prayer. "In the name of ..." Dad leads us in. At the end of the prayer is the time for special intentions to which Dad adds "and for all those people who are hungry because they don't have food to eat tonight" to which, Bob chirps in with "Why don't we send them the liver Dad?" Bam, Bob gets one across the chops and down to our bedroom he is sent, no, dinner for you! As I look down at my plate, bleeding before me very eyes, I am tempted to offer my liver to the poor people too.

## The Vikings

My parents had season tickets to the Vikes, second deck, a few rows back towards the end-zone away from the scoreboard, awesome seats. I think they loved going to the tailgate parties more than the games. They would get there early, meet several friends, grill, veggie trays, cold cut platters, snacks and a full bar. By game-time they were READY. Us boys primarily played catch or football with other kids in the lot. My very first game was the Vikes versus the Bears. Game time temperature zero with a good stiff wind (back then there was not any Real Feel, just cold and damn cold). We literally sat in sleeping bags and would poke our heads out to watch the plays. Dick Butkus was in his final season and though he couldn't run anymore because of his knees. He was an animal! We of course had Fran Tarkenton, the Purple People Eaters, Bud Grant... In 1980, when the Vi-Queens moved into that damn bubble, they ruined the event that was Viking football. All I can say now is GO BEARS!

## President Richard Milhous Nixon (August 9, 1974)

I always liked the name Milhous.

I was in Miles City, MT, the town where my mom was born. Mr. Hickok was taking his son Chris and I out to their ranch in Western Montana for a couple weeks of life on a thirty-two square mile ranch. After being cooped up all day in Mr. Hickok's Thunderbird, Chris and I were playing Frisbee in the parking lot. It was great to run, stretch and breathe in glorious fresh air. "Hey guys, come on in for a minute" Mr. Hickok called. "You are about to watch the President of the United States resign. This is a moment like no other in US history." With that, my nine-year-old brain processed the beady eyed president resigning as a man who looked like he needed badly to poop. Chris and I promptly headed back outside to "burn off the stink" as my mom would say.

## Compliment to Remember – Hickok Ranch, Western Montana (August 1974)

It was about 10:30 or 11:00 p.m. and I could not sleep. Chris and I were in the bunk room, just off the kitchen, a 1930's ranch house that hadn't changed since it was built with its creaky wood floors, old wrought iron beds, lumpy mattresses and a smell of musty age.

In the next room were Mr. Hickok, Ralph and Bob - the ranch hands who were talking in hushed tones. Mr. Hickok was smoking his pipe. Ralph and Bob were hand rolling cigarettes. Bob was a wire of a man, not prone to talking much. He was one of those guys who it would be a mistake to cross in a bad way. Ralph was much older, probably pushing sixty and a lifelong ranch-hand with more experience and common sense than ten city folks put together. Mr. Hickok was a very successful engineer who had married a woman of means and he had been kind enough to bring me along with his son Chris for three plus weeks on the ranch.

As the men smoked, they talked about the day, the ranch, projects and the boys - Chris and I. Bob commented how much of a natural athlete Chris was. Strong, agile and fearless (he truly was all those things). He added that Chris would go far with whatever he set his mind to. Everyone concurred. Now, I was lying on my musty mattress in a sleeping bag, the kitchen door ajar and fighting off sleep listening to the men. Ralph then commented, "That Tom, he just doesn't give up. We were irrigating today and he would go to climb out of the stream, grab a handful of thistle, curse, grab another handful of thistle and haul himself up. That's the kind of determination you just can't teach to a kid."

I smiled, closed my eyes, and nodded off to sleep. The nicest compliment I ever got.

# ACT II

## Pre-teen and Teen (1976-1983)

### Bicentennial (July 4, 1976)

I would be remiss if I didn't mention the Bicentennial, the 200th birthday of the United States of America. It was a huge event, for many reasons. Vietnam was over. We didn't lose, but we didn't win and everybody just wanted to forget it. Nixon was gone. A peanut farmer was going to be our next president. In general, Americans just wanted to feel good about our country and our history (imagine that as a backdrop as compared to the destructive, divisive atmosphere today). The events and fireworks that day were unbelievable. New York harbor was full of massive sailing ships shooting water arcing into the air. Every family gathered for day-long BBQ's and parties that continued into the next day. The whole holiday was a two day national celebration where everybody was upbeat, positive, hopeful and thankful. That night, we went to the fireworks show at Olympia Fields Country Club (Dad had been transferred back to Chicago, and he was not happy about it). The fireworks that night were two to three times longer and bigger than the normal 4th of July show. It was stunning. God Bless America!

### A Young Edison at Work (Winter 1976)

At the Catholic grade school I attended, the hand soap of

choice was dry, pink, grainy sand that somewhat lathered up with water. It felt like washing your hands with sandpaper crumbs and was mandatory after each visit to the restroom, usually supervised by the teacher standing next to the communal hand washing station. That soap sucked. Your hands quickly became dry. They cracked. They hurt. And I swear I think the damn stuff was toxic. No kid wanted to wash their hands but there was no choice.

### Enter Tommy the Inventor.

One day while bored at home, I was playing around when an idea hit me. "Eureka!" Just like Archimedes into action I leapt. It was a simple idea: turn bar soap into liquid form; put it into a bottle; squirt/pump it into your palm; and, *ta da* - simple, effective hand washing for all, no mess and kids would be happy to use it! How did I make it you wonder? I took an empty pump type bottle from my mom's cleaning supplies, washed it well, and removed the label. I then took a bar of soap, shaved it into strips/shavings so that I could jam it into the bottle, added hot water and shook the thing like hell numerous times. After a few hours, I had an awesome liquid soap which I showed to my family.

Everyone I showed it to was impressed and thought it was a great idea.

What should I do next, pondered the eleven-year-old burgeoning entrepreneur? I decided to send my idea to several soap companies and see what they thought of it. In December, I received the following letter, now forty plus years old ago, which still adorns my wall:

*The Procter and Gamble Company*
*December 9, 1976*

*Dear Tom,*

*Thank you very much for offering us a suggestion for a liquid soap in a pump-type dispenser.*

*We are very grateful for your thoughtfulness, and we wish we could accept your suggestion, but we can't. You see, all of the formulas for our products, and their packaging, too, must come from our research and development people here at Procter and Gamble who work full-time in the marketing of the products we manufacture. We count on them for all our products and packaging and do not accept ideas from people outside our Company.*

*We appreciate your letter very much, Tom, even though we can't use the idea you offered us.*

*Sincerely,*

*M.A.Miller*
*Director of Public Liaison*

Quick Post Note: The man officially and correctly credited with the invention of SoftSoap in 1980 was Robert R. Taylor, who died in 2013. Here is an excerpt from his obituary:

> *Told by his daughter Lori - "It was SoftSoap, however, that made his reputation as a business genius. He was just driving to work one day and he had been looking at the soap in the sink and seeing how messy it was and he was like, 'There's got to be a way not to have to deal with that'... through home experimentation and some trial and error, (he) created the soap."*

No bitterness on my end, I was eleven. I had a great idea and took it as far as I possibly could. *C'est la vie.*

### Kevin Denslow and Roller Skating

My best friend in grade school was Kevin Denslow, a smart, cool guy who was unlike anybody else I had ever met. First, his parents were cool, young, and hip. They had a swimming pool in the backyard and Mrs. Denslow who was probably mid-thirties then was really dreamy for an old lady. Kevin's Dad was a Burt Reynolds looking kind of guy. It was different world at the Denslow's than at my "square" house. Loose rules, loud music, a pool and a very groovy 70's lifestyle. I remember when Kevin's parents divorced, unheard of at the time in our circle of friends, I asked Kevin if it bummed him out. His response, "No way, it's great. Now they are both happy again and I don't have to listen them fighting all the time." I was starting to learn that not everyone lived like the Cleaver's aka the Hickey's.

Now if you lived and breathed in the mid-late 70's you roller-skated at Cheap Skate. It was where life happened; guys asked girls to go out. Girls broke up with guys and everything in-between. I mean this was it: pinball, concessions, my favorite air hockey, foosball, mirror ball spinning, music thumping, lights low. This is the shit, man!

Kevin had a very unique approach to getting a girl to skate with him, he would go in front of them and fall down, invariably the girl would tumble on top of him. Being the gentleman that he was, he would help the young lady up and skate off together. It worked almost every time. Smooth operator. I am sad to say that Kevin died in his early 20's, a heart valve defect I believe. I sure loved that guy.

Now my big crush in 6th grade was on Cathy Miner, a 7th grader. The Miner family had dark skin, black hair and in the vernacular of the day—Cathy was smoking hot! Cathy was also a much better skater than I was so I was pretty much screwed from the outset. A snowball is announced where boys ask girls to skate. With the lights down low, the disco ball spinning, slow music playing, I decide it's time I man up and ask her to skate. She is standing against the wall with three or four friends. I start rolling towards her, heart pounding but I am going to do this damn it! As I attempt to stop, I catch my toe stopper on the floor, and I go headfirst into a full splay right in front of Cathy and her friends. Bright red face, I arise and summon my courage. Her friends are laughing at me, but I still ask Cathy to skate. She says no, now humiliated, embarrassed and depressed, I skate away seriously considering the priesthood.

## Bikes and Beaches (late 1970's)

Luckily, I always had my bike. As a kid growing up in the burbs, our ticket to freedom was a bike. As Bill outgrew his bike, it went to Bob. When Bob outgrew it, it went to me. It didn't matter as long as the pedals went around. I could go to: Bennett Field and play home-run derby; Deephaven Drug to work; school; Lilli-Putt Miniature Golf; and most importantly, to any number of beaches on Lake Minnetonka. If you could get to a beach you could get to—GIRLS! Those strange creatures whom I was taking more and more interest in. Usually, we gathered at Deephaven Beach and the guys would play underwater tag beneath the docks. The girls would lie on the beach, tanning oils or baby oil applied, my Lord that is a small bikini. Sploosh—back into the cold water. I shan't belabor the point but bikes and beaches were the greatest freedoms a young lad could hope for.

## Disco with Odalys (Summer 1979)

Hippies were receding, Hard/Acid Rock was waning, and a new sound was pulsating out of the speakers—Disco. The Hickey family had returned to Minneapolis with Dad taking an executive position with Gambles-Skogmo, which meant we were doing extremely well at present. Life was fun and as I entered my teen years, full of promise. My brother Bill was attending Marquette University and his roommate was Francisco Hernandez, a Puerto Rican from New Jersey who was about as different from Bill as is possible. That summer, Franciso came to visit us and he brought his fiancé—Odalys. Did I mention that he brought Odalys?!

Odalys was Puerto Rican, but she most definitely did not look like Francisco. Odalys had a big boofy, black hairdo, almost an afro and how to put this politely? Plump, ample large chi-chi's. Everything else about Odalys was just how it should be! She was joyous, fun, and laughed at every opportunity. Disco is the national rage, and Tom, the geeky adolescent, cannot tap his feet to any rhythm. I am a white cave man, with two left feet. Enter Odalys and her school of disco dancing. I spent the next three days being taught how to disco by a professional Disco Queen. Now let me point out, that at the time, I was eight inches shorter which put my vision and face on a direct plane with the sumptuous chi-chi's from heaven. Every-time I stumbled, I was rewarded with a face full of heaven. Every-time I spun, I bumbled back into a soft, epic bosom of a landing pad. Odalys would respond with fits of laughter and giggles as we whirled on about the living room to the Bee-Gee's pulsing away. Oh, what I would give to take those lessons again today.

### Cut by Digger - South Bend, Indiana (Fall 1981)

We were eating breakfast in the Notre Dame student cafeteria, Paul Foley, myself and my brother Bob who was a sophomore at ND. Foles and I were juniors in high school down for a weekend visit to see college life up close. The cafeteria itself was incredibly cool, gorgeous wood fifteen to twenty feet up the walls and a cavernous ceiling, forty plus feet high. On top of it, the food was damn good (Paul and I had snuck in using other students' meal cards who wouldn't get out of bed for breakfast).

As we dined on a breakfast smorgasbord, my brother was perusing the Notre Dame daily newspaper. Bob happened on an ad in the sports section announcing basketball tryouts that evening in the athletic complex (it is was a NCAA rule that every program must have an open tryout for all interested students) and asked, "You guys want to try out for the Notre

Dame basketball team tonight?"

That evening after dinner, we reported for tryouts, full of optimism at our chances to play Division One basketball. I am 5'10" tall, a short Irish barrel-chested guy with a half inch vertical. Foles, a brilliant doctor today in Denver, was tall, slight and as pale as a white picket fence. Finally, there was Bob, who was on a baseball scholarship at Notre Dame, 6'5" with the elegant moves of a tall white guy with feet of concrete. Our fellow competitors were arrayed in black socks, glasses, grungy unwashed gym clothes, all shapes, sizes and all with high hopes of making a difference for the Irish that season.

The assistant coach gave us a quick spiel about the process and then separated the group into two, half on each end of the court. Time to get in line for lay-ups and show them our game. Standing at the free throw line is the assistant coach with a clipboard and our names on it. One by one he calls off our names and "Hickey, Tom" is called for a right-hand layup. Converse Chuck Taylor's proudly on my feet, I begin my drive toward the basket, leaping towards the hoop, getting at least two to three inches off the floor. I release the ball from my right-hand, and my D1 career is launched, the ball slowly rises toward the basket. It hits the rim (sadly for me, the bottom of the rim) and returns straight down to land on the crown of my head. I glance to my left and the coach is hiding behind his clipboard pissing his pants laughing and my fellow athletes are doubled over in hysterics.

Foles performs better than me. He doesn't humiliate himself and survives the first cut. Bob, due to his sheer height, is a lock for the first cut. Scrimmage time. Teams are divvied up and the game begins. Within the first minute, Bob skies like Kareem Abdul Jabaar and yanks down a rebound. Rather than intelligently pass the ball off to a guard who can shoot, Bob dribbles the ball up like it's his court. He feints right to a wide-open guard and hurls the ball to the left, where the only thing to stop the ball is a brick wall. So ends all our hoop dreams.

Now, that would be good enough but Coach Digger Phelps walks in wearing a full fur coat to watch the end of the tryouts. He gives a non-motivational speech that let's everybody know that if you make it out of these tryouts you: will be on the end of the bench; be lucky to play a few seconds at the end of the game; and in short, be the assistant team manager. So much for the Rudy pep talk.

Given that I have more cojones than brains, I stroll up to Coach Phelps (remember I'm not a student at Notre Dame, I am a junior in High School) and in I go, "Thanks Coach, I wish you the very best this season and thanks for the chance to tryout."

Digger peers down at me and inquires, "You go to school here?"

"Yes, sir," I reply, stepping out onto the thin ice.

With a quizzical look, Digger looks at me and follows-up with, "What dorm do you live in?"

I stammer, and then I stammer, I can't remember my brother's dorm for the life of me (Holy Cross), I just know it is across the lake so that is my final answer "The one across the lake" I say.

Digger is beyond perplexed, obviously wondering what kind of idiots are getting into Notre Dame these days that they don't even know the name of their dorm.

## Down half a Flight (Fall 1982)

This one is going to be tough to write. I signed on to this project so I need to be as honest as I promised I would be. Before I go further, I must say that I loved my dad. He was Superman. He took the bullets for us without flinching and did it for thirty-five years. He was a great man and I think the only mistake of this magnitude, he made was with me.

My Dad, Bill, had worked for Sears for twenty-seven years, Gambles for one year, and was then let go when Gambles got bought out. It was a catastrophic event for him and the family. Dad had done everything to benefit his family. He had been unhappy in his work for years, and we all knew it. Now, both my brothers were in college and my mom had returned to teaching as we needed the additional income.

So, the cocksure young son returns home about 6:30 p.m. from school and practice, no one home except a sullen, brooding Father in the living room. I assume he had a few cocktails under his belt as that would be normal given his despair and stress. Dad asked me a few questions, each one a bit more snide in tone. I answered each one honestly but certainly with a bit of an arrogant air. My life was going great.

For the love of me, I can't remember the question that he asked me that drove him over the edge. I do know that it wasn't a big deal. My Dad was a great athlete and starting college quarterback. His athleticism and achievements were legendary. I was standing at the top of the landing above the stairs and Dad was twelve feet away in a chair. He came out of his chair like a bull out of a gate. I never even moved or changed posture.

Dad hit me with a mighty right, a right that shocks me to this day as I would fly about eight treads down the fourteen-tread stairwell. Now the youngest son was pissed. "Do you want me to come back up there so you can hit me again?" and "Wow, that's great Dad, you can beat the shit out of a 17-year-old!" etc. etc... Each comment stinging my father as he comprehended what he had just done.

I went up to my bedroom and closed the door. I skipped dinner, my Mother, when she got home puzzled what the hell had happened. I laid on my bed and switched between tears, anger and sadness. Sometime about 10 p.m. I drifted off to sleep in my clothes, exhausted, despondent and feeling all fucked up inside.

The next morning at 5:30 there was a light knocking on my door. Sleep-sodden I opened the door with no clue where I was or what was going on. My Father stood in the doorway, tears rolling down his face. Obviously, he was devoid of any sleep before his coming workday. Dad apologized with his heart fully exposed. "I am so sorry for hitting you. That will never happen again."

Dad then stuck out his right hand. We shook hands. We hugged, and the night before receded into the rearview mirror.

Now I must tell you a few things in conclusion. Dad was good to his word, nothing like that ever happened again. I fully forgave him that morning as I knew he was completely sincere. Comparing myself to my father; he was such a better man, father and person than I will ever be.

Love you, Dad

## Son, do you believe in God? (May 1982)

Minneapolis—Back in my mom's blue Chevette, I was headed downtown with my girlfriend, Sheila. We were going into the city on what was then Highway 12 (now Hwy 394) to catch some music or like event. The best part of dating Sheila was that first, and foremost, we were great friends.

So, there we were traveling east on Hwy 12, the sun setting behind us to the west. We were making the last slight turn in the left lane of a four-lane highway, all flowing east into the City. As we round the center median, directly in front of us, coming head on is a massive old Mercury, the kind that weighs several tons. We are in a tiny Chevette—SHIT, you're not supposed to be there. The last thing I see before we collide is a miniature old woman with scraggly, grey hair and the sun shining off her glasses. She looks like a skinny hobbit driving a tank.

Sheila and I brace for the collision. Bam - hit head on at forty plus miles per hour. Bam - hit in the rear by the Honda behind us going fifty plus miles an hour. A dual simultaneous collision at the same millisecond. In fear and incredulousness, I check on Sheila. She's not dead or hurt or bleeding, neither am I. What the hell just happened?!

We hop from the Chevette which is now several feet in the air, trying to get to safety in case someone else plows into the pile or the cars blowup as gas is spilling onto the pavement from the three-car wreck. What happened was just this simple and miraculous. As we hit the Mercury, the Honda which had one of those pointed noses hit us from behind at precisely the same moment and slid under the rear of the Chevette, lifting us up into the air, so that the rear of our car was resting on their hood. Instead of slamming into the dashboard, slamming backwards or nightmarish whiplash, we simply just went up!

Sirens a plenty were howling now, headed our way. Police, ambulances and firetrucks because of the fuel leaks. A state trooper showed up, talked to us extremely kindly and said, hold on a second. He walked over to the skinny hobbit. She was bombed out of her gourd and had managed to swerve through oncoming traffic for half a mile before drilling us. She was quickly cuffed and taken away.

The trooper comes over to us, "You know half a second later or earlier you two would have been human pinballs in there, pointing to the Chevette. Do you believe in God?"

"Yes, Sir" we both replied.

"Good, you should. I have been doing this job for thirty years, and I have never seen anyone walk away from an accident like this."

Quick follow-up notes: The Chevette was totaled, the hobbit's insurance had to pay to replace it. The Honda behind us also was totaled and due to the extreme, severe nature of the accident, the hobbit's insurance company had to replace the Honda as well.

### Fore! Flying Cloud Drive-In (Summer 1982)

As my chums and I turned sixteen, the privilege, the freedom of being able to drive our parents' cars was becoming an ever-present reality. It is hard to believe the zaniness we pulled off as young drivers: making donuts on the icy Church parking lot, racing to school trying to set land speed records if the lights were timed just right going down Minnetonka Boulevard and other such daring, thrilling endeavors. Fortunately, most everybody was a safe driver, not wanting to lose their new precious driving privileges.

Back in those days, one of the few Drive In's left in the Twin Cities was Flying Cloud Drive-In, out in the then "sticks" of Eden Prairie. Routinely, we would draw straws to see who would be the Master "Bater", the poor schlep who would have to drive solo into the Drive-In, looking like a lonely creep with as many bodies as possible stuffed into the car's trunk to avoid buying a ticket to the Drive-in. I remember one time driving from Duff's house down by Lake Harriett, thirty minutes out to Flying Cloud Drive-In with five or six of us knuckleheads crammed in the back of some Dad's black Crown Vic. My head was jammed up to a wheel well and I could not move due to all the fellow sardines packed in tight. By the time we piled out of the trunk we were all light-headed, not because of exhaust fumes but because there just wasn't any fresh air getting into the trunk. Ah, but yet again, I digress.

One of the funniest, zaniest afternoon-evening-night combos I recall began with some golf with Lucke, Marty, and Abes at Interlachen Country Club in Edina. Abes and Marty both worked at the Club so we were able to get on the course for free for some late afternoon fun. I think we played about eleven holes before darkness befell us. Lucke and I pretty much sucked at golf back then, but Abes and Marty had some skills. All in all, we laughed a ton, hooted at the shitty shots and cheered on the good ones. Looking back now, it was truly magical. We were all sixteen years old, full of dreams, hope, health and most importantly, the kind of friendships that endure to this day. I still keep in touch with each of them and love them all dearly.

With golf in the books, the next exploit for the night was the drive-in. Caddyshack was part of a double dip at Flying Cloud and we were in. Dinner consisted of delectable drive-in cheeseburgers, fries, and a coke. By the time the first movie rolled, the place was jammed. I think they had reached capacity. I can't recall what the first film was. It was a dud of some sort, so we just worked the parking lot, looking for pretty girls to impress and dudes we knew from our respective hoods. As the first feature ended, we headed back to our chariot for the main feature. I think it was Abe's blue Chevy that we drove that night, a real beast and we set up our lawn chairs and cooler in front of the hood.

On came Caddyshack and the hooting and a hollering began in earnest. The more noise we made, the more kids who joined us and the louder our laughter became at the "Shack." About halfway through the movie, I came up with a solid idea. I grabbed our golf clubs out of the trunk, teed up a ball and proceeded to hit my best shot of the day, a three iron that bee-lined to the center of the sheet metal movie screen. It struck with a loud metallic thwack and in the light of the projector you could see the ball drop down below, leaving a fresh, beautiful one to two-inch dent in the screen. Bedlam thus ensued and suddenly, Abes, Marty, Lucke and myself are delighting the throng with blasts off the screen. We plunked that screen until we ran out of balls, amazingly not once did management come after us.

To conclude the perfect night, we headed back to Interlachen Country Club where Abes and Marty knew the night security guard. He was another young dude whose job it was to keep out the hooligans, the rabble rousers, you know, the kids like us. The full-sized pool was ours for a late-night melee. Each of us had invited people we knew from the drive-in to join us, so we ended up with about fifteen people on hand. Guys and girls equally divided. People swam in whatever they had. Most guys were down to their boxers to keep our shorts dry to go home in, the girls in shorts and t-shirts. I can still see the glow of the lights, body parts glistening, as kids hurled in and out of the water, full-on belly flops, cannon balls, laughter, chicken fights and in the end, just kids, good kids having fun.

## My Brief Career in the Spotlight (1982 – 1985)

In high school, I was in fantastic shape, averaging about one hundred sixty pounds, exercising everyday including runs as far as ten miles, playing baseball and soccer. At some point, mostly buying clothes from Goodwill with my friend Matt, I even became slightly fashionable. It felt good. The less I cared about it, the more it seemed to work.

In our old neighborhood lived a big wig advertising executive, Mr. Thompson. He approached my Mother one day and said, "You know, Tom has the all-American look: freckles, great shape, broad appeal and some charisma to boot. Tom is what I look for in our ads. He should try modeling. He'd be great at it, and the money could really help pay for college in a few years." With that, Mr. Thompson gave my Mother a card for a top modeling agency in Minneapolis. Things progressed over the next few months and Sha-Zam: I'm a model (please stop laughing now!).

Initially, most of the jobs I got were print ads: banks, colleges, happy rainbow collages of multiethnic and multiracial young people. I remember I had several shoots for Robert Morris College. I was making great bank and damn if the girls weren't smoking hot. Doing a commercial for the military I played a mover; overalls, tight haircut, etc. Lifting some guy in a uniform who was laying on a couch with another mover on the other end, I made four thousand dollars for about four hours work (the ad must have run a ton around the world on Armed Forces Television because half my pay was residuals). One of my favorites was a shoot when they dressed me up as a soldier: helmet, rifle and even camouflage face paint. The photographer looked through the window of the camera and said, "Look scared." I burst out laughing and never was able to recompose myself. Personally, there was a part of me that knew I didn't belong getting clicked at, but what the hell, it beat working at McDonald's.

It was at Brookdale Mall in Burnsville, MN that I did

my one and only fashion show. School was starting in a few weeks and the mall wanted to promote teenage fashion to max out sales. Into the mall I strolled, carrying a hair brush - I got this no problem I thought. In the center of the mall, a stage and a large white tent had been erected. Inside the tent were about fifteen other models, mostly female, most so stunningly beautiful that I doubted I should even be there. Less confidently, I found my table. There hung my rack of clothes for the show and I set down my brush. Every other male and female model had huge tackle boxes or trunks, full of cosmetics, powders, implements, eyelash stretchers, tweezers, pluckers, and anything else you can imagine. No worries - I had my brush.

My role was to be the preppy, brightly dressed student. With loafers on my feet, bright yellow socks and I think even a pink shirt in tow, I filled the part. Paired up with me was Jenny, a blonde bombshell from Edina (the elite suburb in the Twin Cities – you know the one, every city has one). Golden hair, perfect complexion, tanned, white teeth that should have been in dentist commercials and a body that was going to cost some guy real money someday. Jenny's dressing area was next to mine and thank God she was kind to me because I was the new meat who didn't have a clue what the hell was going on. A snarky show coordinator, Patrick, spat out our instructions and kind of left out the locker-room pep-talk in between glares at us. Jenny stepped next to me and said, "Relax, start at this end of your wardrobe rack and work your way that way. If there is a dot on your shirt or sweater that means you and I are walking together." Man, did I ever pray for dots!

Showtime: first outfit, lineup, Jenny on my left-arm, curtain opens, down the runway we go. Remember Patrick had said 'They look at you, you don't look at them!'. Spin. Start heading back. Three hundred plus people watching easy, maybe four hundred was closer. Then back through the tent flap I went and stripped, clothes flying everywhere, bras and panties everywhere, next set of clothing.

"Am I the only guy in boxers?!' I wondered.
"TOM!"

Yes Patrick, right here. Down the runway I go again, this time solo. Hey, I'm the all-American guy so I smile and check out the audience for cute girls then back to the tent and so on and so on. After forty-five minutes of clothing chaos, the donnybrook was over. I thanked Jenny with sincere gratitude and got a hug from a girl who wasn't in my league (she wasn't even in my universe).

I grabbed my brush and headed home, having made five hundred dollars for two hours work in the midst of a bra and panty melee. Tough life.

### Why not in Minot? (Summer 1982)

The Post 259 American Legion baseball team, a cast of colorful characters if ever there was one, headed out by bus to Minot, North Dakota for a baseball tournament. There was nothing too remarkable about the tournament. It was hot and our team did okay, third or fourth place, despite not having a decent pitching staff. So, that puts me in Minot. Time for the story.

John "Hawk" Hawkins was our catcher and a mess. His mother used to have to bring his shoes to games because Hawk forgot them at home, one time he forgot his catcher's mitt on a road trip and had to borrow the other team's mitt, leaving it on home plate between innings. Anyway, it was our last night in Minot and Hawk and I decide to procure some cold beer and see what the night would bring. I was seventeen, a year younger than Hawk, but I always looked older so I was the one to procure beer from the liquor store. The drinking age was nineteen in those days.

Hawk and I ended up at some city park at dusk, happily imbibing the cold libations, sheltered from the light rain that had begun to fall. The rain made Minot look clean with kind of a green tint to everything. After finishing the first six pack, we decided to venture back out into the night and see what the fates had planned for us.

We wandered the streets uneventfully for an hour or so then played some pinball and foosball at the local bowling alley. Nothing exciting going on so we decided to hoof it back to our motel, finishing the remaining few beers off as we went.

The streetlights were on, glistening off the wet payment. It was about 10:30 p.m., and we had walked about a half mile when a white Chevy Impala pulled over. Two girls in the front seat were wondering whether we wanted a ride. Bingo! Hawk and I exchanged happy glances and clambered on in. Hawk got in the back with Wendy, and I was up front with Carissa, a blonde, blue-eyed tan product of the Great Plains. Not drop dead gorgeous, solid frame but hell, she was a lot better looking than Hawk.

The girls offered to take us to the house of Carissa's grandmother who was out of town if we shared our beer with them, of course! Grandma's house was a little white post World War II unit, prerequisite white vinyl siding, gardens and garage out back. It could have been a Hilton. I sure as hell didn't care.

Once inside, we hung out in the living room, drinking beer, talking with a sense of anticipation and excitement in the air. I decided it was time to see if this was headed anywhere and I leaned over to kiss Carissa. Her tongue was warm, full and eager. Within minutes we were in full mash and Carissa said to follow her. Mama Hickey didn't raise no dummy, so I did as I was told.

Carissa steered us into a back guest bedroom. It was a small, paneled room and there was a bean bag on the bed along with many clothes, obviously all Carissa's. Now, as previously mentioned, Carissa was very tan, blue eyes, blonde as blonde gets, wearing a white dress that had snaps down the front, not buttons. We resumed our mashing at which point she opened the front of her dress, revealing the simplest white cotton bra and panties. In retrospect, not sure how I didn't lose it right there. Onto the bean bag we went, her head on the downhill side of the bean bag, leaving me to enjoy the most beautiful form to exist on Earth. As I removed her bra and panties, the white skin underneath was in stark contrast to the dark tan. How did I get this lucky in Minot?!

One thing leads to another and I enter Carissa and the pleasure of a woman for the very first time. I am quite certain that Carissa was well versed in this exercise. Anyhoo, there I am on top of Carissa on the bean bag enjoying the ecstasy of this new thrill ride when the door opens, "Hick, what are you doing?" it's Hawk. What the hell does it look like I'm doing Hawk? This is why I was born I thought. "We gotta go Hick, we are going to miss curfew" adds Hawk. Now curfew was far from my mind, but I tell Hawk that I will be out in a few minutes. I return to the task at hand, Carissa is unfazed and looking for a satisfactory conclusion. I did my job well and it all ends with two, young people shuddering together in unison, life clearly redefined for this seventeen-year-old guy.

The next day, we are on the bus headed home. I am feeling so much Catholic guilt that it is almost crippling. For sure, I am hell bound. As we exit Minot, Hawk yells at me to look at the gas station sign on the left which says, "Why not in Minot?" My mood instantly changes. I smile. I couldn't agree more.

## The Holiest of the Holies (Every March 17th)

Nothing has been or ever will be as easy for me to write about than St. Patrick's Day. Every year I take two days off from work, January 6th - my birthday (it totally sucks to work on your birthday!) and March 17th, St. Patrick's Day. If you added up all the amazing days I have had based on the calendar, March 17th has NEVER disappointed me. My family is 100% Irish, marrying Irish Catholic for four generations until my brothers and I, completely bastardized the Irish-Catholic lineage with marriages outside of the Celtic League.

In grade school, I did go to school but for us it was a day

of wearing the green, mayhem, and revelry. It was the one day you could be certain that my mom - LouAnn, would get very happy via the drink, parades, friends, parties and everything in-between. Dad would have an extra drink or two if it was a work night, otherwise, Dad was in lock step with Mom on weekends. Once, St. Patty's fell on a Saturday and Mom was voted "Ms. Blarney" at our Parish Patty's day party. In quick summation, it was, is and will always be the one holiday that was for us - our branch of the Mick's that had climbed out of the bog with Dennis Hickey in 1861 when he left the Emerald Isle, entering A-Mare-E-Kay via Ellis Island. One of our descendants, Jack McAulliffe, the "Napoleon of the Ring", is in the boxing Hall of Fame, a bare-knuckle fighter who never lost a fight and once had a fight in Boston go seventy-two rounds before the boys in blue broke up the illegal fight. We are pale. We are freckled. We work like dogs. We dream big. WE ARE THE IRISH!

Now before recalling one vintage Patty's day story from my youth, I will list some of the Fenian parades and parties I have attended: Minneapolis - numerous times; St. Paul also several times; Chicago three times; Washington D.C.; Warsaw, Poland (the only Irish Pub at the time in all of Eastern Europe); Denver; and Butte, Montana, truly my favorite choice for a Gaelic fest stateside. Back to my story.

In high school, I never went to school on St. Patty's Day. I went to the parades, either Minneapolis or St. Paul with some fellow pale young Micks. Typically, we would go to Paul McDonald's house overlooking Lake Calhoun, arriving about 8:30 a.m. and hence commence to consume mass quantities of Special Export beer. In the background would be Mac's killer stereo blasting Celtic Rock at a hundred plus decibels. Mac was an amazing drummer and could play along with Zep, The Who or whoever was cued up on the reel to reel tape player. Once properly primed, we headed to one of the parades, always the one my mother wasn't going to, quaffing healthy amounts of additional beer and got our green on. Our first two years we knew bars were out of the question at our age, so we took the bus back to Mac's, kept the party going and slept there. Mac's mom was an angel to us. She delighted having us in the house and fed us well. Most importantly, her love and hopes for all of us was self-evident.

Senior year of high school, shyte, I am to have my wisdom teeth yanked out on March 16th, the day before the High Holy. Being the exceptional individual that I am, I have the worst tooth extraction the dentist has ever performed. My left jaw looked like a black and blue overinflated piece of bad, purulent meat. I could not touch my front teeth to my bottom teeth as my jaws were swollen so badly, the left jaw was twice the size of the right jaw. The next morning my mom is headed to the St. Paul parade, "I'll be fine Mom, don't worry about me." I am to stay home from school to "rest" after the oral surgery from hell. Mom gives me a kiss on the head and off she goes in bright green clothing, shamrocks on her cheeks. That's my ma! LouAnn is gone five minutes and I am up, dressed and headed downtown to Mac's house for the annual festivities and then on to the Minneapolis parade. Hard to have fun with a swollen, ugly mug but Momma Hickey didn't raise no quitter.

Fast forward to around 2 p.m. that day. I am underage in an Irish Pub in Minneapolis trying to eat Irish stew with my distorted, swollen jowls, a pint of Guinness rests in front of me (mother's milk). I glance up and in the Name of God who has just entered the Pub? Me Mum! Feckin Shyte! She spots me and heads my way. 'I'm dead' is all that runs through my head. LouAnn walks over, sits down next to me, a huge grin on her face, "Aren't you going to buy your mother a beer on St. Patrick's Day?" is her query. I'll be damned, I get Mom a cocktail and we have a grand old time, my eighteen-year-old friends now mixed in with my fifty-year-old mother and her friends. A bit later, as she gets up to leave, my mom turns to me with a twinkle in her eye, "For the record, I never saw you here today, and I suggest you be home before your Dad does." Damn straight Mom! And I did just that.

### Louie's Boat – A moment of clarity (May 1983)

There are moments in life, usually extremely brief, when the truth is said aloud and we know that not only is it true, it is insight to ourselves that we will recall forever. This is just such a moment, and no one knew I even heard it.

It was the last month of high school. Everyone was nervous, excited and looking to have as much fun as possible before we all went trotting all over the country to college and life beyond. John Lewis had full use of his family's fifty-foot cabin cruiser on Lake Minnetonka. A couple of bedrooms, bathroom, galley, sun decks, two floors, it was a floating palace.

Louie had invited several of us to head out for a day on the water; beers, sun, girls, etc. It was to be an idyllic day with great friends as our high school days wound down.

Not sure why, but I was the last to arrive at the Tonka Bay Marina. I grabbed my beer, snacks and started to head for the docks. As I made my way, I could hear Louie, Mills, Lisa, Happ and a few others talking about me. They had no clue I was there nor that I could hear them.

At that moment, I heard Louie ask, "What do you think Hick likes more: girls or beer?"

Happ promptly replied, "Well, he has had a lot of both and I would have to call it a tie, he loves them both more passionately then we will ever know."

Laughter abounded as I strode into view.

I was not upset in the least bit. I had heard a truth that still holds true to this day. My friends were merely stating the most obvious fact that no one dared to say. That day has stayed with me ever since. I can still see the blue sky, the turquoise water of the bay, and the feeling that I had just been properly pigeon-holed for the rest of my life.

### Burnin' One Down with Peter Tosh (Summer 1983)

In the early 80's, music was either Disco, which was on its way out, Heavy Metal or a sub-genre of music, one of which was Reggae which was rocketing to popularity. Bob Marley and the Wailers were smoking hot. Peter Tosh, an original Wailer was also in high demand and touring all over the country. Along with the music came the deification of Cannibus (weed, pot, herb or any of a hundred other nicknames). To my parents' generation, pot was for the lazy, the slackers and the people on the bus to nowhere. To my friends who used it daily, pot was a way to: a) relax, laugh and chill; b) a means to alter the mind, seeing things in a new light; c) one hell of an appetite enhancer. (White Castles anyone?)

I was never much of a fan of pot. It made me paranoid, and I was always waiting for someone to punch me in the face. I mostly stuck to my old standby, a six pack of Molson Golden beer, thank you very much. In the summer of 1983, six of my friends had tickets to see Peter Tosh at the Northrop Theater in Minneapolis on the University of Minnesota campus. A most coveted ticket in the Metro area and as fate would have it, one of the guys got sick and couldn't go, thus 'Rasta Tom' got the phone call, "Would I pick up the extra ticket so it didn't go to waste and the guy not going didn't have to eat it?" *Why not?* I thought. I'm into checking out new things and experiences. I wonder what the hell I'm supposed to wear to a Reggae concert ran through my brain.

Off we rolled to the Cyrus Northrop Memorial Auditorium, truly one of the most intimate settings I have been to for a concert. Superb acoustics, red velvet seats, curtains and an ornate interior design with a limited seating capacity of around four thousand. We rolled into the parking lot in Stony's (Tony's) ugly station wagon borrowed from his Mom. Stony was a good guy and the proverbial pothead at our school. I am pretty sure Stony was baked eighteen hours a day. Before our feet hit the pavement, Stony had a massive joint sparked up and it quickly made the rounds. Oh well, when in Rome. I stripped off my preppy Oxford button down shirt, and I was now clad in my beloved Al's Bar Softball T-shirt as I took a large drag of Doobie (cough, cough, cough - always made me cough).

Once inside, two things were abundantly clear: 1) anyone and everyone could light up anytime, anywhere they wanted; and, 2) security was going to make zero effort to stop anyone in the auditorium from smoking dope. Our seats were in the twentieth row right in the middle of the auditorium, dead center to the stage, the only negative being that we were in the middle of the row, a stumble over numerous people was needed to get to the aisle, to the right or left.

I had a few more tokes and settled in with a big soda, some Mike & Ike's from the concession stand, and prepped myself for my first Reggae concert.

The rhythm that pulsed through the auditorium before Tosh came out felt as if it was directed at your insides, lights, the band, and then out came Peter Tosh. I had never felt music that seemed to have a will of its own. I had to sway, had to dance, had to smile, as did four thousand other people.

About halfway through the concert, some people were up dancing in the aisles. Tired of sitting, I followed suit as my party of five remained hunkered down, continuing to keep joint after joint alive (how the hell can they smoke that much?!). I had all I needed, so I headed to the left side of the stage and was standing against the wall at the bottom of stairs to the right of Peter Tosh and the band. It was incredible. I had a close-up view of the band, the mayhem in the auditorium, and charming lasses nearby to sway and dance with.

As Tosh began to conclude his main set, before going onto a few encores, he started playing "Legalize It" the anthem of the pot movement. A huge wicker Jamaican throne was pushed out onto the stage and Tosh sat down and motioned those of us near the stairs to come up on stage. I and about fifteen of my new best friends, were ushered up on stage as the band kept the refrain thrumming. Meanwhile, Tosh had pulled out a joint bigger than any cigar I have ever seen and lit it up with a jumbo flamethrower of a lighter. In front of me there was a cute, brunette in a hemp dress, Tosh passed her the joint and she took a big puff, Tosh's face lit up and I was up next. Here the gringo non-pot smoker is handed a joint by Peter Tosh in front of a highly altered throng. 'Don't cough' was all I could think. I didn't, it was smooth lamb's bread from Jamaica. Thanks Pete!

Afterwards the happy boys all piled in Stony's ugly station wagon, and I was treated as the hero of the night for smoking rope with Peter Tosh. Gladly, we safely made it to White Castle where we ate more sliders than should be legal, helping cut through the effects of the pot. Maybe there is something to this Rastafarian thing after all was what was on my mind that night.

### A Three-Hour Tour (Summer 1983)

My Father's prized possession and truly the only "toy" he ever bought himself was a boat, a nineteen-foot runabout, open hull that could comfortably accommodate up to eight people. It was great for fishing, waterskiing, and tooling around Lake Minnetonka. And naturally it was completely off limits for the boys to use until we had achieved some nebulous level of boating skills and responsibility. My older brother Bill had graduated into the boating secret society. Bob didn't really care I think since he was so busy with Notre Dame, his studies, and baseball. That left me as the outsider looking in - I am sure you know where this is headed.

It is a gorgeous summer evening, a zillion stars overhead, warm breezes and a perfectly flat lake. Having successfully wooed some young ladies at the miniature golf course, my friend Mark "Mitch" Mitchell and I were shooting for a late-night swim, a few cold ones and an enjoyable time with these pretty young things from Pennsylvania. Everybody was game. It was now up to me to procure the keys and vessel. Dropping by my house, everyone was in bed, and I slipped in and out with my excuse prepared if needed, 'I forgot my wallet'.

Down to Grey's Bay Marina we sped, giggly, happy and just plain young. Now in my defense, I really did know how to safely operate a boat. I frequently towed my friends water-skiing and commandeered their boat if they were too "happy from the drink." The craft was prepared for launch. Tarps off. Safety buoys up. Engine warmed and seaweed removed from the prop. "Cast off, Mitch!" I hollered as we pulled into the night at 9:30 p.m. Our first destination was a fifteen-minute jaunt to Big Island, where we dropped anchor and kicked back with some tunes. After a period of youthful exuberance, we stripped down into our boxers or bra and panties depending on the gender. In we dove, the water a chilling wake-up call which we overcame with chicken wars with the girls as the competitors on top our shoulders. Back in the boat, we toweled off, redressed and realized the night was still young, coming up on 11 p.m.

We decided to finish the night in style at the Mai Tai. The Mai Tai was a Polynesian themed bar on the lake another five miles from where we were. Off we sped. Once there, we saw a few friends, chatted and basked in the glow of being young. At midnight, I told Mitch it was time we pushed off. I wanted to have the boat back in the slip by 12:30 a.m. Giddy and care free, we undocked and started the return trip.

About three quarters of the way back, dead center in the middle of the lake, as far from shore as possible, it happened, chunk-chunk-chunk. We were out of gas. Holy shyte! I didn't check the gas gauge before we left. Feckin idiot!

For the next hour, I tried vainly to attract the attention of any boat still on the water while we aimlessly floated in the middle of the lake. There I stand on the captain's chair, waving the emergency flashlights we had on board. As each minute passed, we all got colder and the girls were starting to get really concerned. As the Captain (yeah right), I tried to keep everyone looking on the positive side, knowing full well that a night sleeping on board was a serious proposition and the consequences in the morning with my folks would be like "Dead Man Walking."

At 1:30 a.m. a huge cabin cruiser approached, and they saw we were in trouble. They had large running lights and a massive spotlight that they pointed at us. By now we were all screaming and yelling and the cruiser pulled up close. From the darkness of the captain's seat were words I will never forget, "Tommy, is that you?"

It was our former neighbors, the Stiegmeyer's, who had hit it big with a telecommunications company, moved to a mansion on the lake and had this spiffy new forty-five-foot cabin cruiser. I stammered, "Yes, it is. We ran out of gas over an hour ago. Would you either have some gas or be able to tow us closer to shore?" To their credit, the Stiegmeyer's could not have been nicer and towed us back to the Marina. We said thank you a hundred times, closed up the boat and got everybody home. In the morning, I was up early, back to the boat with gas, cleaning up any debris we missed and hoping beyond hope that my folks wouldn't learn of my escapade.

One day - nothing. Two days - nothing. A week - nothing. A month - nothing. Maybe the gods were going to let me slip by on this one.

Three months later my mom came home from SuperValu having procured groceries, etc. At this point, several months on I have almost forgotten about the boating debacle, at which point my mom looked at me with a twinkle in her eye and a little smirk. "You'll never guess who I saw at the grocery store?" she said. I asked who as I carried the groceries from the garage. "Mrs. Stiegmeyer, she told me all about you out on the boat with two girls and another guy, stranded in the middle of the lake, out of gas. I was just curious, but whose boat were you in?" Various methods for execution came to mind, with my father well versed in them all. The gig was up, I spilled the beans to my mom and she took it all in. When I had fessed up to it all, she looked at me and said, "In a few weeks you start college, if I tell your dad about this we are all going to have a crappy few weeks. So, just this once, this one is between us. If you do it again, I won't tell your dad, I'll kill you myself!"

## Growing Up Homophobic (1970's – 1990's)

I may have escaped growing up a racist but there is no doubt I grew up homophobic.

"Fag, Faggot, Queer, Homo, Pillow-biter, Gay, Cocksucker, Pinko, Lesbo, Dyke, Muff Diver, Queen...." Not pretty words, but they were the words that were used at the time with reckless abandon. Culturally, socially, morally, they represented the fear that "normies" felt for those who were different "us." I am not proud to say it but I did use many of these words in the late 70's and early 80's. They were part of the daily vernacular, part of humor; they were viewed as being okay, permissible because the alternative was "scary." Did I dislike or hate gay people at the time, of course not. Those of my friends who were gay were safely ensconced in a protective bubble at the time, they weren't: a) ready to come out yet; or, b) prepared for the inevitable ridicule they would have to endure when they did.

It would be in the last few years of high school and college that people I knew would start coming out about their sexuality. I didn't care. They were my friends. I just want you to be happy. If that is what floats your boat, knock yourself out. In high school, we knew which of the priests were gay. In college I lived next to a seminary and there wasn't a question of who was gay. It was more of a question of who, if anyone, is straight? My friend's sister came out as lesbian early on. She was strong, beautiful and could handle it without discernible stress. I worried more about my friend Brett. How would he handle the inevitable whispering about his sister? I am happy to report he has handled it well. I saw him a few years back and the love in his family thirty years ago is as vibrant and alive today. His sister is now a grandmother with her partner of twenty-five plus years.

In the interest of full disclosure, I will tell you about my last "active use" of homophobic humor which went shamefully, horribly wrong. It was about a decade ago, and I was in Chicago for some family matter or a Cubs game. An old high school buddy, Pete, was living downtown and said I could crash on his couch for the two nights I would be in town. Damn nice of him and I took him up on it. At the appointed time in the evening we met at a local pub a few blocks from his place, went in and had a few drinks and started telling stories from the interlude since we last saw each other. I ended up telling him about my trip to Ireland, about a joke I heard about God being Gay and screwing Charlie Murphy in Heaven until he was good and dead. Pete's face was ashen, "Hick, I'm gay." I look around the bar, my shame and humiliation written on my face, not a woman to be seen. This was a gay bar, and I just insulted my friend, my host and people who have done nothing wrong other than be who they are. Yes, I still feel shitty about it today. No, I no longer use homophobic language or off the cuff jokes.

It's not okay.

Sorry, Pete.

# ACT III

## The College Years (1983-87)

College of St. Thomas (now University of St. Thomas - St. Paul, MN). Degree conferred - Bachelor of Arts. Field of Study - International Studies: European History and German and the American University - US Foreign Policy Semester Program - Fall 1986

### The College of St. Thomas
### (and busting my arse to pay for it!)

I had applied to five schools: Notre Dame (long shot but every Irish Catholic kid's dream and where my heart was set); St. Thomas; St. John's; Marquette University; and Regis University in Denver. I was accepted to all but Notre Dame, which at the time hurt like hell but I would later be glad about it. I'd have flunked out of there in my first semester. Now the deal with my parents was that they paid tuition which was about fifty percent of the whole bill. I had to pay room and board, books, beer money, gas, etc. Looking back, in 1983, I had to earn about six thousand dollars to cover my half. I don't know how I did it.

In school, I worked way too damn much. It definitely affected my grades. Each summer I worked for a lawn care company called Total Lawn Care "Put a little TLC into your property" (I would ultimately own TLC with a partner). TLC had seventy plus high-end accounts, ten plus employees and simply way too much for a full-time college student to juggle. During the school year, I worked various jobs: washing dishes with "special" people from a nearby group home which meant I had one free meal a day to stuff myself, parking cars at high-end clubs around the Twin Cities for Class A Valet (I parked Prince's purple MG once), liquor stores, (can you say discounts?!) plus any other odd job that blew my way. My family kind of pressured me into St. Thomas for economic reasons, as my dad had a major downshift in employment and income while Mom was back to teaching full-time to make ends meet. No whining, I ponied up and upheld my half of the bargain.

### Academics and my Natural Aptitude for Language

Senior year of high school, just like everybody else, I took the SAT's. My verbal skills were off the charts, my math skills were below the charts. I had always read vociferously and my vocabulary was immense. Math and science were simply a trip to the dentist chair for me. With this as my reality, it is no wonder I ended up in History and Languages. Don't doubt me, I know I am damn smart, smart enough to know that I could coast in school, work my arse off, and have a damn good time when I wasn't doing the first two. Many nights while others were in the library or dorms studying, I was at the bar with friends like Vince Keady, studying, playing pool as we consumed pitchers of malted libations ... sure beat the library.

### Girls and Relationships

After having had a significant relationship in high school as well as some relationships that were far from significant, I went into college with one simple mantra: I want to have fun and I don't want to have to be answerable to anyone in a close relationship. Best damn thing I ever decided. The more

I didn't pursue girls, the more I was pursued. In a short-time, I had gone from the seeker to the sought, why didn't anyone ever tell me it worked this way?! Now there would be some relationships over the four years but each time I never made any commitment beyond having fun today, being honest and upfront in the process, if that's not working for you, feel free to move on. As an example, I had a relationship with an amazing Italian girl Junior year; she drank Scotch, was brilliant, witty, had an incredible body and our private times were simply awe inspiring. After a few months she looked at me and said, "Tom, I need you to need me more, for longer then today and I know you can't do that at this point." Honest, sincere, spot-on, we remained great friends throughout school. In retrospect, Wow, what a body, what a time, what a girl!

## Front Row Seats to the Carnival

Now almost anyone who has ever attended college has been involved in and done absolutely crazy, insane stupid things they would not repeat today. I count myself among that legion so I shall not bore you with countless stories of drunken debauchery, I shall merely give you a few examples to share my humanity with you.

## Day One and 4th Floor Ireland Hall

"Oh God, please don't let me hurl in the next fifty minutes in Dad's new car!" was my mantra of the moment as the sweat on my forehead and back was pouring out of me. In the backseat of my dad's new Buick LaSabre, I sat hungover to the beejessus' belt from having "a few" the night before at the Boneshaker with friends who were headed all over the country to begin new lives away from the nest. My Mother, who had greeted me at the door at 2 a.m. was so angry, that she wouldn't even talk or look at me in the morning. Per usual,

Dad had no clue of the previous night's events. He slept like a rock.

Two hours later, all my possessions were deposited into 413 Ireland Hall. No elevator, just a free stair climber. My parents headed back across St. Paul through Minneapolis and onto the Western Suburbs where they no longer had any boys at home for the first time in twenty-three years (sorry, Mom).

The days and nights on the 4th floor of Ireland Hall were filled with insanity. We tried to stuff 111 students into Happ and Schu's room on 11/11 at 11:11:11p.m., (aka Bones!). There were shower races with large white males stripping as they sprinted to the shower, lather up, rinse and race back to the room (Koenen slipping on the wet, sudsy floor, all two hundred thirty pounds of him sliding buck naked down the marble hallway). Finally, my favorite, the night Schafer aka Shaft, came home wasted again during finals and blasted Zeppelin while stripping down to his bikini briefs. Enough is enough, I led the charge and we tied Shaft up, carried him into the Quad putting him down in front of Dowling Hall, the nearby girls' dorm. We then setoff some old fireworks left over from the summer and ran like hell. It was a beautiful sight as the girls enjoyed the show from their rooms, the coconspirators hid in our rooms and campus security tried to figure out what the hell had just happened. It would take Shaft about seven years to graduate but graduate he did!

## Poker with the Boys (1983-1985)

Freshman year of college, I agreed to be a volunteer in the community nearby campus. Out of the many positions available, the perfect fit for me was to play poker once a week, 3 to 5 p.m. at a local nursing home. I signed on the bottom-line, and I was the dealer to a group of four to six men, penny poker. To top it off the local brewery, Stroh's, donated a case of beer each month for our game. The nursing home provided us with pretzels, nuts or other similar snacks each week. I went in with the idea that I am going to help these guys have some fun, play some cards, and in return I would feel good about volunteering.

To set the mood, let me tell you a bit about the room. It was a little kitchen/break-room: a fridge, sink, kind of ugly grey with massive overhead florescent lighting. It was very sterile, like a hospital space, easy to clean and industrial.

The first player was Fred, a bigger man, black suspenders, collared shirt, sharper than heck. Fred's wife had passed away and here he was, alone but one hell of a good poker player. Fred had been in auto service management his whole life, kids grown, and then he ended up here. It was tough for him to be in the home, yet he looked forward to poker every week, the highlight of his week and soon to be mine.

Next was Ed, post-stroke, very hard for him to talk but as smart as a whip. He was well-dressed and had been a very successful sales man. It was so obvious that he had pride and was always doing his absolute best to present himself well. He had never married and was one hundred percent alone in the world. Ed didn't care if he won or lost. He just liked having something to do and to get ready for.

For Carl, everything upstairs worked, but sadly the body was falling apart. I don't know exactly what he had, perhaps a stroke, but he could speak only in a raspy whisper with his head hung down towards the right-side of his chest. Carl drooled frequently and most days had to have a nurse assist him to play. As challenged as he was physically, it was so very obvious he was ecstatic to be included at the table.

Herb, gotta admit that Herb was really dull. He was a former accountant, but opinionated and an aggressive gambler, even in penny poker. His wife had died of cancer. It seemed like his kids didn't like him much, so for the most part he was on his own. Herb was the guy who would be the most upset if poker was canceled.

Naturally, there were many other players who would come and go in my two plus years of dealing.

It is impossible to understand what a poker game means unless you have had the camaraderie, excitement and continuity of playing cards with true friends. Every one of those guys became my dear friend. I could tell how they felt, I could see when they were ailing, but most importantly, we laughed, we drank our beer, they told stories of their lives, we ate our snacks and in the end, we become important to each other.

Every week, I looked forward to the card game, to being with my friends who taught me so much - I was damn lucky, not them. At the end of my service, I was recognized by the Governor of Minnesota as one of many volunteers of the year, I didn't attend the celebration banquet but I did get the signed certificate. Most importantly, by giving of myself - I got a tenfold return.

### Next on SportsCenter ... (Spring 1985)

In 1985, Bobby Knight, the head coach of the Indiana University basketball team infamously got angry with a referee after receiving a technical foul, Knight then walked over to his bench, picked up a chair and hurled it across the court. Everyone saw it. Everyone laughed. Good old Bobby got fined and suspended for some games then life rolled on per usual.

A few months later, my college, the College of St. Thomas had their usual Spring Games, zany fun events that made everybody gather, laugh, get outside and blow off some much-needed steam after another long Minnesota winter. 1985 wasn't to be an exception, the games would go on and there would be a new event, "The Bobby Knight Chair Toss" out on the main Quad. It was a contest to see who could throw a plastic chair the farthest after receiving a faux technical foul from a dear friend of mine, Vince Keady, dressed up in a zebra shirt with a whistle. The local TV networks caught wind of it and were on hand to record some of the happenings for the evening news.

I know what your thinking - this is setting right up in

my wheelhouse, you are not wrong! Now the initial competitors were simply hearing the whistle, picking up the chair and hucking it, no drama involved. One massive football lineman threw the chair a country mile. Gonna be hard to beat that toss. Coach Hickey's turn, I sit in the chair, Vince T's me up and I go absolutely ballistic. I am standing nose to nose with him, telling him "that was the worst call ever made, that his Mother called and she agrees with me, his children have changed their names, etc." I am beet red and Vince is playing right along, the crowd is howling and the news crews are lapping it up. Over to the chair I madly stomp, pick the bastard up, twirl around 2-3 times and with all my might I fling it with gusto damn you bet. Down she clanks down yonder, I win 2nd place in the competition and several free malted libations on my friends down at Tiffany's, the local watering hole.

That evening, my dad calls me, "Did you see the news tonight?!" he asks in a chuckling sort of way. "By God you were on the news! There I am having a drink and they show you yelling at some Ref, then stomping to the chair and heaving it for all you were worth." He really got a kick out of it - it made me happy he got a kick out of it. So at 10 p.m. my roommates and I watch the local news and sure enough, there I am, beet red in all my glory. But we are not done yet. My buddy calls me into the living room for the midnight ESPN SportsCenter which leads into a commercial break with "Next on SportsCenter, the College of St. Thomas had a Bobby Knight Chair Toss today, you've got to see this." Yea, you got it, there I am one last time, ESPN had grabbed the local coverage and in 10 hours I had gone national. Worth a good chuckle in the midst of Academia.

### The Great Bean Off

When a real blizzard is inbound in Minnesota, you know it. Everything will be closed and down for a day or two. Such was the monster bearing down on the Cities my junior year. I lived in a massive old three-story Victorian that my friend and roommate Dave Olson owned. Knowing what was coming, we did the logical thing - let's have a party! Down to the cellar we went, retrieving empty cases of returnable beer bottles and kegs. As the roads were now impassable, we loaded everything onto two kids' orange plastic sleds and headed off to Marshall Liquors. We had something like $113 in cash from returnables, which we used to procure a sixteen-gallon keg of "Schlitz Malt Liquor - The Bull" plus as much hard liquor as we could afford. Meanwhile back on the ranch, the food team had decided to use two #10 cans of "appropriated" baked beans from the college food service as a base for our meal. They would supplement the pot with more cans of Boston Baked Beans and four dozen chopped up hot dogs. Truly, a meal fit for royalty, I think.

Word quickly spread, that the "Great Bean Off" was on. Adventurous and hearty fools alike donned parkas, snow pants, boots, goggles and whatever they could carry and headed towards 1863 Iglehart Ave, beckoned by a sumptuous feast, libations and hearty fellowship. Late in the night a game of underwear "hide and seek" broke out. Three floors plus the cellar, no lights on anywhere and the seeker(s) were armed with flashlights. I know I sure hoped that Tessa Davenport, a Goddess in bra and panties was in the closet in lieu of some three-hundred-pound meathead. Anyways, come the morning, something unknown to mankind awaited the thirty plus campers on the estate. The stench, the odor, the air was not human, not of this Earth, not something that is even possible to describe to the lay person. This was thirty sphincters, male and female, firing out in unison a medley of beans, hot dogs and "The Bull" Schlitz Malt Liquor. The blizzard raged outside with -10 on the thermometer and winds gusting up to 50 mph. No one cared. Every window in the structure was opened wide, candles were lit, people improvised bank robber masks and many of the survivors fled into the streets to avoid further carnage. Such was the first and last ever, "Bean Off" that I participated in.

## Eroticism v. Pornography (Spring 1986)

Going into spring semester of 1986, I needed one more religion course to meet my religious graduation requirements. Since most of the religion classes at St. Thomas were about as exciting as paint drying (Catholic ideology, snore, dogma, snore, etc), I was not content with the offerings and found that St. Kate's, the all-girls school about two miles away offered a course on "Human Sexuality" that would fulfill me needed religion requirement. Think about it: me, an all-girls school and the class is human sexuality. Where the hell do I sign up?!

The class was big and very popular with about eighty-five students total, twenty five of them from St. Thomas and the balance from St. Kate's. The course was taught by two extremely liberal nuns, no habits, no penguin costumes, just civilian clothes and a sincere open mindedness about sexuality, exploration, discovery and how it all correlates to human interactions within the framework of Theology and Religion. For me, this was like taking batting practice where every pitch is lobbed in and I hit them all for a home run. I remember at one point I had some questions about a recent exam, concerned that I was being too liberal with my views for the professors. I introduced myself to Sister Clara as they did not know our names with our faces, too many students. Sister Clara looked at my paper, smiled and said, "Are you Tom Hickey?" Before I could answer, she added, "We love your work, very refreshing and very honest." A bit red in the face, I said thank you and asked my questions.

Forty percent of our grade was to be a research project on human sexuality. Before starting your project you had to get approval from the professors. With much trepidation, I approached Sister Clara and Sister Mary, "Would it be okay if I did my paper on Eroticism versus Pornography?" The nuns gave me the green light. Now I was on the hook for intelligently defining the difference between the two. Careful what you wish for Tommy Boy.

In being forthright, I have always loved what I consider "Eroticism" tasteful displays of the human body of a sexual nature that may arouse sexual feelings to the beholder but are not perceived as "offensive" by a reasonable general public. I have always disdained what I consider to be "Pornography" aggressive, graphic displays of the sexual act, sadomasochism, bondage, etc. To delineate the two was going to be quite the challenge, especially given as to how it pertains to religion. How do you humans glorify the Creator, should there be One, through sexuality?

My paper was about thirty-five pages long, which I shan't bore you with all the details of. Here is some of what research I did do. I bought magazines: soft-core, hard-core, downright disgusting. I went to art museums throughout the Twin Cities and viewed their art, some simple, some most disturbing. I bought and read a Harlequin romance, then I bought a Penthouse and read the Forum section. Lastly, I went to two XXX porn movie houses: one in St. Paul for heterosexuals; and, a homosexual movie house in Minneapolis. Extremely sticky floors grabbed your shoes, making that thwunking noise with each step, as I reluctantly creeped to my seat. Seats I didn't want to touch, (I sat on my jacket) men sitting solo usually with large coats on, at the Minneapolis theater, men in groups of two to five. As I watched the films I felt revulsion, zero arousal and kept constantly waiting for the forty-five minutes I allocated to each theater experience to end so that I could get the hell out of there. I also positioned myself in the back of the theaters with a wall behind me so that I didn't have any unwanted guests. After both experiences, I went back to my house, took a long shower, trying to forget what I had just seen but cognizant that I had to document it all in writing.

In addition to academic research, I poured all of my feelings and thoughts into my paper. After turning it in, I was less concerned with my grade as opposed to being branded a complete pervert. Sister Clara and Sister Mary loved my paper and I got the only A+ in the class. In fact, the nuns asked if I would mind reading excerpts of it to the class. Tepidly, I said yes and recounted my experiences, feelings and thoughts to my classmates. To my great surprise, it was well received by my peers and lead to very interesting discussions with wide ranging views. I even had several students ask for copies of my paper.

Finally, the difference between Eroticism versus Pornography that I found is the finest of lines - one that must respect the beholder but also that values society, especially in regards to protecting children. In this beholder's eyes, standing before "*The David*" by Michelangelo in Florence, Italy is viewing erotic art. It is something that may or may not be stimulating yet is inherently beautiful, thus glorifying any divine being that may exist. Whereas three people engaged in aggressive sexual acts with the intent to purely stimulate a sexual response regardless of depravity and perversion is my definition of Pornography. I am glad that I don't have to argue this one in front of the nine Justices dressed in black in Washington DC who just know pornography when they see it.

## One Happy Boy Toy (Fall 1986)

Rose Gillian Ashworth is a name that will stick with me until my final exhale. Rose was a full-time student at American University in Washington, DC, where I was studying US Foreign Policy for the fall semester. As fate would have it, Rose and I met at the campus grille. How best to describe Rose? From Knoxville, TN, she was a stunning blonde from old money who dressed, smelled and smiled like a million dollars. Rose wore only the finest clothes, her body was absolutely perfect, slight with medium size perky breasts, a smile worth going to war for and an infectious personality that drew people to her like bees to a flower. She had a composure and confidence that was well beyond her years, derived from her knowing what exactly she wanted and how to best go about getting it, a very rare quality. Just being near her was a heavenly treat.

With my lunch tray in hand, I took a slice of pizza, a side salad and a Coke to the only open table in the student grille. Ms. Rose and her friend Ginger strode up and asked if they could sit at the two open seats at the table. Incredulous at my luck, I quickly obliged. For the next hour I became enamored with these young Southern ladies and their stories. I shared my own saga, which they found entertaining, especially the stories of Minnesota winters, frigid cold and mountains of snow. As time passed, to my amazement Rose and I began to make an intimate connection, smiles, laughs and glances full of queries. Ginger must have sensed this was leading somewhere as she excused herself to go study or some excuse like that after about thirty minutes. Rose and I chatted merrily on, giggled and at one point she reached out and put her hand on top of mine. Thank you, I am happy now.

Before leaving, Rose invited me to a party the next night, Friday, at a house just off campus. Being no dolt, I gladly accepted, still not believing this was happening to the gregarious, stout Irishman of the great Midwest.

The party was fun and the bonding with Rose continued. I did well at being accepted by the diverse, wealthy guests primarily from the Eastern seaboard and South as I was welcomed as a part of the reverie while consuming my share of malted libations. The party itself was at a super wealthy, classic old house. There were maybe thirty people on hand, a roaring fire in a massive brick fireplace, expensive oriental rugs on the hardwood floor, comfortable yet authentic antique furniture and a luxuriousness that bespoke of old East Coast tradition and money. Afterwards I walked Rose back to her dorm, I gave her a peck on the cheek and I made a date for Sunday afternoon: sandwiches at Dupont Circle and a walk-in a nearby park.

Our park bench meal was simple, peasant-like but joyous, two young people enamored of each other, quick to laugh and in Rose's case, beaming with beauty and grace that was visible to all in her vicinity. With Autumn unfolding all around us, we kissed in the park for several minutes. Rose was the best damn kisser I ever happened upon. She smelled heavenly: shampoo, soap, and perfume. Rose was an olfactory smorgasbord. Even her lip gloss tasted exquisite, a slight hint of peach, soft and supple. Damn it Tommy, just roll with this, don't think!

Two days later, I was studying in my room and my roommates were downtown working at their internships on Capitol Hill when there was a light knock upon my door. Opening the door, there stood Rose in a plaid wool skirt, silk white shirt, red wool P-coat, pearls on her neck and pearl earrings. She was so stunning that I was speechless, which was fine because I didn't get to speak. Rose stepped forward, and we melted into one. How to describe the rest of that evening and yet remain a gentleman? We found the bed five feet into the room, the campus night lights streaming through the window. My spartan, ugly dorm room just became instantly beautiful by just adding one Rose. Our passionate embrace grew and garments were slowly removed or parted. Satin lace bottoms, an exquisite lace brassiere, a wool skirt lifted, my lower body bereft of clothing. The entire evening was purely poetic, two young bodies united in ecstasy, sensations indescribably culminating in that moment, that moment of utter bliss.

Afterwards, we lay in each other's arms, content, happy, giggling, and the only two people on Earth that were this contented. Rose looked at me and in all sincerity said, "You are going to be my boy toy for the next three months." I promptly agreed that whatever she wanted from me, she would have it. Gratefully, Rose was true to her word, and I would be her toy for the rest of semester. We did keep in touch after I left DC, and we even hooked up a few times in the coming year. In the end, Rose returned to Knoxville where she fulfilled her destiny, marrying some guy who also had gobs of money, a family to create, raise and hopefully the memory of her college boy toy once in a while.

### The day everything changed (October 1, 1986)

It had been a cool and crisp Autumn evening in the Washington D.C. area. I had taken Rose down to Dupont Circle to get a couple sandwiches for dinner and to get off campus for a while. Upon our return to the American University campus, we went our separate ways; time to study for a bit and perhaps hit the bar later for a few libations, games and socializing. Strange how our lives can change and we just never even see it coming.

As I entered my dorm room, my roommate Doug was there with a very uncomfortable, dire look on his face. "You are supposed to call your Dad right away" was the message he delivered with a pained expression. Back in those pre-cell-phone days, our entire floor shared one coin-operated phone. I headed into the little, dark blue cinderblock phone room, closed the door and dropped in enough quarters to talk with my dad for several minutes. It wouldn't take that long.

On the first ring he answered, this just ain't right my brain screamed, what is going on?!

"I don't know how to tell you this other than, your mother is dead," my father said.

Suddenly, I was against the blue cinderblock wall trying to process what I had just heard and not collapse with the whole building.

"Your Mother was on her way to a women's church group to deliver a talk when she was hit by another car on Interstate 494. She was killed instantly and did not suffer."

At this point my dad started to break down and lose his grip on things. I was the last of the family he had to tell. Now that he had completed delivering the news that his wife, partner, lover and soulmate of thirty-one years was dead, the complete devastation set in.

I mumbled something about that I would get home the next day somehow and we hung up.

Across the hall from the phone room was Karen and Shelly's room, two caring, warm girls from Minnesota as well. Without knocking, I entered their room, fell to the ground and began wailing and screaming at the top of my lungs. My mother had been the glue in my life and in our family and just like that, she was gone. "My mom is dead" I kept shrieking over and over as my hysteria turned into shock. Shelly and Karen were at a loss as to what was wrong with me but they were kind and compassionate, getting down on the floor with me, holding me and slowly getting the story out of me as I rocked back and forth in a fetal position on my knees. A friend, Cleighton, tried to help by giving me a pull of Vodka from a bottle he had. I promptly spewed the Vodka across the room, so much for that remedy.

The rest of the night centered on booking flights in the morning back to Minneapolis, packing what I would need, talking with a few people and worrying all night long about getting home ASAP. To attempt to be comfortable and get through the night, I spent the night with Rose in her room. There was no sex of any kind, but I have never been as appreciative to have the comfort of a woman's breast than that night.

### Home to a Non-home (October 2, 1986)

In the a.m., I caught a bereavement flight out of Dulles headed towards Minneapolis - St. Paul. Upon landing I found waiting for me was about twenty of the saddest, most sullen, wonderful college friends I could hope for. They had heard about my mom's death and stayed up all night telling stories about her, talking and having a libation or two in her memory. Hugs and tears abounded, I swear they were as tired as I was as we wound through the airport. I can't recall everyone who was there that morning but it was the best greeting committee a guy could ask for given the circumstances.

A couple guys drove me out to my house, and we had to pass the location where the accident had taken place the day before. It just didn't matter much to me, she was gone and she wasn't ever coming back. Once home, I entered the living room where my dad was a shell of his former self. I believe my brother Bill was there, as were a couple of close family friends. The complete lack of life and energy was palpable. Without sleep for thirty plus hours, I headed downstairs and got a few restless hours of sleep on our old couch.

That evening, I started to get a fuller picture of what had happened. Mom had been headed south on Interstate 494 and was to give a talk on "How wonderful it is to be alive" to her church group. As she traveled south on the interior lane of 494, heading north on 494 was Scott Johnson, who lived a block and a half from our house. Scott attempted to pass a semi and didn't clear the front before trying to merge in front of it, thus clipping the front of the semi and spinning out of control into the grass median. Interstate 494 has a large grass median dividing the two travel lanes that goes down in a V at the center of the median and then ramps back up to the other side, maybe thirty to forty yards wide. Scott's car was now sent spinning down the median at 65 mph and rocketing up the other side to literally fly into my mom's driver side window, killing her instantaneously. No pain, perhaps no awareness, probably just a glimpse of an airborne car and then fade to black.

The irony that it was a neighbor kid we played with was mind boggling. The fact that one to two seconds either way and the vehicle would have missed my mother was another trip. And finally, that my mom was on her way to give a talk about "How wonderful it is to be alive" was the ironic cherry on top. All that said, nothing made her less dead or eased the pain we were all feeling.

## The Rest of the Week:
## The Wake and Memorial Service

My mother was buried in the purple dress that she wore to my brother Bob's wedding. Looking upon her in the casket, it simply wasn't my mother. The bruising, contusions and facial bone damage were clearly visible. I was only capable of a brief look. After the wake, there was a memorial service in St. Therese Church. Since my mom was a seventh-grade teacher at the school, the students were understandably distraught and grieving. Thus, the Memorial Service with more than four hundred people had tears aplenty, with more than enough emotion and breakdowns to drive my father nuts. He simply wanted a traditional Irish Catholic mass and burial, not 7th graders blubbering at the microphone. I simply was numb, a non-factor in any planning or active participation. Everyone knew that I had my mom's 'cry at a sad cartoon' genes and asking me to speak at such a time was a disaster waiting in the wings.

### The Funeral

The next morning, the funeral mass took place at St. Therese with a full church before more than five hundred mourners. There really was nothing that stood out about it to me. It was a standard Catholic mass with prayers, incense, readings, etc. I do remember that when they went to wheel my mom out of the church, I completely lost it. This would end her time here amongst the living and confine her to a grassy hill cemetery where leaving isn't an option unless there is an exit to somewhere beyond.

### The Burial

As we headed to the cemetery, there was an overwhelming sense of fatigue. This whole debacle was coming to a close and it had to, no one had anything left to give. The rites and ceremony were quickly over, the setting and location was serene and peaceful. As if sensing that it was time to step back from this week, people offered their condolences and headed back to work, family, bars or whatever was their destination.

### Back to American University

By week's end, my dad was sinking into a sullen depression and was adamant that I get back to school, insisting that it was what my Mother would have wanted. Both my brothers were married by this time and had young children at home, thus the youngest son was to carry on alone, half a country way. Honestly, I didn't mind. Home was now gone, Dad had a lonely road to travel for a time and he sure didn't want any company at this point. So that weekend I boarded a plane, changed forever, and headed back East, to cope as best I could with the new paradigm of my existence.

### Tommy Tuba

Upon my return from Washington D.C. and American University, I had one semester to go to graduate however I needed to pick up one extra credit since one of my History credits in DC transferred back three credits instead of four. Hmmmm? What class could I take that would get me just one credit? Music, brilliant! After surveying all the possible instruments, the answer was unequivocal, the Tuba. I enrolled with high hopes of how much fun this was going to be at parties. Unfortunately for some poor musical Doctor at the University of Minnesota and a member of the Minnesota Orchestra, he would have listen to me burp and blat for six lessons, fifty minutes at a pop, making a complete mockery of his profession. My playing was a cross between fart noises and a goose being strangled. But I digress. Quickly, I became known campus-wide as Tommy Tuba and in high demand for public performances, let me retell the most infamous performance of the Tuba Man at the house on Grand Ave.

Up to the second floor of the house I went with tuba in tow and switched into my stage costume: aging white Chuck Taylor's, my Everlast red and white boxing shorts, no shirt, exposing my overly furry torso and a pair of mirror sunglasses. Two of my friends put on their sunglasses, white T-shirts and would serve as protection from the hungry horde that craved the Tuba man. Out on the stereo, Bon Jovi was blasting, I believe it was hedonism weekend on MTV. Out to the landing we stepped, my bodyguards positioning themselves on the stairs, Tommy Tuba looking down on the throng. To everyone's credit, all played their pretend roles well, the girls screamed and rushed the stairs, lighters lit up, guys quaffed beer and laughed at the spectacle, meanwhile the nut job Tuba man was really blowing his brass, squelching out notes to "Living on a Prayer" when it happened, something I'll never forget. I somehow released the spit valve on the Tuba by mistake and the stored saliva went straight down over the railing, landing in the TV vents and before you knew it, the TV literally, shorted, smoked, popped and blew up. Chaos ensued, security rushed me to safety, the owners of the house were pissed, they found an empty beer cup on the top of the TV and assumed someone had spilled it onto the TV in the mayhem. As a live performance artist, who was I to dispute their beliefs, especially since the pyrotechnics show was a great end to my performance!

# ACT IV

## The Kerouac Years

### Bullwinkle heads to Jackson Hole (May 1987)

The summer before my senior year I had planned to work with my best friend, Dave Lucke in Grand Teton National Park or Yellowstone National Park as seasonal workers. Dave ended up bailing, understandably since he was getting serious with his girlfriend at the time, Ellen, and would be headed into the Air Force and the Gulf War shortly thereafter. Thus, I tabled my plans to go West for one year.

In the spring of 1987, I came across my dream vehicle, an old brown mail jeep for $500. With its big moose decal on the door, I promptly dubbed it Bullwinkle. Enhancements were quickly made. Astroturf replaced the ugly carpet. Add a stellar stereo with cassette deck (state of art, baby) and a pair of new seat covers. There was no key for Bullwinkle, just a skinny fishing knife that you stuck into the ignition and turned to fire up the rocket. The knife was stored in the defrost vent in case a large walleye ever attacked. I took every penny of my graduation money, about $2,000, and bought the best camping gear I could: North Face tent, Feathered Friends down sleeping bag (still got it today), cook stove, pocket knives, fishing pole, etc. I had everything I needed to start my new post collegiate mountain man life.

As perfect as Bullwinkle was, it couldn't really go above fifty miles an hour. No worry, I was in no hurry. I drove state and county roads from Minnesota to Wyoming with the front doors rolled wide open, giving fellow travelers a full view of my chariot. Some men want a Porsche, I'll take a mail jeep. On the third day I rolled over Togwotee Pass, east of the Tetons and began my descent into Jackson Hole. Now if you have ever driven this route, I am sure you will concur that the views coming into the Grand Tetons are so stunning it seems surreal. I had made it, and I was going to stake my claim. Little did I know I'd still be here over thirty years later.

Jackson Hole in 1987 was unlike Jackson Hole today. There were shoulder seasons then when the town just dried up and went into hibernation. You could go to Shervin's Independent Oil to fill up and there would be two dented pickups being filled up by guys with cowboy hats, jeans, dirty boots and a belt buckle. One of them would be a ranch worker. The other would be a millionaire ranch owner. Distinguishing between the two was impossible. I spent the first few nights sleeping in a friend of a friend's basement before heading up into the Gros Ventre to camp for the next eight weeks. Within a few days, I had finagled a couple of jobs, morning shift at Jedidiah's House of Sourdough as a dishwasher/busboy. By night, I was a bouncer at the Shady Lady Bar at Snow King Resort.

The Shady Lady was the teeny bopper bar, the drinking age being eighteen back then which meant sixteen and seventeen-year-olds with good fake IDs could get in. It really was insane. If the band playing for the week was hot, the place would be packed to the rafters through Saturday. It was thus on two memorable nights that summer.

In the first instance, I was working the upstairs back door and keeping tabs on the balcony section to my right. The band is wailing, the crowd is dancing, jumping and loving every moment of it. Out of the corner of my right eye, I see this tall, skinny whacked out guy climb onto the table right in front of the balcony railing. As I head his way to get him down, he is dancing badly on the table top and flooop over the railing he goes, falling twenty plus feet to the main floor below. Down the stairs I haul arse. The bastard is lying on the top of a now collapsed table. Fortunately, he did not drop on anyone, just the table which was now in multiple pieces. It is thirty minutes to bar time, so I tell the band to wrap it up and for the crowd to head home. When the paramedics get there, he is still out cold and they wheel him out. The next day I would learn he was on PCP, dope, booze and God knows what else. Since he was so messed up, he landed like a wet noodle. He was fine other than some bumps and bruises.

The other classic night was when this drunk son-of-a-bitch was bothering a guy and his girlfriend at the bar. The girl was getting nervous about things and came over to alert me. The drunk guy (we will call him Johnny Rotten) was getting boisterous and threatening, so I called Hans over, another bouncer. We told the guy it was time to go. I grabbed his left arm and Hans grabbed his right arm, and we headed for the door. Now Johnny Rotten is far from done and Rotten yanks his right arm free from Hans in time to punch the boyfriend in the side of the head at the same time trying to spit on the girlfriend. Okay, I have seen enough, I put Rotten in a side headlock and the bartender, Eddie, jumps over the bar and with his right shand grabs Rotten's nuts. Hans, sorry to say, just wasn't much help. We are now hurtling towards the big swinging oak door that opens into the lobby of the resort. No time to open the door, I use Rotten's head to ram the door open. We all go spilling out into the lobby, me screaming for the front desk to call 911. The dude who got sucker punched came out and threw a couple of rights into Rotten's face and Eddie is back there holding onto Rotten's nut sack. I must say, Rotten didn't put up much of a fight with me bulldogging him and Eddie keeping the family jewels safe.

A few quick other things from that summer. There was a massive Summer Solstice party at a historic old dude ranch at an in-holding in Grand Teton National Park. The bonfire was at least thirty-five feet high. There was access to a full array of mind altering substances and gorgeous mountain women abounded. The party went for about 48 hours and once you were on site, there was no reason to go anywhere. For a while, I skip-peeled logs for Callum McCoy, a tough as nails, smart old Scot. I got paid 31 cents a linear foot, and it was by far the hardest work I have ever done. We dined at Dornan's Dutch Oven cookout every night. Later, we slept under the logs with a tarp in bad weather. Sunday night the whole town went out to the Stagecoach Bar where everybody got stinking drunk and danced. I used to go up to the top of Teton Pass with an old ranch-hand, Wally. We would put back some Rainier beer and discuss life before going down to try to get a dance or two with a pretty philly (back then Jackson was about a ratio of five to one guys, so getting lucky would have to be with small livestock). This was all the adventure I had dreamed and hoped for all my life.

### The Dead - Park City, Utah (August 1987)

Charlie was a bartender at the Silver Dollar Bar in the Wort Hotel, Jackson, WY. One fine summer evening, Charlie and I traveled down to Park City to see the Grateful Dead in a single act mountainside show. The day could not have been more glorious: warm, sunshine, mountains, mellow hippies and happy people a plenty. It was shaping up to be an epic evening.

Charlie was from Iowa, but he had lived in Jackson Hole for about five years. He was a Midwesterner who presented himself well, gave great customer service, and earned awesome tips. Charlie was also one of those guys who once you were friends, would walk through fire for you. In short, I was in a great place, with a great friend, and lined up for a magical evening.

Once parked in the open field lot, we consumed some shrooms, drank some beers, made some friends and watched as the drug vendors worked the lot. "Shrooms, tabs, joints" was their perpetual chant as they peddled their products.

Hard to believe that in America the police weren't out closing down these sales. There was an otherworldly feel to all that was going on.

As the chemicals we had ingested began to take effect, Charlie and I began the hike up the mountain to enter the performance area. The views were breathtaking, we could look to the setting sun in the West, green mountains alive via a yellowish-red sun, Charlie and I both pulled up short, looked at each other and commented how epic what we were seeing was. Unbeknownst to us, a dude looking like Moses strode up behind us, dressed in a burlap tunic, sandals, dreadlocks, baked blue eyes and a staph in his right hand. He looked at the sunset, turned his gaze us, and said, "God is happy, his children are coming home." Charlie and I looked at each other, incredulous, and realized that this event was far beyond us, real or imagined.

The next couple hours were perfect. The Dead mountainside with long drawn out melodies and hippies swaying like seaweed, and there was not a single, uptight person to be found. Maybe these counterculture folks had really figured something out. Anyway, the show would pass without event; a few beers, a gorgeous night, a plethora of stunning, lovely girls and Jerry and the boys playing away.

It was during the first encore that I started talking with some smart looking, tall guy, dressed in a white oxford. He was a chemist from MIT out traveling with the Dead for the summer. He offered me a tab of acid, one he had made in the lab. What the fuck I thought, this has been such an amazing evening, how could this hurt? I thanked him, popped it into my mouth and within a second realized, "Holy shit, how long is this gonna last?" I asked him that very question and he replied that I should sleep sometime around noon tomorrow, thirteen hours away. Holy shit!

As the Dead wrapped up, Charlie drifted away to somewhere, probably some bonfire where hippie women offered their comforts. I knew what was coming my way and knew I had to get into a safe harbor ASAP. I headed for the $400 tank of a station wagon I bought a few weeks earlier. Once bedded down in the back, sleeping bag and pillows arranged, I got as comfortable as I possibly could.

Within the hour, I was seeing the most spectacular meteor shower that had ever occurred in astronomical history. These stars were ripping across the entire sky, beautiful at first then becoming terrifying after that. Oh crap, the tab had kicked in and the trip had begun. Paralyzed with fear, I stayed huddled in the back of my wagon, watching the heavens for as long as I could.

About 3 a.m., I was crispy and had to do something, so like Lazarus, I arose. Nearby were some dudes sitting by a fire, strumming guitars, passing around a bottle of Jack and staring into the flames with uninterrupted intensity. I joined my fellow trippers and assumed the position. Some earth worn looking cowboy type handed me the whiskey bottle. He said it would help to cut the acid effects down. I would have drank battery acid to achieve that end.

Somewhere about 4:30 a.m. disaster struck. I had to shyte. Not just a minor urge, this was a need to be addressed immediately or experience the dire consequences. Lacking toilet paper, tripping off my rocker and being in the middle of a grass field parking lot, I set my sights on the 7-11 about a half mile back down the road. My quest was underway, all the while paranoid, nervous and withdrawn from all contact. Now I just needed to keep the turtle head in my pants from poking out.

Up ahead, intense, the garish lights of the 7-11 gleamed out. Parked in the parking lot were three squad cars, damn it, this wasn't going to be easy. Summoning up my altered state courage, I had to go in. Once inside, there was a long line of Dead refugees lined up for the shitter. No way could I wait through that line.

There was also one new wrinkle on the scene, my vision was impaired by the psychedelic drugs so that everything was now in cubes. Whatever I saw was broken into at least 100 cubes, like an insect's eyesight, this sucks! With cops standing by the door, it was time to implement plan B, procure some buttwipe and make my exit. I was able to locate the shelf with toilet paper on it, there was one 4 roll pack left on the shelf. I swept it up and held it tight to my chest like I had found the holy grail. Now to pay for this and try to get out of here without Johnny Law interfering. At the counter, the teller who was some Middle Eastern dude, rang up my sale. In addition to seeing the hundred cubed screens there was a new development, I could not speak. So, like a mute I slapped down $5 and headed for the door, not even waiting for the change.

I made it passed the boys in blue and once out of the store, I picked up speed and headed into the darkness towards a small stand of trees. The turtle was coming! Well, what happened in that small stand of trees was simply Homeric. I shall spare you the fecal details but it was as close to a religious experience as a person gets.

Sometime around 8 a.m., Charlie straggled back to the wagon, looking no better than me. Charlie had spent the night with a band of Deadheads and hooked up with some unshaven woman, Juniper or something like that. It was obvious that when Charlie had woken up next to Juniper, she had either: A) looked a lot better last night; or, B) had gotten ugly overnight.

So, we breakfasted at a Technicolor McDonald's (at least it was Technicolor to us), and we headed north for the four-hour drive to Jackson Hole and some much needed rest.

### A Eurail Pass, $20 a day, and Adventure Awaiting (Fall 1987)

Paris was just too damn expensive. Upon our arrival in Paris, we stopped at a small cafe, about $8 for a tiny coffee and a micro sweet bun, this was not working into our budget of $20-$25 a day. With this in mind later that day, Brian who had studied in Paris told us about a street vendor who for about $7 sold a big peppery sausage in a roll, topped off with a ton of French fries. That was enough food to keep us fueled for a full 24 hours. So, off we marched to the Metro in search of sustenance.

Just like Brian had predicted, there was the vendor in the student section of Paris and his product lived up to all the advertisements. The area was old, a bit worn but incredibly quaint. With our bellies now full, Brian mentioned that a few blocks away was the cemetery, *Pere Lachaise*, where Jim Morrison was buried. Mr. Mojo Risin' was in the neighborhood? Off we traipsed to pay our respects to Jim.

*Pere Lachaise* cemetery is massive, one hundred nineteen acres, about ten square blocks. It was unlike anything I had ever seen to that point, massive grave markers, tombstones, overgrown trees invading the plots, cobblestoned pathways winding through the graves, all you could see in every direction was tombstones and mausoleums. Some graves were so old that reading the inscriptions was impossible, the elements wearing down the stones over the centuries. It was eerie and comforting at the same time. These people were very good at being dead.

How to get to Jim's? Easy as pie, just follow the spray-painted signs on the massive monuments "To Jim - this way" Wow, these are some seriously dedicated Doors fans. Winding our way through the cemetery, we knew Jim was close, graffiti everywhere and the sounds of music wafting in the air. As we turned the final corner it was truly a sight to see. A bust of Jim with a joint stuffed in his mouth by a devotee atop the grave, multi-colored like it had been tie-dyed, about twelve hippies/groupies/vagrants and us all surrounding the grave. The smell of pot hung heavy in the air, wine bottles were being passed around freely. The guy playing the guitar had long hair and wore leather clothes that looked like he had been wearing them since Jim died. There were a few hippie chicks swaying to the music, singing occasionally, appearing to be advocates of free love. It is almost hard to believe but the three of us, despite having been on trains for days and certainly tarnished, were the cleanest ones at this daily tribute.

It was a surreal sight. We hung around for about forty-five minutes, paid our respects to Mr. Mojo Risin and drifted away from the fellow worshippers. We did see Chopin's and Edith Piaf's graves on our way out. Fortunately, our tour guide Brian knew of a cheap bar nearby and we quaffed a bottle or two of nice red wine in Jim's honor.

## Ninety minutes with Eve in Eden, Cannes (September 1987)

Our travels led us to the Mediterranean. And as much as one can be on the *Cote d'Azur*, it was a rough morning for the three Amigos after a late night. Brian was still pissed about our lost luggage. Dave was asleep or had wandered away. So, left to my own devices, I decided to head down to the beach for a swim. At twenty-two, I still looked good in surf shorts thanks to years of athletics and most importantly, youth.

A quick comment, what follows was simply a ninety-minute chance encounter: sweet, magical, beautiful and most importantly, innocent. It is a glorious memory for a man in his fifties to recall when the bones ache, the weather is bad, or I am just simply having a crappy day. Yet I digress, back to the story.

What a perfect day: the Mediterranean displaying numerous shades of teal and a high hot, massive sun above. Simply put, it was as good as it gets. I waded into the sea, relishing the chance to cleanse away the pollution of last night's revelry. In the distance I saw a white swim platform some ways out to sea. Perfect, a good swim will be just the thing to clear my head and loosen my tired muscles and frame. Away I went at a steady pace, reaching the platform in about fifteen minutes.

Once there, I laid out full, absorbing the sun's rays to dry off and was near to dropping off to sleep when someone else climbed onto the platform - Can't be real - just can't be real I kept thinking. There stood a nineteen-year-old Swedish bombshell sporting a hellacious tan, aquamarine blue eyes, mid-shoulder length blonde hair, a small, tailor made red bikini bottom. Her body was long and lean, toned and perfect, large breasts and nipples that would make any man wish to suckle. If I am dreaming, please dear Lord, don't wake me up.

Introductions ensued, her name was Kalli, on vacation from Sweden with her family, staying in some Villa overlooking Cannes. She was in-town for a few more days while I was headed to Italy tomorrow. Kalli was obviously from a very wealthy family, I obviously was not. How do you talk to Athena standing in front of you with folded arms supporting the most beautiful breasts pointed directly at you? Somehow, I was able to use the cool water to control my Irish Zeus.

For the next ninety minutes we talked, laughed, joked, and luxuriated in this glorious moment of karma. A game of diving tag ensued. The joy of being in her presence was immense. We bonded as much as two people from different worlds can in ninety minutes. When the time came to swim back ashore - me to the north - Kalli to the south, we hugged and I gave her a light peck on the cheek. Kalli was first to dive in. I watched her swim away then turned and dove back into my reality blessed with a lifetime memory.

Ms. Kalli - wherever you are today - Thank You!

## A Shooting in Roma (Fall 1987)

We were somewhere near the Spanish Stairs in Rome headed to catch a bus out of the city where we had a camp site reserved for the night. It was an ideal night, about 70 degrees, not a cloud in the sky, Rome was a damn expensive place but at least the weather was phenomenal. Down a sidewalk we strolled crossing an alley, when on our right-hand side there were popping noises echoing down the high stone walls of the alleyway. I quickly turned my head to see a man about twenty yards away, a blue oxford shirt, black pants, black hair with a pistol in his hand, arm held high at eye level, pulling the trigger as fast as possible. The gun was pointing down the slight incline of the avenue and what he was shooting at was out of my sight line.

Smoke rose from the muzzle after each shot. After his hand recoiled, the shooter recalibrated his aim, his body and head unmoving. People nearby him were crouching or scattering, arms above their heads. My eyes focused on a mother attempting to shield her child in a stroller on the other side of the avenue. "Go!" my brain said. I dropped my backpack and ran towards the shooter. Before I got halfway towards him, he glanced at me and ran back up the avenue away from where he had been firing. What the hell was I gonna do? Damned if I know but I sure as hell didn't like seeing the mother and kid anywhere near the shooting spree.

Once through the alley way I stopped, crouched and peeked both ways. Nobody hurt to the left. Whoever he was shooting at got away uninjured. Turning the other way, I did not see the shooter to the right. He must have been scared away by my bearish shuffle coupled with my intimidating lack of any weapon with which to threaten him other than my rugby-esque figure.

All of that in about five to ten seconds. Yet it is indelibly etched on my brain for a lifetime.

### Oktoberfest - Munich, Germany (October 1987)

The massive finale of the Eurail trip of 1987 was attending the Oktoberfest in Munich. Dave, Brian and I arrived in the first week of the fest. No accommodations, no plans, just a desire to drink great Bavarian beer with our best friends we had never met. All things considered, it was shaping up to be a beautiful experience.

Forgive me for starting with snippets of the fest. At night, post-fest; we slept in the train station, pulling out our sleeping bags, toiletries, and personal items out of the coin lockers. We then started to get as comfortable as was possible on the cement floor beneath our lockers. Thankfully, we were so inebriated that it wasn't a difficult challenge. At 6 a.m. we awoke to the calming tones of German Shepherds barking in our faces while their police handlers kept repeating, "*Raus, Raus, Stehen zie auf*" (Get up, Awake, Stand up). It was not a warm fuzzy wake up call. One day, Dave and I were so tired, we hopped on a train leaving Munich and slept for two to three hours, we then boarded the return train to Munich, again sleeping en route and went straight back to the Oktoberfest refreshed and ready for another go around.

Oktoberfest is three weeks long. Different nationalities attend during different weeks. In week one, the Aussies and the Kiwis attend, a raucous event if ever there was one. It is illegal to display either country's flag, sing national songs or sleep with women from the enemy (I made up the last one). Anyhoo, we are in a giant beer tent with three thousand plus of our best friends when some Aussie nut job inflates a balloon from a canister in his pocket, hoists the Aussie flag and runs across the tables. Bedlam ensues. Coasters, beers, paper and any other suitable projectile are being hurled at the offender. He is determined to elude the security for as long as he can, making it across several tabletops. After much mayhem, security tackles him and hauls him away. Order is quickly restored and revelers return to the task at hand: consumption of mass quantities of malted libations.

On our last night at the Oktoberfest, we were in the Lowenbrau tent, getting ready for another evening of drunken adventure. More than a hundred partakers are seated just at our table which is much like a giant picnic table with benches. Starting on the second or third stein, the anthem toast of the fest begins "*Ein Prosit, ein prosit, ein gemutlichsheit....*" Everyone stands to sing and clink steins. Standing next to us are some Polish guys, completely rinsed, and as we all go to clink steins, one of the drunk Poles slams his stein into mine, breaking my stein and sending the heavy glass bottom towards the table and my left index finger knuckle. Suddenly, the table turns red with my blood and there is a serious gash on the top of my left index knuckle.

From nowhere appears a beer Frau, a massive server who could carry a dozen beer steins at a time and still play left tackle for the Chicago Bears. She wraps my hand in a bar towel, promptly tucks it under her armpit, my hand resting on her massive bosom. Helga is now charging through the tent, bowling over potential tacklers to escort me towards the exit. As we emerge from the rear of the tent, a short trot ensues to the medical tent where I am promptly left to the care of a Munich MASH unit.

As I get my bearings, the scene around me is surreal. One dude got so drunk that he fell head first into the urinal, cracking open his forehead on the porcelain. Another lush got into a fight and took a stein to the back of the head. There are numerous sots in the MASH unit in various comatose stages. A cursory exam of my hand by the medical team determines that I warrant a free ride to the Munich hospital with several of my fellow revelers. Thus, about fifteen of us are loaded into a stripped bare meat wagon (I think it was so that they could hose out the vomit and urine easily) and off we went.

Since I was the closest to sober, I got to go first at the hospital. The doctor took a look at my finger and determined that: a) they would have to remove any glass they found under the skin; and, b) my tendon had been severed at least 70% and that if I wanted to use my index finger the rest of my life, they would have to do a microsurgery to sew it back together. Gratefully, the surgery went well, I was outfitted with a silver bowl thing for my hand to keep the finger bent and the tendon extended, wrapped in ace bandages and the doctor asked if I wanted pain killers or to return to the Oktoberfest to consume alternative liquid pain killers. I chose the latter.

Upon my return to the fest, Dave and Brian were absolutely hammered and singing, swaying and drinking with the

Pole who had cut my finger. Obviously, there were no hard feelings. I got in a few more steins before closing. A quick note: when I awoke in the morning, my hand hurt so fecking bad I thought I would hurl. A few Advil and a few beers and the world was right again.

## Le Havre to Rosslare:
## An Adventure at Sea (October 1987)

Dave and Brian were headed stateside: Dave to the Air Force, and Brian to a job with a family soon to follow. That left me on my own in Paris then headed to the northwest coastal town of Le Havre, France. From there, I would catch the ferry to Ireland in search of more adventure and hopefully employment in Cork as a security guard at a Jazz festival (or so I had been led to believe by a drunk Irishman I had met in a pub over a few pints).

I really liked Le Havre. It was a sleepy coastal town, nothing fancy, but gorgeous views of the sea. Right by the docks was a classic little cheap hotel. It was old, worn but as comfortable as any five star hotel for a vagabond like me. My room was on the third floor, small, Spartan, with views of the quays below, gulls circling everywhere and the immense sea off to the northwest. I unpacked, did my laundry, showered, a lovely experience and headed out for a square meal and a leisurely stroll about town. Within a few kilometers thanks to a "Let's Go Europe" recommendation, I was eating the most simple, handmade meal I ever had; fresh bread, cheeses, mussels and a fish that had rode in on a local fishing boat that morning, all exquisite. A stroll about town and I turned in for a heavenly night of slumber.

The next afternoon it was time to head to the Ferry for the voyage to Rosslare, Ireland, the weather was gorgeous, not a cloud in the sky, and not knowing what to expect, I thought it would stay that way - I'd soon learn. The ferry was not small. It looked like a medium size cruise ship with multiple decks, movie theater, bar, etc. For those travelers like me who had no berth, we were allowed to store our bags in the corner of the bar/viewing room, which would also serve as our sleeping quarters for the night. Basically, above the bow was a large room with windows looking out at the sea, a large open space and against the back wall, a long bar, not attractive, but very functional. It doesn't take much imagination to figure out what happened next, all evening long the bar grew in population with like-minded young idiots and maidens from all over the globe including Irish, English, French, Italians, Africans, Gringos like me, and many others. It was a veritable potpourri of thirsty mongrels. The Guinness and shots flowed while dancing pulsed until 2 a.m. which was bar time. By the time the bar closed, we were steaming south down the English Channel. I unrolled my sleeping bag in the middle of the bar/viewing deck in the midst of a hundred other "sailors" for a solid night's rest.

7 a.m. - What the hell? - Shyte, I feel like shyte - Is that puke I smell? – Oh, my head hurts - Wham, what the hell was that? - God, I just want to sleep. Sploosh, seems like up, down, then wham. Slowly I open one eye. Holy shyte! Massive waves are breaking over the bow - that feckin guy over there just puked in his sleeping bag, nasty. Down we go again. I could feel the heavy pressure of water slamming against the windows. Those damn waves are traveling ten feet over the bow and slamming onto the windows thirty feet away. Oh, God, Tom get up now before you puke in your bag too!

Like a punch drunk boxer, I arise but damn if my legs ain't working right. I hold onto a support pole in the middle of the room and try to take one-step. Useless as another wave hits the window. The boat dives downward along with me to the floor. My queasy stomach is really roiling from last night and this fun ride is not helping. Time to exit stage left, ASAP! On all fours, I crawl like G.I. Joe to the exit door and see the corridor that will get me to the exterior door then out to fresh air on the deck.

Pulling myself up there is a railing in the hallway which can support me for the forty feet to the exit. I'm gonna make it. Halfway down the corridor, suddenly a stateroom door swings open and a sweet sixty-five-year-old woman takes one step out of her room, looks at me and projectile vomits like Regan in the Exorcist onto the opposite corridor wall. That's it - I'm fecked! Grabbing my mouth and running as fast as I can to avoid her voluminous bile on the wall and floor, I burst through the door to the deck and promptly deposit my bodily contents into the English Channel for all to see, the Queen included - just remember I didn't vote for you!

The next eleven hours were spent on the top deck, outside, cold, wet until the sun came out about 3 p.m. Somebody said that a steward thought it was one of the worst transit crossings he had ever been on. By mid-afternoon I was nursing a few beers down with some of my new mates. There was only one thing I couldn't do. If I so much as set foot inside that damn boat, I was immediately seasick again. In the late afternoon, we crossed the Irish Sea under a blue sky, calm seas. About 7 p.m., we docked in Rosslare. I had survived to return to the land of my ancestors. Dennis Hickey had left here in 1861. Mom, I'm home!

### Three Days on the Dole (October 1987)

Despite the bowl on my hand from the Oktoberfest, I managed to get to Cork, Ireland where I had been promised a job working the Jazz festival. This is going to be sweet. I telephone the guy who promised me the job, no answer. I go to the site of the festival, no luck. "Well, this sucks," I say to myself.

To distract myself, I catch a Cork Dolphins Rugby Match, brilliant and I talk to the trainer about catching on with the Dolphins. He is most welcoming. Now I just need money, and I can make a go of it. Two days later, no job, no dude from the Oktoberfest. It's time to end this expedition with almost all currency gone. It's code red. I hitchhike back to

Dublin. I am there in two rides and about five-six hours.

With less than a hundred bucks to my name, I gotta buckle down. My return ticket to the States is from Amsterdam, so somehow, I have to get there. Once in Dublin, I head straight for the US Embassy, I need $200 for a flight to Amsterdam, that'll get me home. I phone my Uncle Ed, this request is way outside of his comfort zone, he freaks. Plan B, I call Joan, my father's 2nd wife who is a total sweetheart, she will handle it, and I know get it done (my dad had just had heart surgery in the last few days and was out of the loop, part of the reason I wanted to get home ASAP). So, $200 will be on the way and it will take up to seventy-two hours to get to the Embassy in Dublin.

With the help of "Let's Go Europe" I found the cheapest hostel in Dublin, about $20 a night. I paid for three nights, and headed up to my quarters which were well worn but very clean; certainly, a decent place to spend the next seventy-two hours. I then head to the grocer, where I procure: three cans of beans and one large round loaf of bread. Gonna have to milk this for three days.

Each morning I woke up, got dressed, and headed down to Trinity University where I would walk and read "Trinity" by Leon Uris. Often times I would sit in the sun against the library wall and grab some rays, reading, nodding off and simply glad to be there.

As 2 p.m. approached, I would sidle over to St. James Gate, home of the Guinness brewery and take the complimentary brewery tour. I wasn't so much interested in how they made the product, I was interested more in how the lovely drink tasted. That aside, I gave them forty-five minutes to educate me to get to the tasting room, cheese, crackers, fruits and an opportunity to quaff some draught of excellence. I would take the tour three days in a row. By day three I was on a first name basis with Eamon, the bartender who was kind enough to over serve me on a daily basis based on my deplorable economic condition.

In the evenings, I headed to my bunk at the hostel, got in my sleeping bag and read until my eyes sagged. A couple of sweet young lasses from Scotland took pity on my plight, and as they left they gave me their leftover food: sardines, tinned meat, tea and some bread - Thank you, Lassies!

## A Salty Tar (October 1987)

It was my final morning in Dublin, my ticket back to Amsterdam secured thanks to Grandma Joan. I had hours before my flight home and a few pounds in my pocket so I thought that the best use of my time would be to find the cheapest pub I could and have a few pints of Guinness. It was a grey, damp, cool morning, the kind that makes you glad to have a heavy Irish sweater.

Towards the sea I strolled, down to where the merchant and fishing fleets rolled in and out. Seagulls, thousands of them, were violently vying for fish scraps or any other available morsel. They dove in and out around the masts making the most raucous of noise. I had found where I was supposed to be.

Now, I really wish I could remember the name of the pub, but I'd be lying if I said I did. Suffice to say it was a monstrous wooden door, high vaulted ceilings, not much light and a competition between cigarette smoke and human/fish smells as to which stench dominated.

In the middle of three pub rooms, I found a barrel table with one chair and made myself at home, backpack and all. The Guinness was cold, the perfect elixir to a weary Yank going home. I opened up Trinity by Leon Uris and set to reading and imbibing.

It was about my third Guinness when I started to notice an elderly Gentlemen grunting and growling a few tables away. The wrinkled, thinned hair man was easily seventy years old, dressed in what I assume had to be his only white shirt, collars askance, an old Navy v-neck sweater, several days worth of stubble on his mug. The most disturbing aspect about him were his eyes. One could look at you while the other was watching the other side of the bar. Today, the one that could look at you was looking at me. Shyte!

Over the next ten minutes his grunts and groans became louder, his intent one-eyed stare focused on me. What did I do? I looked like any dirty, stinky backpacker, definitely not dressed as an American - didn't need that hassle. Finally, he tried to get up with a roar and rush me, thankfully his friend held him down.

Meanwhile, another compatriot of the Cyclops came over to me. He was a kind, worn out Irishman. He extended his hand to me and handed me a five-pound note. Speaking softly so only I could hear he said, "You remind my friend over there of someone he didn't like very much forty years ago. If I were you, I'd take that fiver and get a fresh pint somewhere else." Yes, sir - I didn't need to resolve a forty-year-old feud with some disturbed tar. I loaded up, thanked the man for the fiver and ambled out to find a new watering hole.

**Homeward Bound**

On the third day, my funds came in, and I was on my way to Amsterdam. Once in Schipol, the Amsterdam airport, the wheels came off. I didn't have a reserved seat with TWA so I was on standby. Flight after flight, no open seat. There I was sleeping under chairs to have darkness, some cover and after 30 hours in survival mode, a kind TWA booking agent took mercy on me and bumped me up to first class, the only open seat possible.

My $200 ticket was now letting me fly first class, a $1200 seat. I strolled towards my recliner (it really wasn't a seat), and I knew I smelled like a Billy goat. Off to the bathroom I trotted attempting to clean up as best I could and determine which of my four T-shirts stunk the least, it was a close call. The man in the seat next to me was a businessman from

Houston. He was awesome, loved my story and had no issues with the stinky guy next to him. I had two glasses of champagne, the beef dinner and reluctantly, yet promptly fell asleep in my chaise longer, missing out on seven hours of first class treatment. A fitting end to my first trip abroad.

## Archie and the Road Show
## (late October 1987 to January 1988)

Winging my way back to the States from Amsterdam to New York to Minneapolis, I had a whopping zero dollars in my pocket. I didn't have a quarter to make a phone call for somebody to come pick me up. Ah, it will work out. It always does and lucky for me, KLM had complimentary drinks in flight. Why yes, I think I will have another fresh Heineken. About halfway to Minneapolis from New York, I heard this guy a few rows ahead of me loudly talking in a heavy East Coast accent about going to sell World Series souvenirs in the Twin Cities, as the Twins were in the series for the first time in twenty-two years. This guy was loud, fat, obnoxious and from Jersey. He made his living going around the country selling souvenirs and had set his eyes on the Minneapolis - St. Paul metropolitan area. On a trip to the header, I introduced myself and told him that I had grown up in the Twin Cities. Archie extended his corpulent hand, we shook, and I was yet again gainfully employed (with the promise of twenty-five percent of whatever I sold in cash). He even gave me a twenty spot to get me home so that I would be ready to work in a few days when the stock arrived from his nefarious Jersey warehouse.

How to explain Archie? Have you ever seen those blow-up sumo suits? That was Archie. Two feet, a head encased in gristle, and easy a four-hundred-pound round mound in the middle. He was the kind of fat where he had to rest his hands just under his boobs. I don't know how the hell the guy wiped his arse, nor do I want to know. Archie's business was to buy some legitimate authorized souvenirs so the tables looked legit and then he bought good looking knockoffs from some warehouse/printer in Jersey. Everything was cash with Archie's wallet being a long white tube sock. The most cash I ever saw him have was $110,000.00, all in bills in a huge wad and crammed in a tube sock. Archie's ability to eat was simply mind-blowing. He could easily devour two full racks of baby back ribs or an entire deep-dish pizza. He would prop himself up on his hotel bed, his gut as a table and eat until he passed out. He was Monty Python's Mr. Cresole come to life. But I digress.

Two days after returning home, I set up a stand in Minnetonka at the corner of Highway 7 and Williston. I paid the station owner $50 a day. The first day I cleared $400 cash. Say again, $1600 gross sales with $400 for Tommy Boy. Within a week I was out of debt from my European jaunt and putting money away daily - $200 to $500 a day depending on the weather. The Twins won the World Series, two more weeks of serious bank. I remember going out for meals; lobster, steak, oysters, whatever I wanted and it was all a business expense. Other than having to look at Archie - this was quite the gig, I even brought some friends on board to share in the gravy train.

Archie's next destination was the Orange Bowl in Miami. Archie wanted to make it kind of a vacation, party trip. I think he just really wanted to see my girlfriend Elsa Eckstrom and a friend, Katja Berg - a Dutch model, wearing bikinis in Fort Lauderdale. Whatever the reason, we were provided with gas and meal money plus accommodations, $100 per day cash even if we didn't sell a thing. Into my late 60's Plymouth Valiant we piled, Elsa, Katja, me and Jack, the boyfriend of my stepsister. Road trip!

After two days to get there, booze & beer a plenty, Elsa and I seeking out every opportunity we could to play hide the sausage. To Elsa's credit, she was a strong Norwegian gal, blonde hair, blue eyes, athletic, strong body and a large appetite for sex. Perfect for me I might add! Katja was about six feet tall, huge fabulous boobs, amazing smile, svelte and making serious bank as a top model in the metro area. She was dating a great friend of mine (and I even witnessed their wedding, which was more for citizenship purposes than for true love). It did not matter where you went, who you were with, everyone stopped and focused on Katja when she entered a room.

Now Archie is determined to have access to the girls, so our living arrangement in Fort Lauderdale is a vast room shaped like an L with beds enough for everybody. It was one of those spring break specials, across from the beach, sleeping eight to ten, with a little kitchenette. Elsa and I shack up in the only bed in the place with a semblance of privacy, Katja next to us, then Jim and finally Archie by the door. To Archie's credit, he stocked the place with beer, booze, food and snacks. We were set.

The surf was absolutely monstrous, the weather not good, cold and cloudy for the most part. Didn't matter, the Northerners were on the beach. Jack and I body surfing like crazy. The waves got so big that there were surf warnings. We never should have been in the water, screw it, gonna get me some. So, I catch this one massive wave and it flips me over, feet over head and the undertow is roiling. I start swimming for the surface, bam - I hit my head on the bottom of the sea. Oops, massive launch towards the surface, badly needing oxygen as I break the surface.

One night, feeling a bit romantic and wanting some privacy, Elsa and I head up to the roof of the hotel, which is unfinished other than some basic patio furniture. We barricade ourselves on the roof, a candle, some cocktails. Elsa was in a purple sundress (for a while). I was in a T-shirt and shorts (for a while). Now we are on the chaise lounge. Elsa on top. She is loud (damn this is fantastic). At this point I look up above me and there, five floors higher in the next building are five guys on a balcony watching the spectacle below. Thumbs up, high fives, fist pumps, all in silence as they don't want the show to end. Elsa and I labor on, reaching a most happy ending when the cheering section above erupts in applause. To her credit, Elsa took it well and frankly, I don't think either of us cared.

The trip ends with us at the Orange Bowl with 1988 Oklahoma Sooners National Champions T-shirts, (Archie's alma mater). The Miami Hurricanes beat the Sooners by six and so ends our trip with Archie. I would go onto Denver at the end of January for the Super Bowl however the Broncos got drilled by the Washington Redskins by more than four touchdowns, thus ending my lucrative souvenir sales career.

## In Pursuit of Adventure, Purpose and Change (Spring/Summer 1988)

What to do? Applications had been submitted to: 1) The Peace Corps; 2) Habitat for Humanity; and, 3) Brethren Volunteer Services. Within a few weeks, I was accepted into Brethren Volunteer Services (BVS) before I could even complete the approval process with the other two organizations.

The Church of the Brethren is one of the three peace churches that relocated from Europe, the other two are the Quakers and the Mennonites. BVS offers placements all over the globe as well as across the United States. I was just stoked to know I had a plan, a way to support myself for a two year commitment, and a wide open adventure that awaited. The rest would take care of itself.

In the late spring of 1988, I attended the BVS orientation on the South-side of Chicago. It was an old Catholic Church that had closed and was now used as a community center. It was in one poor, rough and tough neighborhood. I had already expressed my interest in going abroad and at the end of orientation, I was offered three options.

First, would be volunteering in a Peace Center in Dusseldorf, Germany. Since I am fluent in German, it was a logical choice but just sounded too dull given that I am not that much of a kale eating, "peacenik" guy.

Second was working in a Youth Community Center on the Shankill Road in Belfast, Ireland right smack dab in the middle of the "Troubles." This was during the days of open warfare between Protestants and Catholics. I knew my dad would completely stress out if I was in Northern Ireland as a Catholic. So, I took a pass on Belfast. My friend Nick who took that position, ended up getting seriously injured - an injury he would never discuss.

Third was teaching English as a second language at a higher academic institution in Poland. I would live as Polish Professor and Polish PHD's would study and live in the US. It sounded exotic, foreign, intriguing and challenging, I was in - I signed on the bottom-line.

I would spend the summer of 1988 working at a BVS summer youth camp in the mountains of Central Pennsylvania. It was fun, easy, and beautiful. I even got to play slow-pitch softball on a top-tier local team. All told, the summer of 1988 was great; a great setting, pretty ladies all around, softball and the excitement of leaving in the fall for Poland. This was the life I had dreamed of for myself.

### Lights, Camera, Action - Take 1 (August 8, 1988)

It was to be a historic night in Wrigley Field. After decades of squabbling with Major League Baseball about having night games at Wrigley. Baseball had given the Cubs the ultimatum, either put up lights or any play-off games will have to be played at Comiskey Park, the dreaded home of the White Sox on the South side. Thus, over neighbors' objections, the City of Chicago passed an ordinance approving lights at Wrigley for the first time.

To say it was a festive atmosphere would be a gross understatement. The Governor was on hand. Harry Caray, Steve Stone, and Bill Murray liberally passed out cold Budweisers from a cooler he had managed to sneak into the WGN booth. It was the most coveted ticket in years in Chicago and my cousins, Mary and Aileen had finagled four tickets through a friend at WGN. Joining us would be a dear old family friend and powerful Chicago Attorney, Pat Mahoney.

Each fan received a commemorative hat. Libations were flowing freely all over Wrigleyville as the Cubs got ready for all the pre-game ceremonies and a game with the Philadelphia Phillies. The official lighting ceremony took place with Mayor Daly officiating. The National Anthem was sung with the color guard presenting the flags. It was truly a spectacle which only a major city can produce.

The teams took the field, the lights were on and they played 3 1/2 innings before the flood gates opened and a torrential downpour occurred. The fans, us included, continued to have a good time, singing songs, talking, etc. until it became clear that there was no way that this game would resume tonight.

### Lights, Camera, Action – Take 2 (August 9th, 1988)

So, with all the pomp and circumstance out of the way, the first official night game would be the next night, August 9th. My cousins were able to finagle me a ticket but this time I would be flying solo. I was close to departing for Poland and just biding my time until departure.

I hit several of the local haunts like Murphy's Bleacher, the Cubby Bear and others to properly prepare for the adventure. It felt much better in Wrigley the second night, as it was way more of a baseball crowd. My seat was under the second deck overhang behind home plate. Once again, I had a great view of the broadcast booths. About the 4th inning, Harry Caray comes out of the booth and heads to a private bathroom above me. Now Harry was in there a longtime and I started to get worried about him and thus I began the chant "Go Harry Go! Go Harry Go!". By the time Harry emerges, about 2000-3000 fans with a view of Harry are in unison "Go Harry Go!" Harry was up there waving and smiling at us like the Pope and we were in St. Peter's Square.

The Cubs would go onto win that night 6-4 versus the New York Metropolitans.

## Towards, Into and Beyond the Iron Curtain (August 1988)

My itinerary was set, Pittsburgh to New York City, on to Lucerne, Switzerland for an overnight with four of my fellow Poland bound volunteers: Amy, Paul, Don and Pete. This was in the day before wheeled luggage so Pete and I both had backpacks. Amy had two of the largest, heaviest suitcases ever known to man. Of course, Paul, Pete, Don and I ended up schlepping my bags to the hostel where we overnighted. It was a gorgeous, magical evening in Lucerne. Clean cobblestone streets, light refracting off the slightly damp streets, the adventure was finally under way.

The next day we would take the train to Geneva to meet with the European project coordinator. Many instructions were relayed, most importantly safety and evacuation plans in case martial law was declared again in Poland. Should that occur, we were to grab what we needed, our passports and hightail it to the US Embassy in Warsaw. Once there, we would be flown back to Geneva to wait things out or get reassigned elsewhere. It all was very intimidating to think that we might become refugees in a communist country and could be trying to run the gauntlet of martial law on the streets.

In the morning, we loaded up our stuff including Amy's bags of bricks and hopped aboard the train to West Berlin. All wheels were in motion.

Now, I must be frank. Writing about West/East Berlin at that time in history is a daunting task. We crossed the East German border about midday. The train was descended upon by soldiers with AK-47's, guard dogs, and control agents. There was zero kidding around. Every compartment was checked. The undercarriage and roof of the train and our documents all double checked. It felt so very eerie to know that one hundred percent of our fate depended on visas, documents and these dour soldiers in the blandest color green uniforms I have ever seen. Once all the T's were crossed and the I's dotted, we were underway for West Berlin, not a single stop anywhere in East Germany and it was abundantly clear that this was a direct travel corridor with the population kept at a distance from access to the tracks.

On we rolled, transiting through the West Berlin border, a breath of fresh air, efficient, kind border guards and into the Zoo Bahnhof. We had survived the travel ordeal, found our hostel, dropped off our bags and headed out to explore West Berlin, get a meal and more than a few beers. A few hours later we turned in, tired, and prepared for the final leg of our journey to our new homes in Poland.

Up at sunrise, we again dragged ourselves and Amy's bricks to the Zoo Bahnhof (the central train station in West Berlin). Everything was completely spotless, well lit, with all clocks ticking in unison. It truly was a stunning station and quite the contrast to about what we were about to experience.

We loaded onto the commuter train and began the journey back towards East Berlin and onto East Germany. The crazy thing was that the commuter train terminated at the city border, we then decamped onto the platform and went through the whole control process with the East German officials again. So, imagine you are riding a Chicago El train, it stops and you walk 100 yards and you are in another country, a communist one, riding the same rails, in essence the same train.

The instant that the East German train started to move, it was obvious that we weren't in Kansas anymore Toto. Absolutely everything turned grey. The walls outside the train were bullet ridden, having been that way since WWII. As we emerged into daylight, absolutely every building, every street, even the air itself was gray or dinghy white. As we gazed out the window of the ancient train, we looked at each other and started to wonder what we had signed up for. The game was on.

## *Nicht Sie!* (Not You!) (Fall 1988)

Another train story as long as we are at that station. Pete and I were again transiting through West Berlin, via East Germany and then south, headed to Trier, West Germany for the annual Brethren Volunteer Services retreat. Politically, everything was precariously unstable, no one knew if the Russians would crack down on the Democratic uprisings surging through Eastern Europe. East Germany was the frontline for the Warsaw Pact and the tension was palpable.

It was late afternoon when Pete and I found our train, clambered aboard and found a comfortable unoccupied six-person cabin (sweet). About ten minutes later, this dude, Ronnie, wanders in and takes a seat with us. Ronnie emitted a serious bad vibe. He was dressed in black from head to toe with a small black Fedora atop his noggin. Pete and I exchanged glances knowing that we would have to make the best of it. A few minutes later, the train began rolling south and we hit the East German border where guards, machine guns, dogs descend on the train and a huge guard stepped into our cabin.

"*Stehen sie auf, gehen sie aus.*"

Being the only German speaker, I tell the other knuckleheads to step out into the corridor because our belongings are to be searched. 'God damn it Ronnie, if you have drugs with you, I will kill you myself' ran through my head. Now the movie Midnight Express did not take place in East Germany, but at this exact point in my life, I'm not exactly quibbling about details. Out Pete and Ronnie go, when Fritz, the Guard puts a monstrous finger in my chest and says, "*Nicht Sie*" - not you! He then leans over and draws the curtains on the cabin and closes the door.

### SHIT! SHIESS! GLOWNO! CRAP ON A STICK...

Fritz then begins to question me in German, "Why do I speak German? Where are we going? What am I doing in Poland?

What is the purpose of our trip? Do I know both of the men in the cabin? How long have I known Ronnie?" And on and on. At this point, I may have been answering all his questions well, but I am sweating bullets. Fritz wants to go through my possessions, which he does meticulously. My books, my writings, my passport, my stinky dirty clothes and so on. Now the thought hits me, Oh God, curtains closed, just him and me, is there a strip search coming? A body cavity search? A plant of something into my belongings? Fritz finishes with my bags, pats me down and lets me step out into the corridor. I am dripping wet with sweat and my hands are trembling.

Fritz then brings Ronnie in and does the same process with him, except Ronnie speaks no German, so it is all hand gestures. Pete and I talk in the corridor, "I think they believe that Ronnie has drugs on him or is a drug runner." Pete is now tense as he doesn't want to be a black man alone with Fritz in case Fritz wants to plant something on him. We vow that if either of us goes somewhere, both of us go together so that there is a witness. And if one of us is free, he can get to the embassy in West Berlin and get help ASAP.

Another couple of minutes and Fritz exits the car. Ronnie passed the test. But Ronnie's first words to us were, "Good thing I left my dope with my friend in West Berlin last night. I think the dog smelled my luggage which reeked of the clothes I wore smoking weed last night. That must be how they got onto me."

You think Ronnie?! At that point Pete and I switched cabins, bought some beers from the steward rolling down the corridor and looked forward to the freedom of West Germany in a few hours' time.

### Big Brother is Listening (Fall 1988)

Entering Poland after East Germany was like going from a police state into Wisconsin. The border guards and controllers were laid back, perfunctory and pleasant. Pete would hop off in the Western City of Poznan, originally a German city that was redrawn into Poland by Stalin, Churchill and FDR at the end of World War II. Amy would get off in Warsaw, where she would work at a university, Don was off to Kracow, an architectural haven, Paul and I would head onto Skierniewice, a city of about 100,000 located 70 kilometers southwest of Warsaw. Paul was assigned to Instytut Sadownictwa and Kwiaczarstwa. (The Research Institute of Horticulture and Flowers) I would be at Instytut Warzywnictwa (the Research Institute of Vegetable Crops) and share a two-room apartment. Both of the Institutes were formally palaces for Polish royalty and were stunning in their architecture and elegance.

Even though the East German gestapo was hundreds of miles away, living in Skierniewice, Poland there were always reminders that we were living behind the Iron Curtain.

My roommate Paul was a white-Jesus-looking-guy from UC Davis. Paul and I had been warned that our apartment was most certainly bugged. There was a ninety percent plus chance that the secret police, the intelligence agencies and perhaps the Soviets would be trying to ascertain if we were CIA plants this deep behind the Iron Curtain. Our suspicions were promptly confirmed. I would exit the apartment building and an orange *Maluch*, a tiny little car, would be sitting across the street, the driver "reading" the paper (yeah, right). I'd walk to the train station a few kilometers away, and as God is my witness, there was that same *Maluch* and the same guy parked near the entrance to the train station. How did he know I was coming here? Onto the *Osobowy* (commuter train) I boarded and once in Warsaw, a green *Maluch* would tail me about the city, noting where I went, who if anyone I talked with etc. Back to Skierniewice, same orange *Maluch* awaiting me, but this time there was a different driver behind the wheel. Must be different shift time - those sneaky little bastards!

Just to mess with them in the apartment, Paul and I would often talk in rapid fire, non-sensical banter, lots of numbers and American slang. "Dodgers won today in 14 innings, 7-2, repeat 7-2, attendance 41,462."

I'd blurt, "Shakespeare has decided not to attend the event in June."

"He has other obligations," would reply Paul, and so it would go.

After a few months, the surveillance came to an end for one of two reasons: A) The Cold War was about to end, and they had better things to do with their time; or, B) they finally figured out that Paul and I were just two silly Americans who posed no threat whatsoever to the greater good of the Communist State (little did they know that just my mere presence brought the Wall down in and of itself - no need to thank me folks!).

Another person who seemed to seriously invite suspicion was Pete, a black man in a world of lily white. Pete lived in Western Poland and was my main adventure/drinking companion at the time. He was a black belt in two forms of martial arts, had a background that didn't run too deep, and easily had the brains to pull the whole spy thing off. Last, I heard Pete had his PHD and was teaching in South Korea. Coincidence?

### Life in Communist Poland (1988 – 1989)

It is impossible to sum up in a few words what life was like in Communist Poland because it was so different from life as I knew it. However, people are still people and we all need to meet our daily needs. The best way to describe my life in Poland, is simply to show you my life in Poland.

**Ration Cards:** At that time, almost everything was rationed. Each month I was given a meat ration card that allowed me to purchase up to 8.8 kilograms of meat, broken down into pork, beef and chicken. So that is a little less than twenty pounds of meat for the month. Prices were subsidized by the government. It was possible to buy meat at the open markets, but prices were double to triple the government price. I took many students on to learn English, not so much for the money, but to receive meals and/or food.

**A store devoid of product:** As the uncertainty of which way the government would go with Solidarity's efforts to reconstitute, people were hoarding foods and goods left and right. I once walked into a grocery store (not anything like an American grocery), and there was nothing on the shelves. The only products left were in the infant/mother section which I didn't qualify for. The first four to five months of my stay were concerned with trying to subsist on whatever I could find. Had it not been for my coworkers and students I would have never made it.

**Obiad - (Dinner):** In Poland people consume numerous small meals throughout the day with one large meal at 3 p.m., usually provided by your work. On my first day I went to the cafeteria for Obiad, knowing full well that this is 90% of the food I will get today. In I go, hungry and ready, dinner is being served by women in white aprons who look like they could play offensive line for any NFL team. I look down, dinner is a watery bean soup, mashed potatoes, beets and LIVER! I hate liver. Okay, Tom, shut up and shovel that in or you will be hungry for 24 hours. Somehow, I ingest the meal. The second day I come back and the menu is again similar but this time I think it was chicken liver! Again, pinching my nose, I chew, choke, gag and swallow the dreaded liver. This is going to be a fun two years.

**Laundry:** When it came time to do laundry, it was a non-complicated process, throw your laundry in the tub, add hot water if you've got it, and dump in some detergent. Then hop in the tub and start stomping on your clothes like you are crushing grapes. Once adequately trampled, hand rinse your clothes in the tub and then find anywhere to hang them up to dry. It did not take long to figure out that wearing clothes multiple days was a necessity.

**Beer:** When and if beer was in the store, usually a brand called "Warka". It was necessary to check every bottle of Warka due to the fact that the beer was not pasteurized. To check a beer, you inverted the bottle to see if there were "floaties" active yeasts growing in the bottle. If there were, the beer not only would taste bad, it would usually cause a major upset stomach. The other place to go was a worker's bar on the West side of town. To call it a bar is a stretch, it was a grey wooden shack with only outdoor sitting. There was no running hot water, just cold water that a stout, short woman would use to rinse the beer steins, no soap, no sanitizer, just cold water. Other than the woman working the shack, I never saw any other female there. The patrons were all men usually just getting off work at 3 to 4 p.m. and stopping in for a drink or six on their way home.

**Water and Electricity:** Both were commodities that could come and go at any time of day. Often times the government would ration one or both to save money throughout the day. There might be water in the morning and no electricity, that afternoon the two might flip-flop and there would be no water for four to five hours throughout the evening. The critical lesson to be learned was always to have a bucket of water on hand in the bathroom in case the water went off. One time I was bathing (no showers, which was common), and I had just lathered up with soap when the water was turned off. As you might guess, I had not filled the gallon bucket, thus I was stuck trying to wipe soapy lather off with a towel.

**Toilet Paper:** TP was a precious commodity, either at home or on the go. (No pun intended!) The paper was a grey, recycled product that had the texture of a medium grade sandpaper. It wasn't always available and so stockpiling it was a critical necessity. Also, in my backpack I always carried a small quantity of TP just in case. One time I was traveling to Warsaw, and I was traveling on an "Osobowy" a commuter train. Sure enough, I was caught short, no paper. So, into the bathroom on the train I go which was nothing more than a stool with a piece of duct work that went through the floor and the waste would simply fall onto the exposed tracks below. When seated, the wind would blow across your backside while doing your business (a refreshing experience during the six months of cold weather). So, there I am have evacuated my bowels with no TP in sight. At the time, I was reading *War and Peace* by Tolstoy and was reduced to using the first several pages to accomplish my clean up. It worked well. Sorry about that Leo, I loved the book!

**Salary and the Black Market:** My initial salary was $17.00 a month in the Polish Zloty. Since it was still fully a communist economy with government subsidized prices, I actually was able to live on seventeen dollars pretty well when I could find products to buy. In Warsaw, it was extremely easy to change dollars on the black market with money changers usually hanging out in transport areas. The going government rate at the time was eleven Zloty per dollar, on the black market you could get triple that rate, about thirty Zloty per dollar.

**Shopping and learning Polish:** I went into Poland with a Polish vocabulary of about ten words, I now lived in a town of 100,000 where maybe 100 people spoke English. Hence it was full language immersion, 24 hours a day. All night I left the radio on and listened to Polish radio, a very effective learning tool. To buy produce and farm products, I would go to the town farmer's market to buy staples like potatoes, rice, flour, etc. Most often, I would say to a short, rotund Babcia, "*Prosze, po kilo ziemnacki* - Please, half a kilogram of potatoes." At this point, if the woman understood me at all, she would tell me how much I owed her which was extremely difficult to understand as numbers are long and fast in Polish. I would then take out my money and hold it out to the woman in my open hands for her to take whatever I owed. Usually, she was smiling, wondering who is this strange gringo at her stall. I honestly don't believe I was ever taken advantage of. It would take me about six months to master basic Polish and a full year to become fluent.

The items above were common occurrences in my first six months. Once the Berlin Wall came down, things improved substantially, especially stores, products and basic living conditions like water and electricity.

### Some positives of life under Communism

Yes, I know, here is where I lose readers talking about politics. If you wish to live with a closed mind, that's your call, it may work in America. But elsewhere on this globe, you have play the cards you are dealt and make the best of it. There are positives everywhere, and there are negatives everywhere. The United States is the best thing going, but failure to steward it forward in the bests interests of all will culminate in the fall of what it took two hundred and forty years to build. Yet I again, I digress.

**The family:** Under Communism, your family was your safety net, your advocates, and those who would make your life possible. Most families bought dirt or apartments that would take up to fifteen years to be built and completed. Got some extra cash? Buy $300 worth of bricks and add a few more layers of brick next year. Finish the first floor, and enclose it. We will get the second floor done in the next decade. Credit was not an option, everything was cash. How will you spend your holidays? With your family. Great homemade food that was saved up for a month plus, add a few bottles of Vodka and the happiest party you ever saw ensued. Someone is sick, you have 24/7 care from your family, whatever it takes. No nursing home here unless your own home counts. Dying a horrible death, your family is there every step of the way. In summation, like'em or not, that's your family. You are joined at the hip until death. Family was a given and the foremost reality of existence.

**Health Care:** Sick - no worries, go to the doctor and get the best care available. Most visits resulted in a trip to the *Apteka* (Pharmacy) where your meds were prepared and handed to you at the astronomical price of free. Most times a cold, a flu, an illness of any kind resulted in a prescription from the physician sending you home for a week or more. Turn that prescription into your employer and you received 100% pay for the time out of the office. Now I know many of you may be thinking this cannot be efficient. Let us take Ed, a grocery worker, who has a nightmare cold. In the U.S., he is headed back to work ASAP, healthy or not because he cannot afford to be sick. What if Ed is home for a week, not infecting others and most importantly, healing and regaining his strength? Which one benefits society most?

**Crime:** Not really an option. For the most part everybody knew that if you broke the law, the cost would be far beyond the price you were willing to pay. The court system was not merciful. Jails were a major deterrent in and of themselves. What's my point? I felt safer walking in Poland than I ever did in most American cities. How many of my friends had been mugged in DC, Chicago, Minneapolis? One hundred percent more than what I experienced in Poland. Now, I am not advocating a harsh, brutal criminal justice system here. I am merely saying that when criminals are scared to commit crimes - I am okay with that concept.

**Stress:** Now I know I am pitching a losing battle in sharing my thoughts about Communism/Socialism with so many Americans. I am not trying to sell you; I am just sharing my observations. Under communism, stress was extremely low.

Why? You had a job, you had to work extra hard to lose it, then you get a crappier job at the same pay. You had a baseline compensation that ensured your most essential needs were met. As I mentioned, when I arrived in Poland in 1988, my salary was the US equivalent of $17 a month. Two years later, after the wall had come down, I was making $248 a month. I lived better on the $17 pay rate. It was a society with low expectations, a low reality and yet a basic comfort level of existence imbued with family. Work hard, don't rock the boat and things will be okay.

### My Roommate - Jerzy Frykowski (Fall 1988)

One of the perks of being an English teacher abroad is that people covet having you come on their English language camps. Such was the case in the fall of 1988 when I was invited to stay at a Communist spa and retreat. This place was not built for the proletariat. The spa had beautifully manicured lawns, shrubs and trees finely trimmed, indoor swimming pool, sauna, steam room, tennis courts, etc. etc. etc. It was a plush secret hidden amidst a country of grey.

The Polish media had invited me to attend with TV personalities, movie stars, directors, producers, and so on. It was a who's who of the media, all gathered for a week to work on their English by day, drink vodka by evening and perhaps hook up for a tryst. Being a fuzzy foreigner, I had no clue who was who so I didn't have to be impressed.

The first evening I went up to my room which I was to share with a Polish man attending the conference. The room itself was very nice by East European standards: green carpet, not big, two beds on each side of the rectangular room, a small balcony with gorgeous views of the great lawn. At least I knew I was going to eat well for a week.

About halfway through unpacking my stuff, my roommate arrives and introduces himself as Jerzy Frykowski, a cog in the film industry (Jerzy even has his own Wikipedia page with all the films he produced and acted in). "Nice to meet you Jerzy" I say as we shake hands. He is in his late 50's, quiet, and yet there is something about him that is a wee bit off.

After dinner we were invited to one of the six vodka parties about to start but I was tired and didn't want to survive a wild first night to be miserable the rest of the week. Jerzy felt the same so we grabbed six beers from the ever-stocked fridge and retired to our room.

Per usual, beer and being comfortable made for good conversation. We had talked for a bit when out of the blue I asked, "Jerzy, you ever been to the States?"

"Why yes I have" he replied.

"Where?" I inquired.

"Los Angeles. I spent two months there."

"Did you get to the beach much? Disneyland? What was your favorite part?" I plodded on, unaware that he was getting quieter and quieter with long pauses before speaking.

"I was there for a trial. I represented my family at a murder trial in Los Angeles. My brother, Wojciech Frykowski, was killed by Charles Manson and his family."

Time-out here I thought. This is nuts. Not wanting to push Jerzy, I let the pauses do the work and in time Jerzy continued.

"My brother was in Roman Polanski and Sharon Tate's home when the Manson family attacked. My brother was on the couch downstairs and put up a serious fight before they killed him. Once it came time for the trial, I was chosen to attend the trial on behalf of the family."

Finally, I had to ask, "What was the trial like? What was Manson like?"

"The trial was full of lawyers, police, etc. The only thing that was psychotic was the Manson family. It was obvious from the outset that they were beyond disturbed, illogical and under the sway of this crazy guy who did have a powerful charisma."

In the end, the Frykowski family were the only ones to get a judgment against Manson for monetary damages.

## Old World Farm Life (Fall & Winter 1988 & 1989)

Ania and Zbiszek were a young married couple who worked at the same Institute where I was teaching. They spoke excellent English. The couple kindly invited me to Ania's family farm, two hours southwest of Skierniewice. This was a great opportunity to get away for a couple of long weekends, see the countryside, experience rural life first-hand on a non-mechanized farm. I didn't need to be asked twice. On a Thursday evening, we jumped on the train south and hopped off in the middle of nowhere. At the stop there was a small platform with a tiny building which was no bigger than twenty feet by twenty feet serving as the train station. When we arrived, it was pitch black. With no lights to pollute the view, there were a zillion stars above. Waiting for us was Ania's father and brother in a horse drawn cart. We would ride in the back of the working farm cart on hay bales wrapped in heavy wool blankets. Edward, Ania's Dad, gave each of us the obligatory three cheek kiss. Before departing, he opened a bottle of Vodka from which we all took long pulls. Nestled into our places on the hay bales, the strong smell of sweaty work horses, manure and fresh air all swirling around, we trotted off into the night. It felt as if I had peeled back a century or two - well, good evening there Mr. Dostoevsky, good evening Mr. Tolstoy.

After about a twenty-minute jaunt, we were home at the farm for the weekend. The farmhouse was tiny, ancient, and immaculate. The coal and wood stoves were burning warm. Ania's mom was a bright red cheeked hobbit with about six front teeth missing from a life of hard labor keeping the farm. She radiated warmth, health and love for her family and now her new Gringo guest from the West. The country villa had three rooms total plus a small kitchen. No indoor plumbing

- out to the outhouse with you. I would be staying in the attic space with Zbiszek which was accessed by a ladder on the wall leading up to a trap door. We shuttled our bags up and fired up a few candles and a lantern. My bed was a straw mattress on the rough, hewn wood planking. Standing up was only possible in the center of the room due to the slope of the roof. My bedding was a twenty inch thick down comforter called a *pierzen*, down pillows, and the cleanest starched sheets I have ever slept on. In short, it was beyond rustic, beyond charming. It was Dostoevsky-esque, and I loved everything about it!

The next three days would be spent helping out around the farm: milking cows, slopping the pigs, putting hay up in the barn loft for winter. It was laborious, hard work but exhilarating at the same time. I knew then as I know now; I was experiencing something that was about to expire. Progress would come and this simple charming place would fade as the 21st Century rolled in with "progress".

About 3 p.m., we would stop for *Obiad*, dinner, and that would be it for the work day. Then of course the feasting and vodka would begin in earnest. The best homemade chicken soup ever, with kluski, fresh egg noodles, wild pickled mushrooms, pea salad, a pork cutlet, kielbasa. And on it went. Neighbors, family members, all coming and going, the house warm, joyous and full of laughter. Everyone got a kick out of my attempts to butcher the Polish language. But to my credit, I was learning fast and could convey basics. I could get what I needed and when tired, zone out for a while and listen to the steady hum of their Polish banter. On the second night, old Zbiszek got so hammered that he couldn't climb the ladder up to the attic, I threw his blanket and pillow down and he slept like a dead man on the floor in the hallway.

There is one sad incident from those weekends that stands out to me this day. It was on my second visit. We were out in the horse drawn sleigh, it now being full on winter. Through a huge forest preserve we emerged and went through what supposedly constituted a village, maybe four to five hovels clustered together. As we drove up, people were gathering to watch Staszek, the man of the house, who was violently inebriated beyond measure. It is impossible to relate that level of intoxication here but East Europeans will know what I mean, Staszek was on a rampage. He had kicked his whole family out of the house and now they stood in the front yard in a foot and a half of snow, watching their father/husband throw every single possession of the mother's out of the window: shoes, bra's, blouses, hats, you name it, all of it was flying out, drifting down, to the snow-covered ground below. It was a sad sight to behold. It was rural domestic violence at its absolute ugliest. Other men had been and were trying to talk with Staszek, to intervene, but if they went too far, Staszek would brandish his hunting rifle. We would learn the next day that some men went in to drink Vodka with Staszek until he passed out and then took him to his brother's so that the family could go back in the house for the night.

### Skiing the Tatries (New Year's 1988)

A group of college students from Lodz were headed on a weeklong ski trip in the Tatry Mountains of Southern Poland for New Year's and invited me a long as a tutor to help improve their English skills. In return I would pay for - nothing! Free lodging, meals, rentals and lift tickets. A deal too good to pass up. So, per usual, I signed on the bottom line and would ski the Polish-Czechoslovakian border for a week. Tough duty but somebody had to do it. I was driven over to the university where I met about twenty-five excited coeds (and yes several pretty young ladies), and onto the train we load, headed south. In Krakow, we boarded a commuter train with three or four cars behind the locomotive. Up we start to climb into the mountains, always uphill and only stopping every six to ten kilometers to let people get on or off. There are no roads up here, too much snow in winter. To compensate, everybody travels by skis or by horse drawn sleigh. What have I gotten into now, I wonder? Up we go and after about an hour of slowly climbing, it is our turn to disembark. Off we pile onto a platform in the middle of a forest. Everyone puts on their ski boots under one of the two lights on the platform. Then click, on go the skis and we literally start to cross country ski in alpine gear through the dark forest. Is somebody kidding me? After about ten to fifteen minutes depending on ability, we emerge from the forest. There up above us is the farmhouse we will be staying in. It is big, looks great but we have a solid uphill slog to get there. Once there, ski's outside, and boots downstairs with the farm animals. Yup, the basement of the house is the barn. I am loving this. You can't make this up!

In the morning, we were served a hearty farm breakfast. Everything harvested on site (talk about living green). We put on our ski gear and slide another ten minutes to a ski run going down. We schussed down and were on the ski mountain with chairlifts, lodges, etc. I don't believe this kept running through my head but it was all novel, new, and a blast. My favorite run was right on the Polish-Czechoslovakian border, using the border markers to make my slalom run. I must have skied in and out of both countries a couple of a hundred times a day without a single passport check. The groups of students I was with were awesome, friendly, playful and yet most sincere. They really wanted to have decent lives using their education to their best advantage and they studiously practiced their English with me.

There is one conversation from that trip that is branded into my brain. It was at the New Year's Eve party in the farmhouse. All of us happy, Vodka, beer, some of the girls had champagne but it wasn't a raging bash, more of a fun, quiet, muted alpine New Year's Eve. Anyways, I can't remember what the conversation was but I must have said something very "American" (easy to do when you are um, American). This one guy, Gregor, who was extremely smart and generally quiet, paused for a moment and looked at me.

"That's the problem with you Americans. You think you can fix everything. That life is fair and all you have to do is try and it will get better. Take the water that we drink everyday of our lives. Do we know that it is polluted, that it is unhealthy, that it will have negative health consequences and that we will die earlier because of it? (most water at that time was filled with heavy minerals, lead and other toxic goodies). Yeah, we know what's in the water but we don't go around freaking out about it. We accept it. We have no choice. It's what we've got. We live our lives and we don't waste time worrying about something that is beyond our control."

Now I know there is a happy medium out there, but when I hear many Americans bellyache, gripe and demand instant remedies about the most banal of things, I drift off to that Polish farmhouse high in the Tatries...it's New Year's Eve.... and I don't want to waste my time worrying about that which is beyond my control.

### The City that was Berlin (Fall 1988-1990)

In my travels across this orb, I have never experienced anyplace like West Berlin prior to the wall coming down. It was an island of freedom surrounded by angry drab people, armed with machine guns and turrets filled with sharpshooters. The wall itself had two walls with a no man's land in-between. All buildings on the East German side were shuttered, abandoned and decrepit. Any attempt to cross those walls, that space was met with lethal force.

West Berlin exuded freedom, joy, and a constant realization of how lucky you were to be on this side of those walls. In bars, restaurants, the streets there was an energy that pervaded everyone and everything. A simple visit to a pub made every patron feel connected: 'We are in this all together, we are the lucky ones. Why yes, I'll have another beer and I'll buy my new friend, Wilhelm one too.' It was unlike anything I have ever experienced, and I am sure that today that vibe is gone in the reunified German capital.

**The Kufurstendamm - (Ku-Damm)** - A gorgeous, old treelined street that was home to the finest shops, shopping centers and fashions of the West. After spending months in the grey tones of Eastern Europe, just a walk down the Ku-damm was a luxury even if I never had the money to buy a thing. Beautiful women shopping, brand new BMW's, Mercedes, Audis, etc. All of it revolving around the Ku-Damm. If there ever was proof that Communism was doomed, it was after spending time on the Ku-Damm. Hard to believe that a walk down an urban street could bring so much emotion and thought, but that was the reality of the moment on the Ku-Damm.

**Kaiser Wilhelm Memorial Church** - Right in the center of Berlin, close to the Zoo Bahnhof, sits the Kaiser Wilhelm memorial Church, massively bombed in 1943 and never rebuilt, it serves as a memorial to World War II. It is stunning to behold, a spire roof mostly gone, walls clearly gutted by the bombs that had rained down during the around the clock bombing of Berlin. In front of the church is a plaza with benches, where we would pass time, playing cards, drink a beer or two and eat breads, cheeses and dry sausages while we waited for our train back to Poland. As long as someone was awake, the Police would leave us alone and it became the most historic hangout I ever was a part of.

**The Olympic Stadium** – Now, I am not talking about an Olympic Stadium. I am talking about THE Olympic Stadium - Hitler, Jesse Owens, the Nazi rallies, etc. If there is any place that echoes the "myth and pathos" of Adolf Hitler, it is this stadium. I visited it as often as I could. Every time I did, it always felt as if the torch carrying Nazis were about to enter at any moment and that the echo of Hitler's barking oratory still reverberates. The Stadium itself is surrounded by massive monuments made with stone the color of the Pyramids.

They speak to the "greatness" (some might say depravity) of the Aryan race, the prowess of athletic competition and an onerous feeling of impending hatred and death. Often, I just would have the most eerie sensation that there was a presence here (even though I don't believe in that stuff). The Stadium itself is huge, cold, austere and hard. The spot where Hitler spoke and watched the Olympics is clearly marked. Looking at the oval track, it was with great pride that I thought of Jessie Owens circling the track and then accepting the gold medal, Hitler forced to watch.

I could ramble on about Berlin, the Reichstag which Hitler had burned, the severe Soviet War Memorial, Checkpoint Charlie, Hitler's Bunker where he committed suicide (now an apartment complex), and on and on. Next to me here in my room/office, I have a small bag of stones and rubble I gathered as people demolished the Wall, letting freedom out and opening the door to a historic challenging, transitional era of history. Just looking at these little fragments I broke off brings back all the emotion, energy, fun, tension and passion that was West Berlin. Guess I just got lucky. I was there to see it firsthand and be a part of history.

## My visits to the Black Holes of Humanity (1987 – 1994)

Everything that follows is solely my recollection. The horrors of these places are historically well-documented. Do not count on my opinion to be authoritative in any way. It is my intent to merely share with you what it felt like for me to be in these spaces, what I saw, learned and took away, a man changed forever.

**Dachau:** In the fall of 1987, I visited Dachau while in Munich. It was very hard to get a feeling for the place for me as so much of it had been razed. There were some rebuilt quarters on site, many concrete foundational footings and an eerie silence.

While all of it was disquieting, I did not feel a personal connection, a historical connection, absolutely. The city had fully enveloped Dachau and it was slightly bewildering to walk in and out of the gates. In short, I knew where I was, what I was seeing but the impact was mitigated by how much wasn't there.

**Majdenek:** Majdanek was a worker's camp in Lublin, Poland that I visited in the fall of 1988. It was vast, windswept, austere, and severe. Much of the camp remains and the "slave labor" aspect was abundantly clear. Work until you die, next. Don't feed them, more are on the way. Anything but 100% cooperation and effort, next. It was a palpable feeling of pain, suffering, and death. Everybody from Jews, the Roma (Gypsies), dissidents, racially impure bloodlines, and anybody else who just wasn't "liked" by somebody, were sent here to be underfed, overworked, treated like a void and ultimately to die, to be burned, to not be inhabit this Earth anymore.

My blood ran simply cold. This was an economic harvest machine. No need for diesel; we've got blood. Money was the currency. Human life was how you obtained it.

In one section of Majdanek is a domineering, massive, concrete dome that covers the unfathomable ashtray of human remains stored there. I stood there and looked at the grey mass of 150,000 people all reduced to a cone of ash. Deposited here after the war and the largest UFO in history erected above it by the Communists/Soviets. Are there words to describe the ashes of 150,000 people in one place? Mom's, Dad's, Grannies, Grandpa's, kids, cripples, gays, non-desirables, and on and on and on.

If there is one iota of humanity in a person, this is a spectacle of life altering import.

**A Secret Camp outside of Warsaw:** In the fall of 1989, I was taken by some friends to a very small, remote camp in the forests outside Warsaw. This was where political dissidents, suspected spies, enemies of the state and anyone else who simply needed to "go away" were taken. It was not a mass murder facility, it was a surgical elimination facility (sorry, but for the life of me I can't remember the name of the place, just the trees, the leaves and the shocking, quiet, saddening beauty of this mass murder site). There were some German housing units, a massive razor wire to keep them safe, but no need to build housing for the prisoners. They won't be here that long.

As we tromped through the crunchy autumn leaves, I was led to what I will call a dry well, about sixty feet deep. It had never had any water other than the rain. What then was it used for? Once a prisoner had been interrogated, they were led here and pushed in, alive. Once at the bottom of the well, there was no possible means of escape. The only food source were the people before you who were pushed in - beneath you. It was said that the Germans took delight in listening to the cries from the pit at night. It broke the silence for them.

Shortly thereafter, I was led to a four by four cement platform at the bottom of a ravine. Taking my place on the platform, I was told about how this was where you caught the endgame bullet to your skull. The goal was that you would confess whatever you knew before being shot, if so, you were promised decent treatment. However, it didn't matter if you said anything or not. You still got a bullet between the eyes.

## Auschwitz (1987-1994)

This place needs its own chapter. Between 1987-1994, I visited Auschwitz five or six times. What I saw, felt and learned in Auschwitz changed me forever. It disturbs me to this day. And the worst is that when I try to explain it, most people are indifferent or unconcerned. I feel like it perhaps included the death of a part of humanity.

Given its proximity to Krakow and visiting American's desire to see it, I became a tour guide of death. A bus or train ride into Oswiecim (Polish) deposits you a few blocks from the camp. Nobody was hiding this thing. Auschwitz is in the center of the town. A convent abuts the perimeter. Nuns hanging their laundry on the line. There is no way that people didn't know this was here. The smokestacks of the crematoriums are visible to all. So, we walk in silence down the streets, enter the brick gates, and continue on to a place like no other.

Once you have paid your admission, a noble donation in and of itself, you hit the iron gate with these infamous words: *Arbeit Macht Frei* ("Work shall set you Free"). Passing underneath it, thinking of those who went before you, the realization that you get to leave is the most comforting thing you have ever known. Now most of Auschwitz is intact, buildings, crematoriums, experimental labs, etc. What I will share with you now is an amalgamation of my multiple visits and personal knowledge acquired from some of the Poles I know. Into a barracks you go, something like two hundred foot long filled with shoes. They are shoes harvested from "visitors" next building, same thing with suitcases, names, addresses attached. Next building, eyeglasses piled up twenty feet high by forty feet long; next to it, toothbrushes in a similar pile. In the dentists' building there are teeth where gold fillings had been mined for the cause. The next building had overcoats from little girls up to giant men. And on and on...

Human fabric, made from harvested human hair, exceptional clothing, well-made for the "acceptable" populace. Beyond imagination and I shall not deign to say anything more, human skin as a product tool of luxury goods, lampshades and other horrors.

My God, I wish I could stop here!

Shut up Tom, you must share their story to the end.

**The Shower Rooms:** The first thing that struck me was the narrow entry to the shower room. If you were claustrophobic, this was a horrible place to be. Packed in beyond tight, how did people breathe? But these were made for function. The doors open into a massive, dark room, shower heads above, room to spread-out depending on which treatment you shall receive. The pipes are slate grey, several feet above your head with no way to touch them. Water/Cyanide/Water/Cyanide whatever you got, you got. As I exited the room, off to the right was the gas room with canisters of cyanide ready on site should this facility go back into production someday.

**The Furnaces:** Just like baking bread. Slide 'em in, clear out that damn ash, and load up again. It must have been so damn hot in there. I assume the loaders were all shirtless. I stood there and tried to imagine the production process. This process was labor intensive and grossly inefficient, thank God. Once the snap-crackle-pop was done, blow out the ashes, NEXT! The fires to run these things were beyond massive: coal and/or wood. Please think of just one corpse, please multiply it six plus million times, now you are with me.

**The Courtyard of Bang:** There are two buildings, red brick, two and a half stories high. In the middle a courtyard with a high brick wall connecting the two buildings on the exterior side. In the center of that wall, there is a fourteen foot by ten foot wall of concrete and wood. Once you were in the building on the right, your fate was sealed. One by one, all day long, undesirables were marched to the courtyard and the interior wall. This is where you caught a bullet between the eyes or to the heart. Ammunition was a valuable commodity compared to humans, so much so that if you didn't die in one shot, you would bleed to death. Your fellow campers would serve as the labor to remove the corpses or temporary survivors to carts that would haul you away to mass graves. At the end of each day, the "laborers/campers" would be shot as well, no need to have them foment fear back in the barracks.

**Medical Experiments and Torture Facilities:** There is a giant, cold cistern in a courtyard. Fill it with water. Drop in a few undesirables into this icy bath and let's see how long they survive at 20 degrees in the name of science? How best to sterilize men and women? Well we have plenty of "volunteers". Let's trot them in and find out. On and on I could go on with the "medical" experiments, but they are well documented in the "Rise and Fall of the Third Reich." I shall return to the troubling personal narrative.

There was one building more infamous than all the others. It is the site of mass torture, depravation of humanity and as vile as humanity is capable of. Into the basement of this building I ventured with a Pole who would explain its significance to me in detail. This was where the Nazi's would go to any length to break and kill anyone who they deemed "too important" to survive. Blackened cell after blackened cell we visited, human excrement accounting for most of the blackened cells. In one cell there is a plexiglass cover of a priest's etching of the cross and scripture scratched in the wall. He had volunteered to take another person's place.

Into a torture chamber I am led which consists of cement phone booths built along the wall. Each has a small slate of air at the bottom and top of the booth. No phone here, wrong number. On average six to eight people would be shoved and locked into each phone booth. The door would be locked, and remain so for seven to fourteen days, no food or water provided externally. At whatever point the Nazi's deemed it appropriate, the door would be opened and the contents examined. If anyone was still alive, they would have gained weight. No food or water provided, what did they eat to gain weight? Clean this stall, let's try it again!

**The Russian Liberation Movie:** At the end of each visit to Auschwitz, I mandated that anyone with me watch the movie made by the Russians on the day of liberation. It was stunning, raw, honest and exceptionally done. Black and white footage; bodies, children, furnaces, mass graves, humans as stick figures in rags, a complete lack of any joy. How could you express anything but desperation if you survived this Holocaust. The film, in addition to what you have just toured, makes the viewer feel that not only have you visited, but you have witnessed this horrible place in action. You felt it in your bones. And that no matter whatever happens in your life, the worst humanity is capable of, is now imbedded in you as a witness.

**Leaving Auschwitz:** Leaving Auschwitz is intensely personal. Each time I did, I was incapable of conversation for many hours. The weight of the experience demanded reflection. All words were shallow in comparison to the reality. It was as if a switch had been flipped and a time of contemplation was required to come back from "there". Today, decades later, I can go back in the flash of a second. To the many survivors of these camps that I have met throughout the years, you are what makes life possible, if you can live past "The Final Solution" then humanity will endure, I know I couldn't do it.

### Solidarnosc' (Solidarity) and the ZOMO (January 1989)

It was as grey as grey can get, a raw January cold day. Yet seventy kilometers from where I lived, there was to be a protest march through the streets of Warsaw by the leaders of Solidarity seeking the re-legalization of the outlawed trade union. Lech Walesa was to be there as well as the top brass of Solidarity. It seemed like a great place to be and see some history up close, so a friend of mine, Janusz (John), and I caught the train into the city.

Everyone gathered in the old city center, not far from the Warsaw Ghetto. There were songs, chants, speeches and tons of energy to have things change in Poland now. The only thing nobody calculated was what the Communist leader of

Poland, General Jaruzelksi, and most importantly, the Russian Politburo would do. Would there be another major communist crackdown again to squash the uprising? Nobody knew.

After a few hours of Slavic language assault on the ears, it was time to start marching. Janusz and I hung back, more as observers than participants. The procession headed through the narrow streets of the Old City and headed towards Stalin's gift to Warsaw, the Palace of Culture (most Poles always joked that they would like to give it back).

As the streets widened and we hit more open space, I looked down an alley on my left, there was the dreaded Polish Secret Police - the ZOMO. At least a thousand men in full riot gear, batons, shields, helmets and masks, etc. Behind them were these strange massive tank looking things, almost something out of Star Wars. But these weren't movie props. They were water cannons. On the right side of the alley were men with tear gas canisters and bazookas ready to launch the gas, if need be. To say I needed to change my diaper would be an understatement.

As I looked right a half block down, same setup in another alley. But now they were in motion towards the street. Since Janusz and I were in the back, we knew we were at the highest risk. One empty beer bottle tossed at the ZOMO, and we would be the first to get hit with batons. I grabbed my US Passport, held it high and told Janusz to follow me posthaste. Off at a sprint we went exiting the march in a few blocks and headed for the Intercontinental hotel where I knew we would be safe. We spent an hour or two drinking *Piwo* (Polish for beer) and processing what we had just witnessed.

The confrontation never escalated beyond a few minor skirmishes with a few dudes getting clubbed in the head but it was real enough for me to understand the courage it takes to change history. However, three months later, Solidarity would be legalized and the inevitable fall of the iron curtain had begun.

## May Day with the Communist Party (May 1, 1989)

Overt displays of Communism in late 1988 and early 1989 were few and far between, there was an overall sense that "the perfect workers state" wasn't working out so well and the prevailing winds from the East were being overcome by fresh breezes from the West. This being the case, there were two remarkable spectacles/experiences I was invited to be a part of that would soon disappear.

In May of 1989, I was invited by Jacek, a dedicated atheist, scientist, and card-carrying member of the Communist party to attend the illustrious May Day celebrations in Warsaw. Jacek confided in me that he was in "the Party" because it had benefits: better housing, better pay, and perks like the one we were about to attend in Warsaw, tickets for what would be the last Communist Party May Day event. Here I am, a twenty-four-year-old student of International History who has read Marx and Engels in the native German and I am to be a guest at the most important annual gathering of the Communist Party. To state that my feelings were surreal and incredulous would be a gross understatement. I was just glad that Joe McCarthy wasn't around anymore to harass me as a budding Commie. Into Jacek's late model Skoda and we are off for the ninety minute ride to the Palace of Culture, Joseph Stalin's domineering landmark and his gift to the people of Poland.

In an effort to look my best, I mangled my one white button down shirt with a borrowed thirty pound iron, pressed my khaki's as best I could and wiped the dust off my hiking boots. Jacek was dressed to the hilt in a really ugly soviet era suit, an ugly brown knit tie that ends in a square. He was shod in comfortable, practicable footwear, a trait of a good Communist I suppose.

The next three hours is somewhat unremarkable except for the fact that I was there to experience it. Into the largest Sala (Hall) we stride, ornate, gilded with plush blood red velvet seats, surrounded by a solid five thousand of Poland's best comrades including the Politburo, Prime Minister and visiting Soviet Dignitaries, a program is handed to us which intimidated me from the outset. Damn, this is going to be a long program. I really suck at sitting still for five minutes. Too late Comrade Hickey, it's game on. Jacek had outlined to me in advance how things would go: a few officials would get up and go do the greetings, introductions, etc. Next, a large stout woman, Poland's leading Opera singer belted out some arias that I am sure were heard back in Moscow. Now for the main speaker, some devout Communist who could really orate, I mean he went on for an hour plus, raising and lowering his titanic volume as his message demanded. Even with my rudimentary Polish skills, I could pick up what he was putting down: Communism rocks; the West was all just moral degenerates (me included); and, it wouldn't be long now and the Party would be taking victory laps, etc. etc. My ears hurt for God's sake, his face was purple as he finished and the crowd rose en masse. The best part was next, the cultural portion of the program. Out trotted Poland's most celebrated folk dance troops dressed in traditional regional garb, stunning, colorful costumes. Beautiful women abounding and spry men a leaping. It was beautiful, poetic and all the while I was simply happy that nobody was yelling at me anymore. Children's choirs, poetry and other such delightful fare ensued to the delight of my fellow Reds. To this day I am so grateful that I experienced this spectacle: an intimate birds eye view of history and living dogma that was soon to be swept away by events unfurling about me.

### Workers Road Trip to Prague (1989)

Another Scientist at the Institute named Piotr (Peter) was a low level researcher with cockeyed wire rim glasses. Piotr was always disheveled with brown hair tousled and a shitty, cheap Soviet cigarette dangling from his lips. We got along swimmingly. He loved to laugh. He loved his family infinitely. And there were no pretenses about him. Piotr had to road trip to Prague for a combined work and family jaunt and asked if I would like to attend. I'm in, Spring Break communist style. Our transportation was vintage, a 1968 Orange Skoda which was completely beat to hell. I loved it! It looked like a VW Beetle that a giant had stepped on, Piotr kept Irina (Irina was Piotr's name for his car) running with tape, glue, mystery fluids and whatever else was needed to keep the ancient Irina purring.

The first leg of our journey would be to Katowice, an industrial city in Southern Poland - decidedly not a tourist destination. We would be delivering some documents to Piotr's sister, grab some parts for her brother-in-law's car, and drop off some delectable cakes and torts that Piotr's wife had baked. We would also be overnighting with them and then onto to Prague the next day. The apartment was in the ugliest building imaginable. Some really twisted architect had diligently worked to design a structure that was beyond hideous, downright scary and without an iota of warmth. Up we traipse to the micro two room apartment on the eighth floor. It was two dollhouse rooms with a small kitchen-living room and an equally small adjacent bedroom. Piotr and I would be crashing in the first room, I on a couch that was eight inches too short for me and Piotr on the kitchen floor on a pad in front of the oven. In hindsight, Piotr had the better setup to actually get some rest. One thing I recall from that night, (yes, we did get treated to a few liters of Vodka) was that everybody had the most horrendous teeth. Piotr's sister, in her early thirties had black teeth with several missing, the kids teeth were no better, nubs and stubs of yellowish-brown, melting from the municipal water they were provided for every facet of their daily lives, a silent predator. For me, coming from the land of Colgate Fluoride MFP, it was mind numbing to comprehend that their water tap was enemy #1.

The morning would arrive completely devoid of the adjective "refreshed." It felt as if I had slept on a midget's couch with iron springs forged in a dragon's lair (quit your sniveling, it's Spring Break Hickey). Into Irina we pile, a glorious seventy-degree morning bereft of clouds, and on we go. Piotr smoking at a vicious pace, me gulping copious amounts of fresh air. The Polish-Czechoslovakia border was running slow, so we conserved petrol by pushing Irina forward through the long line of fellow spring breakers. Sometime about noon, we hit the border guards. Passports checked. Piotr's belongings gone through thoroughly as he had so much scientific gear and the spare parts for the brother-in-law who lived about ninety minutes from the border. And yes, it was still Czechoslovakia back then.

We turned off the main highway and were travelling country lanes from millennia ago. Charming farms being tilled by horse drawn plows, people hand scything grass and putting it up to dry, kids playing who were too young to work the fields, and women hanging up the laundry to dry out back. It was truly charming and glorious, but I had no idea what was about to come. Somewhere around 1 p.m., Piotr turned Irina down a rutted drive next to a substantial forest and we arrived at brother-in-law Jerzy's hovel. It was a grey wooden structure, probably three hundred years old, the whole structure cockeyed, crooked windows, uneven thick slab wood floors. No need to take off your shoes -this was the definition of rustic - I loved it!

Well, since I am an American gringo it is time to kill the fatted calf. Jerzy and his wife Danka slapped together a feast for the guests with me as the guest of honor. Jerzy heads out to his stone cellar and comes back with a jug of hooch. It was literally nestled in hay, in a wire basket, a large stopper pulled out and this brown liquid poured forth. I was told that it was homemade plum brandy (it may have been brandy but I am certain it could be used as aviation fuel, drain cleaner or a myriad of other industrial applications). The gala was on! Brown liquid, open faced sandwiches, stories, car parts, toasts aplenty - *Nozdrowia*! The next three to four hours were spent in such manner, faces red, laughter, soviet cig's, questions for me about

America, where everything is perfect, without flaw according to those inquiring. In the end, Piotr is just too shitfaced to drive anymore and we fall asleep in the ancient old barn on top of loose hay. Somewhere about 11 p.m., Piotr starts puking to beat the band. As 5 a.m. rolls around, we have to get on the road to get to Prague by mid-afternoon for Piotr's first scheduled meeting. I've slept on a shitty, tiny couch and in a barn - cross those ones off; hell of a spring break so far!

Up early, off we went, a bit worse for wear, especially Piotr – that truly was the East European version of white lightning. Once in Prague, we located the Institute where we would be staying and in Piotr's case, working, and I would have a solid three days to ramble the streets of Prague to my heart's content. Now, I could write a book about Prague in itself. It was the greatest surprise city I have ever been to. It was as beautiful as Paris, cheap beyond measure back then and immaculate, one of the cleanest major cities I ever happened upon. I was and am in love with Prague. I would love to spend half a year there just wandering about, stumbling upon surprise after surprise. For three days I had free reign and it stole my heart.

Piotr and I shared a functional, spartan, room that through some architect's complete oversight, didn't have any windows. It was a fine place to sleep, sip a delicious Czech beer before going to bed but that was about it, thus I was on the prowl. Piotr was busy from early in the morning until ten at night, spending the evenings as a guest with his colleagues. I was off seeing the Charles Bridge, Prague Castle, St. Vitus Cathedral, the Old Town and more than a few bars and pubs. Each day we partook of an incredible occurrence, the workers main meal (*Obiad*) in the Institute's cafeteria which was paid for by the State just like in Poland. The cafeteria was red brick, stolid stainless steel, hearty, hale and most functional. Each afternoon, four hundred researchers and scientists gathered, camaraderie and good will abundantly on display in this soon to be gone culture. A sample meal would be roasted chicken, beets, chunky mashed potatoes, soup and the elixir of the Gods,

Pilsner Urquel which was the finest of products from nearby Pilzen that has been brewed since 1842. Unequivocally, my favorite beer of all time. So, there I am in Czechoslovakia and everyday there is a sumptuous feast accompanied by the divine nectar, thank you Lord! After three days of living large on a micro budget, Piotr's work was done, and we were ready to pile into Irina for the return home.

The voyage home would have us stopping for a night in Bratislava as Piotr had some research documents to drop to a colleague. We arrived mid-evening and would be off in the morning, thus there would be no sightseeing. In fact, although spending the night there, I never even saw the city which is the Capital of Slovakia today. But don't you worry, we were about to experience a cultural event of Homeric heights. We lugged our bags and a case of Pilsner Urquel into the Soviet era hotel, a white concrete structure seven stories high that placed function far ahead of form. Luckily for us, we were on the top floor. More important, the architect had graciously included windows that even opened.

As we crossed through the lobby I was struck by every wall being covered by a form of art I had never seen before - Industrial art. More on that in a minute. Piotr and I take the elevator up to the 7th floor, drop our bags, bust open some pretzels, beer and recline like kings. Within the hour we are joyous, the last night of our Proletariat Spring Break, the cold beers a balm for our travel weary souls. At this point, I mention the art in the lobby and Piotr educates me on the genre known as industrial art, a Socialist's praise to progress, taming the environment and most importantly, glorifying the worker. I am just incredulous, I must see this and so out into the hallway we go, taking in paintings of smokestacks churning out thick black smoke, coal dust covered miners removing the black gold from the Earth, blast furnaces, massive piston driven engines, lumberjacks clearcutting vast swaths of forests, women working the fields, joyous to be productive for the State, dams blocking pristine rivers. It was simply

Orwellian. It was indescribable, art glorifying Industry that wantonly polluted the environment and as I had come to learn, the exalted worker who was to benefit from the industry. There were seven floors of such art and we took all seven in. On about floor four, there was a moment of madness, of hysterical laughter, of clarity, the irony of it all, an experiment of massive proportions, Communism, the worker's state, it hadn't worked, in fact it had been a colossal disaster and it was deteriorating everyday all about me. I was a witness to the failure and the madness.

### Cultural Barbarians (June 1989)

As the first year of teaching English as a Second Language in Poland concluded, Pete (my African America partner in crime as opposed to Piotr my spring break buddy) and I decided we should celebrate with a road trip to Amsterdam where we could stay for free with another BVS volunteer, Tracy. Of course, we did not have much money, so we strategized on how we could make extra dough to fund the trip. Our resourceful plan included buying bottles of Vodka, two each was legally allowed, small Polish toys and dolls, those little wood jobs that have multiple hand painted dolls housed within the first doll and sell them all at the open bazaar in Berlin. Truly a perfect, well-thought out plan per usual.

In Poznan, Western Poland, Pete hopped on the train and we bought our passage to the German border in Zloty, the Polish currency. The normal means of getting to Berlin for us was to bribe an East German conductor on the train. Usually, $5 each guy, $10 total would get us the three-hour trip to Berlin where we would then hitchhike to the Autobahn and to wherever we were headed: Munich, or parts unknown. It was always a crap shoot and an unbounded adventure. This time we were heading to Amsterdam.

Off we trod to the open market bazaar in Berlin where Eastern Europeans were hawking their wares to West Germans who were incredulous at the cheap prices on goods. There we were, a large, pale Midwestern guy and a skinny, black-belt, black Easterner vying for space and attention. There were Babushkas selling bras that would fit most small nations, men selling tools and army gear from Russia and other East European countries. It was truly a pell-mell of activity so Pete and I fit right in. Our stroke of genius was the Vodka, it sold at premium prices in about ten minutes. The chachki dolls sold, but not nearly as profitable or easily.

Off we went to get near the autobahn and found an office building with an open back door that allowed us access to the exterior, enclosed stairwell. We were in the stairwell but could not enter the main building (score!). We had our gratis housing for the night, sales profits stuffing our pockets, off to the nearest bier-hall we ambled to celebrate our success. Cold beer, a warm, dry place to sleep in our sleeping bags and camp mats. Life was blessing us amply.

Next morning, our gear was packed up, teeth brushed and the adventurers were ready for more. The A2 Autobahn was a few kilometers away. We slogged to the Autobahn entryway only 656 kilometers (about seven hours) from Amsterdam. Our luck continued to hold, and we caught a ride with some guy making deliveries a couple hundred kilometers along A2 - sweet! A little after midday, the driver deposited us at another entry ramp and out went the thumbs. In practice, hand-waving is the norm for hitchhiking in Europe. Our luck turned. No rides, no bathrooms, hungrier than hell other than a few cookies and some stale bread. As the hours passed and our progress continued to be impeded, we resorted to the one bottle of Vodka we had left, stored in one of Pete's black socks. We took turns trotting into the weeds to take a pull off the clear stuff. Within an hour, we were again giddy, in fine spirits when fortune struck. A touring band of hippies/folk musicians rolled by in a school bus about half the size of a US school bus. It was decked out with bean bags, couches, beads, tie-dyed curtains and about twelve troubadours, mostly long-haired, leather clad, skinny as wire folks and a few real Earth Moms. We gladly shared our bottle of lightning with them. They shared their food, music and laughter. On top of it all, they were headed home to Amsterdam so our tickets were punched. After a bit, Pete and I curled up in the back, each on a bean bag and slept the sleep of the dead. Hours later we woke up in the center of Amsterdam. Thank yous and hugs were exchanged along with a few dollars for gas to our new friends.

The next morning, Tracy had to work so Pete and I were free to roam at will about Amsterdam with the promise that cold beer would await Tracy. Pete had not been to Amsterdam before, so I played tour guide. We started with a visit to the Van Gogh Museum (mind-numbing!). We even sat in on a lecture by a Van Gogh scholar about the art markets, trends and economics of artists in Van Gogh's day. Next, we were off to Anne Frank's House for a tour of where she was hidden all those years (a few years ago in Jackson Hole, I heard the woman speak who had hid Anne in her house). The final stop on our cultural spin about town was a tour of the Heineken brewery, which of course was a challenge for Pete and I but we managed to make the best of it.

Time to get back to Tracy's, procure some beer, cheese, crackers, bread, etc. as a means of showing our gratitude. I remember the beer to this day. It was Grolsch flip-tops from the market across the street, in a green plastic returnable crate. It was tied for the best beer I ever had with Pilsner Urquell in Pilzen, Czechoslovakia also a brewery tour I suffered through. Ah, but yet again I digress and the next paragraph must be up to the beauty of that afternoon.

Tracy's interior courtyard was a garden of beauty, cobblestones, trees, tables, chairs, benches, flowers, etc. It was as splendid of a simple spot as I have ever seen. Surrounding the courtyard on four sides were apartments of young Dutch artisans, tradespeople, musicians and so on. The afternoon sun kissed the courtyard, the table had been as nicely prepared (as best as Pete and I were capable of). Tracy arrived and we took turns bantering on about life and sitting in silence soaking it all in. Soon, other residents drifted into the courtyard and joined us. Beer, wine, food, music, laughter all liberally exchanged. A few times in life I have been present for such magical experiences - this moment was right up near the top.

Now, you are probably wondering why the subtitle to this book - Cultural Barbarians. Allow me to explain. As this impromptu event progressed, Athena arrived. This natural, stunning, kinky blonde haired Dutch young woman was a vision, a vision so enamoring that of course Pete and I were drawn in like moths to a flame. Her actual name was Hannika, she was so simple, elegantly beautiful that we were entranced into her spell without thought. Then she started to ask Pete and I questions. Where are we from? How is Poland? How did we get to Amsterdam? What are we doing while we are here? Just as Arlo Guthrie did, we told our story in four-part harmony. We told of our other adventures about Europe, about Berlin, Poland, Italy, etc. She listened attentively, enjoying the mayhem of our travels.

When we finished, Hannika looked at both of us and said, "So, let me see if I get this right, you guys tramp all over Europe, seeing and engaging in significant cultural activities; art, history, architecture and then in the late afternoon you get properly pissed, is that correct?"

Exchanging glances, Pete and I nodded affirmatively in unison and said, "Yup, that's us!"

"Sounds to me like you are both Cultural Barbarians," she said without a trace of positive or negative attached, just recognition of who we were.

Pete and I exchanged glances, high-fived, danced, hugged, laughed and even got hugs from Athena aka Hannika. We had been correctly identified, labeled, and henceforth we were and are the "Cultural Barbarians."

## Is that an ICBM or are you just happy to see me? (Fall 1989)

It was a cloudy, dark night after a cloudy grey day. The windows of my second story flat began to rattle about 3 a.m. and the roar of a semi came within earshot. What the hell is that I wondered? The noise grew steadily louder leaving the option of sleep a fleeting memory. I arose in my boxers and T-shirt to see what was the matter. As I looked below, a realization came upon me that truly was one of the most unnerving feelings I have ever experienced.

In 1988, President Reagan and Mikhail Gorbachev had negotiated an Intermediate-Range Nuclear Forces treaty. Twenty feet below me was the first of six intercontinental ballistic missiles (ICBM's) that were being pulled back from East Germany and Western Poland to the Soviet Union. Each of the missiles below me was capable of killing hundreds of thousands of people. Each missile was covered with a camouflage netting and was being moved at night in hopes that they wouldn't be visible to "eyes in the sky."

The idea that a weapon of mass destruction was right below me, being driven by a shitty 1960's Soviet truck with a bad muffler was beyond disturbing. The parade was moving at 5-10 miles per hour and the sheer size and length of these monsters was mind-numbing. Suddenly, the realization of the pinhead that the World had been balancing on since 1945 hit home for me. Good night, sleep tight.

## *Amerikanen ma Pilka* (The American has the ball) (Spring 1990)

To do justice to this one I need to lay a foundation to make this story come together. My freshman year at the College of St. Thomas I went out for the rugby team. I made the team but I really wasn't the right size for any position. I was too light for the scrum and too heavy for the backs. So I played some "B" matches but it just wasn't clicking.

By my Junior year, I had beefed up considerably and was lifting weights like a madman. In short, I had become a 225-230 lb beefcake who was an Irish barrel-chested guy. I went back to rugby and not only was I good at it, I was excelling. My position was loose head prop, meaning that I was in the front-line of the scrum with my right ear free to the outside and my left ear into the scrum, the triangle of humanity that hooks up with the opposing team's scrum (triangle). I played very well, loved the camaraderie and the game itself.

My senior year, I spent the fall semester at American University in Washington D.C., playing loose-head prop for the AU Eagles. This was serious rugby. We played all over the Northeast, the most memorable being when we went to Annapolis in Maryland to play the Naval Academy. It was one hell of a match, I think we lost by three but played great as did the extremely well-trained cadets. After the game, we went into a small clubhouse, and some naval muckety-muck came in and said, "Gentlemen, congratulations on a wonderful match today. In the corner is a sixteen-gallon token of appreciation. That said, this was never here, you may not leave this building for two hours, guards will be posted. Cadets, you will return to your quarters in exactly two hours, roll will be taken. To our guests, you will have two hours and fifteen minutes to exit this structure at which time your team bus will return you to the AU campus. Good match today, enjoy yourself gentlemen." With that he left and the vultures of both teams descended on the barrel of happiness. Damn good time!

Thus, once I was in Poland, I had the desire to play some more rugby. The closest team was *Orkan Sochaczev* (the Tornado from Sochaczev) about forty-five kilometers from where I lived. I visited the squad a few times and inquired if they were interested in having an American loose-head prop to join the squad. "Love to have you was the response" so I was now a Tornado. *Orkan* was a semipro team at the time so it was extremely competitive rugby with skilled guys at each position. I bought a mini-bike that I could ride to and from practice and matches.

Now being on a semipro team had its perks. We traveled all over Poland for matches. I dislocated my right index finger at a match in Katowice. When the Doctor yanked it back into place I raked the nurses shin with my aluminum cleats, drawing four lines of blood down her leg (sorry). I am happy report that I recovered enough in time to join the team for the post-game Vodka gathering. Another classic was just before our match, two of our bigger guys were in the locker room and spoke zero English. My Polish was passable at the time, anyhoo, these guys are sitting there with these two vials of amber fluid. They can see I am watching them, curious what's up. Stanislav holds up his vial and says, "Ben Johnson" then smiles and drinks the fluid. Of course, Ben Johnson was the first major Olympic athlete to get caught doping in 1988. My teammates were doping. What the hell? I guess I hope it helps, I thought.

Time for the main story. The Soviets sent over a team to take on the Tornado on our home pitch. They brought these 1950 speakers, a small camper thing with an extended arm to lift the speaker twenty-five feet. The speakers themselves looked like they had come straight out of M*A*S*H. The match was to be broadcast live on site as well as being broadcast back in Russia. Let's just say, the Russians weren't small, but we had an edge in speed. Through the first half it was a close match and we led by a few at halftime. Early in the second half I stepped up to intercept a pitch by a Ruskie, and I had nothing but forty meters of daylight ahead of me. I start sprinting for the try line (end zone) as fast as my stout legs would carry me. Over the loud speakers I can hear the Russian announcer bellowing "The American's got the ball, the American's got the ball." (He sure as hell didn't know how to say Tom Hickey) "He's at the thirty-meter line, the twenty meter line, the ten meter line." I am starting to actually believe I might score, similar to a fat lineman in the NFL punching one over. I get to the five, the two - Wham! Some tall, fast, Ruskie ran me down. I am knocked out of bounds with no clue what just happened. My teammates are picking me up, game on!

We would go onto score and to win. The post-match party was a display unlike anything I have ever seen, these Russians knew how to seriously consume distilled spirits in mass quantities. This truly was a day of *glasnost*.

To end my rugby career, I would play a couple of years with the Jackson Hole Moose until age, body, and family dictated that I cease such intense combat.

# ACT V

## HALINA, TWO YOUNGINS AND A CABIN IN THE TETONS

### "Are you married or are you single?" (December 1988)

The holidays were near, and I was settling into my teaching gig just fine. From basic English for beginners to discussions of agriculture and literature with PHD's who had studied in the states, it grew on me. A couple of days a week I had class in a building off the main campus (palace grounds more like it). So off I strode to where the testing labs, a kilometer or two away, where the experimental fields were located.

Most of the students in this class were all lab assistants who helped prepare agricultural papers and monitor experiments. To my delight, they were mostly women who giggled a lot. It was a beginning English class and the only textbook I had was a crappy British English book that was donated by the British Embassy. It was stuffy and stilted, but it was all I had.

About mid-month, a new student came back from a three month exchange in East Germany at another AG Institute. Enter Ms. Halina, stunningly beautiful, blonde hair, blue eyes, thin and gentle. Sadly, she was wearing a wedding ring though - damn my luck! As my freshman English teacher, Dr. Lippert, would say, "But I digress, back to the text!"

About the third class Halina attended, we were doing an exercise in the British book answering basic questions. I would ask the questions in order and the students would reply as best they could. As fate would have it, when the question came to Halina it was "Are you married or are you single?" I swear it was just luck she got that question, I did not rig it - I already thought she was married. Halina looked at me, blushed a little and with a heavy accent said, "I am single." What? Hold the presses. However, having to maintain classroom decorum, I moved onto the next student "Do you like ice cream?" or some other inane thing.

As class came to a close I drifted out to the hallway to chat with the students and when Halina strolled by I said, "Ms. I don't think you understood the question, you said were single but you have a wedding ring on?" as I pointed to her left hand.

She raised her right hand, blushed a little and pointed to her ring finger which was empty, "In Poland we wear our wedding rings on the right-hand."

Then she turned and headed down the stairs and back to work.

Bingo - winner, winner, chicken dinner - Amen, Hallelujah - I'm not worthy! etc.etc.etc.

Note: All of my "students" were "workers" and most were older than me, including Halina.

## Supporting Characters (1989)

No accounting of my years in Poland could be complete without including two incredible characters and the fascinating lives they led. I was truly fortunate to become part of their lives and ultimately their family.

**Gruba Bacia (Big Granny)** - Halina's maternal Grandma, known by all as "Fat Granny" or I think more appropriate in translation would be "Big Granny" Gruba Babcia was a short, stout fascinating woman. She lived on the family farm with her son, sleeping in an unheated room off the back of the house. Gruba Babcia slept under a twenty-inch-thick *pierzen* comforter so on the coldest winter night, she was toasty in bed. The farm itself had no running water, no plumbing, and no heat except for the wood stove in the small kitchen attached to the barns which was heated by coal or wood.

The farmyard was surrounded by buildings on three sides with the fourth side opening to the fields. Tiny by U.S. standards, it was probably about ten acres in size, but plenty enough to grow all you needed to live off of. It was the original version of living off the grid. In the out buildings animals were housed which included pigs, chickens, dairy cows, workhorses, sheep, ducks, and farm dogs. It was a self-sufficient Noah's Ark, impervious to what the Communist government might be doing out there.

How to describe Gruba Babcia? She was about four-foot-eight inches tall and had shrunken in time with osteoporosis as so many in the old World did. She was round and stout, not fat but certainly solid. She was in her eighties at the time, wearing mismatched clothing and an eternal smile. She never complained about anything, and everything she ever did was for her family. Her hands were a marvel, large, calloused, meaty and warm from a lifetime of hard manual labor. She was full of charm, practical wisdom and lots of rural superstitions. Always adorning her head was a kerchief worn in the babushka style. Her blue eyes didn't work in tandem with the left eye tending to wander. When she smiled at you or held your face in her hands, there was an instant feeling of peace and love.

Each morning at dawn, Gruba Babcia arose and tended to the animals, hand pumping water from the old iron pump in the farmyard. As I get to know her and love her, I knew that I was seeing into a bygone world which was soon to disappear. At our wedding, Gruba Babcia and Pradziadek sang to us an old folklore song about the things a new married couple would need to know to be happy. It was bawdy, witty and charming, the guests were roaring with laughter. At the conclusion, dear sweet Gruba Babcia handed me a large bowl with a plate covering it. She sang how the secret to children and a happy life was enclosed, warily I lifted the plate and saw a large sausage with two hard boiled eggs each strategically placed at the base of the sausage. The crowd erupted. Gruba Babcia kissed me, and I knew I now was part of the family.

**Pradziadek (Great-Grandpa Jozef)** - The first time I saw Pradziadek he was coming off the local train wearing a suit and carrying his bike on his shoulder headed up the stairs to cross to our side of the tracks. He was 90 years old. There was not a hair on his head except for a stout mustache that made him resemble an old Italian photograph. His grip was like a vice; the strongest hands I ever happened upon.

Jozef was Artur's father and Halina's grandfather. He had lived his whole life within a hundred-kilometer zone. He attended school through the fourth grade, learning just enough, as Artur would joke, 'to learn how to count money'. Jozef was a shrewd and brilliant businessman. He bought tracks of forest land, set up his own lumber mill and was always ready with cash if a good deal came along. He was like the Village Don. If somebody needed or wanted something, Pradziadek was who they went to see.

As World War II raged, Jozef kept to himself and kept his lumber business going. One day he was driving some logs to the mill with his horse team when a German Staff Sergeant came up in his open topped Mercedes, Jozef was halfway through the dirt road intersection when the Staff Sergeant came up to him, yelling about the lumber cart blocking his way. He then drew his pistol and hit Jozef on the side of the head with the pistol butt. Grandpa was deaf in that ear the rest of his life with a dent to prove it. What the Sergeant did not fully comprehend though was, that although Pradziadek was too old to serve in the army, he wasn't too old to fight. For the rest of the war, strange things would happen in Jozef's forests, no German was safe and several mishaps befell anyone in a German uniform.

As a student of history, just listening to Jozef tell his stories was an incredible experience. His life was full of hard work and success, which he shared with his family and gratefully with me.

## Decision Time (April 1989)

Okay folks, until now I have walked down the street naked for you, filling in blanks as I went. Here, I shall discuss my wife of almost thirty years and soon, our two children. All three are taboo and off-limits other than general stories in this narrative. I owe them their privacy, their own lives and destinies.

My first real date with Halina was in mid-December 1988, I made Chinese food at my apartment and as decorum would dictate, another couple joined us so that Halina would not be alone with the "sleazy" American. I did an admirable job of preparing a meal with basic ingredients. Halina arrived in a fur coat, white gloves, a grey blouse and skirt, high black leather boots and dark leggings. I was 100% absolutely certain that she was wealthier than crap, and that I had no chance in hell.

Everyone was a bit tense, with me being less tense because I usually am. The highlight of the evening was when Gosia, the female in attendance asked Halina what she thought of me, to which she replied, "*On jest bardzo sympaticzna*" (he is very likable). Damn, I was in the game!

My first dates with Halina entailed me taking the train fifteen kilometers to her home in Radziwillow Mazowieckie, a former hunting ground of Polish royalty and a heavily wooded area. Halina's family home, a three room lower floor of a duplex was right across the tracks from the train station. Initially, I always had to bring my Polish-English dictionary so that I could communicate with Halina, her sister Lilka, parents Artur and Basia. About six months into my time, I could safely leave home without my "slownik" (dictionary) and navigate everyday life.

Halina and I fell in love pretty damn fast. Let me repeat,

we fell in love. This was an exotic, fun, fluid relationship. We enjoyed being together and everything being new, we longed to be alone, to have simple time, sitting on a bench, practicing Polish on the couch, or cooking together. The relationship with her family was a no-brainer. If I may be so bold, I think they knew I was a decent man who would always take care of their daughter. In a short time, my heart was given, accepted, and reciprocated.

In April of 1989, a Polish friend, Gregor (Greg) pulled me aside. His inquiry was what are my intentions with Halina? Huh, perplexed I asked what he meant. "Look Tom, Every American has the same reputation, dirtbag. You come here, spend time with a Polish woman, time runs out and you all go home. The Polish woman has just spent significant time with the sleazy American, her reputation is ruined meaning no Polish guy wants to ask her out, and you Yanks are back in the States moving on to the next girl."

I totally got where he was coming from and all of its ramifications. The last thing I wanted was to hurt Halina or her family. It was time for some soul-searching and introspection. There was a big park in Skierniwice with the entrance close to the dairy store, *Mleczarnia*. I walked the park for hours, considering all options. End it and move on. Stay in the game and see what comes. Think Tom - this is a big one you lummox! As I strolled towards the *Mleczarnia*, the answer was crystal clear. I can imagine my life with this woman. I can't imagine my life without her! Damn the torpedoes, full speed ahead...

### Stateside and Mom's Ring (August 1989)

Things with Halina had progressed to the point where I knew I wanted to marry her if she would have me. I hadn't come looking for a bride when I came to Poland, but I had potentially found one. With the summer break upon me, I flew Stateside in August to retrieve Mom's wedding ring which had been left to me after her death. The only issue was that the ring was in my father's care and that meant I would have to ask him for it. I knew what was coming.

Back in Minnesota at Joan's house, I asked Dad for some time to talk. He deferred me to cocktail hour, obviously wanting a good stiff drink for this one (not that I could blame him). So the summit is set and at 4:30 p.m. I report to the living room, beer in hand. Dad has a bourbon on the rocks that he managed to get a few ice cubes into.

"Dad, I am going to ask Halina to marry me, and I would like to get Mom's ring, please."

My part is done, now I can drink my beer.

And Dad is off, "Now just hold on there, you don't have any money, no job, and you have known her less than a year," he started. "How are you going to support a wife? Where are you going to live?"

...and on it went.

After about five minutes, I had heard enough "You know Dad, when the day comes when my adult son tells me he is getting married, I hope I just stick out my may hand, congratulate him and wish him the best" was my rejoinder.

He softened but quipped, "We aren't there yet" a couple more minutes and he had had his say.

Seeing I was unswayed by his arguments, he accepted the situation, shook my hand and then we had a good stiff drink together.

As a quick addendum, when Dad met Halina a year later, it took him about ten seconds to fall in love with her. She completely won over his heart. Dad loved Halina unequivocally, and I am quite certain that until his untimely end, that he thought that Halina had made a big mistake in marrying his youngest son.

### Engaged Polish Style (September 1989)

Back across the pond I jetted, ring in tow and a woman waiting who will hopefully say yes. When I got back, I made dinner at my place then went out on our beautiful little balcony, got on one knee and asked for her hand in marriage. I had the ring fitted to her size in the States with one of her other rings that I had swiped. She said, "Yes" which I thought was fitting since I ran the gauntlet with my dad and we were now engaged, or so I thought. The next day at work, no one would talk about it, acknowledge it or even say congratulations. 'What the hell is this, I thought?' After work I saw Halina, and she gave me very specific instructions. On Sunday I was to be at her house at 1 p.m., bring flowers for her mother, sister and for her. I was to bring a bottle of Vodka for her father. Wear your best clothes, chocolates would be well received and don't be late.

At the appointed hour I arrived and was escorted into Room #3 (remember, only three rooms in the house). I sat down with Artur to discuss our plans. Oh great, another grumpy dad I thought. This was a piece of cake, Art in a suit and tie wanted to know that I would be good to his daughter, to take care of her and any future kids. He asked some basic questions about our plans and with that we intertwined arms and had a shot of vodka - I had a new Dad. Into Room #1 we went. A massive feast was laid out. Close relatives were on hand with more distant relatives to stop by later. Vodka bottle after Vodka bottle was opened. Course after course of food appeared and sitting together, beaming, Halina and I were soon to be wed. On top of that, in a little over a year, I had integrated into a different culture and now had a huge, extended family. Couldn't have mapped it out better if I had tried.

### Weddings Polish Style (January 20th, 1990)

Engagements in Poland are brief compared to the States. So once the engagement was on the books, things started to move quickly. January 20th was selected as the date, just four months away. The church was reserved, a banquet hall was booked and the civil wedding was put on the docket. Back home in the States, both my brothers, Bill and Bob booked tickets into Berlin. And to my surprise, my cousins Mary and Aileen and even my old neighbor, Ted Freese, would also make the trip. Not an easy undertaking given the challenges of travel in Eastern Europe, crowded trains, people jostling and not a single one of them spoke a word of Polish. All in all, it took a lot of guts for them to attend, and I am grateful that they did. Due to medical care issues and his recent heart surgery, Dad would not be able to make the trip, I fully understood.

Now the parties and celebrations would go on for days, meaning I was the host with the most who didn't get any sleep for seventy-two plus hours. It was brutal. On Wednesday night, the American teachers in Poland plus a few other BVS volunteers from across Europe made the trek to see the big guy go down the aisle. We had quite the bash that night in the Hotel Cudko, a communist structure made of concrete and art promoting the workers state. It was ugly, comfortable, except for the lower floors where Mary and Aileen would stay where cockroaches had made their homes close to the kitchen below. All in all, lots of beer, some Vodka and little sleep for Tommy Boy.

The next night my family was arriving. We would meet them in a city called Kutno about 11 p.m., ninety minutes from Skierniewice. To welcome them properly and to make it easy for them to see me, I took a bed sheet and wrote on it "Welcome Cub Fans to Eastern Europe." As the train rolled into the station, I knew they would be nervous as hell that this was the right place. Bill stuck his head out the window and was yelling my name. I yelled back and confirmed that not only had they survived, but they had made it to the right place. Now the train was packed, corridors jammed with people standing. Getting them all out of the train was going to be a challenge. The guys started handing me the suitcases out the window, Mary and Aileen held tight to their purses and just like the Chicago Bears front line, they just plowed right through the sea of humanity. Within ten minutes we were all assembled, bags and people piled into a couple of friend's cars who had agreed to help. Yet another night, little or no sleep for me.

The next day was the big family get together dinner at Halina's house. Basia, Halina's Mom, had been preparing for a month for this three-day gala. Family one meets family two, for the first time without a common language other than yours truly and Halina acting as translators. Fortunately, there was vodka which coupled with copious amounts of food loosened everybody up. My brother Bob, not a big drinker ended up having perhaps one to two too many vodka shots. He was shitfaced! He locked himself in the bathroom by mistake and pulled a plant off a shelf dumping dirt all over the floor. His voice went up an octave or two and the piece de resistance was when Basia asked how he liked the Flaki, a traditional Polish tripe soup, a dish that Bob wouldn't eat in a hundred years, he nodded his head saying "very good" which meant he got two more ladles of tripe from Basia. I thought I would wet my pants. It was a memorable, fun evening with the best part being able to share Poland and Halina's family with my family. Yes, not much sleep for yours truly and tomorrow is the big day.

Saturday morning came and since the Communist government did not recognize Church weddings, we would first have a civil wedding in the morning presided over by a Judge. I had a suit made for the occasion, Halina had a new business type dress, simple yet refined. We produced all the needed documents and Bill stood in as my best man. The ceremony was brief, straight forward and over within about thirty minutes. A little champagne on the steps of the courthouse, and off we sped to get ready for the main event, the Church wedding.

Halina's church is a beautiful, 450 year-old structure with stained glass windows immortalizing Poland's hero, Pope John Paul II. In the history of that Church, no American had ever been wed, so most of the villagers turned out to see the gringo give it a go. In most churches in Poland there is no heat. It was January 20th and you could literally see your breath. I am in a rented tuxedo. Halina is in a beautiful satin dress made from material that a friend's mother sent over as a gift. Poor Halina was so frail and the dress not providing any heat that she was literally shivering, the flowers in her hand quaking. As the service progressed, the Church did get warmer just due to body heat from those in attendance. I only made one mistake, I was supposed to say, "*Ja nie bede opuszic ciebie*" literally, "I not will leave you." I said, "I will leave you not" putting the negative at the end, which no one heard because everybody gasped, all they had heard was "I will leave you." Anyhoo, the priest had me say it again. I got it right and we were pronounced husband and wife.

Now my dad was feeling bad that he couldn't be there and wanting to be a part of things, he had sent $2000 with my brother Bill for a dinner on him. What he didn't know was that our entire wedding party would cost $1800 and here is what we got for it: the wedding hall; a band that played for fifteen hours with breaks for food and Vodka; seven meals, yes, I said seven meals spaced out from 6 p.m. to 9 a.m. the next morning; two bottles of vodka per person, I think we had one hundred sixty bottles of vodka in all; a couple of cases of beer for the gringos; and, flowers for the table settings. Now tradition dictates that the only people who aren't allowed to drink at a wedding is the bride and groom. So, I got to watch all my friends and family have a raucous time, and I drank Coca-Cola. Bob was still green from the night before but he was in rare form at the reception. About 1 a.m., I look over and I see Bill doing shots with Halina's Grandfather and Uncle Charlie, a massive guy. All were so rinsed and didn't speak each other's language that they were signing, smiling, and drinking heavily. At one point, Bill and Grandpa Jozef were doing the traditional three cheek kiss of friendship and they missed - kissing each other right on the lips - still one of my favorite memories.

About 2:30 a.m., my family pooped out and I sent them back to Hotel Cudko in a classic, vintage Soviet van I had rented for the occasion. About 4 a.m., I gave up on the Coca-Cola and had some vodka and beer, I'll be damned if I will miss my own wedding. By 8 a.m. I was so tired I just wanted to go sleep, but Halina would have none of it. About 10 a.m. the party shut down and we headed back to the hotel where we had a room for a couple of days. We were going to sleep but nature took its course, no sleep for me but at least I was happy! Back to Halina's house we went and the second day party was in full swing, close family continuing right on with the libations and feasting, incredible. Halina and I then headed to Warsaw to get my family on the train to Vienna. All were weary, but glad to have been a part of the momentous occasion.

That night Halina and I stayed at a beautiful Holiday Inn in Warsaw. We finally both slept a good 14 hours. From there we were off to the Tatry Mountains in Southern Poland for a sixteen day honeymoon. We had a great time as most people do on their honeymoons. The best part was we had nothing we had to do, so we just relaxed, recuperated, ate well and well, you know!

### How to exit a Hospital? (June 1990)

We were now six months married, and Halina was a few months pregnant. Initially, our plans were to go to Norway and pick strawberries for the summer but we couldn't have been happier to have a child on the way and a chance to get a family started.

A few months into the pregnancy, Halina experienced some spotting, or minor bleeding. To make sure all was okay, we went to the Skierniewice Hospital and had Halina checked out. The doctor wanted to admit her for a few days for observation, just to make sure everything was all right. Thus, a maternity ward built for twenty patients, admitted a thirty seventh patient, my wife, who would have a bed in the hallway due to the overcrowding. The maternity ward had two toilets, not bathrooms, so two stools for thirty-seven pregnant women. I'll just let you picture that scenario.

At the time, patients in the hospital did not get meals, that was to be taken care of by the immediate family. Thus, I worked up a schedule with Halina's folks to deliver food three times a day plus whatever Halina wanted: fruits, juices, breads, etc. Amazingly, Halina kept commenting how kind the people were and that she was just fine. Hell of a better trooper than me if I was sleeping in a hall.

Three days go by and Halina is feeling fine. The spotting has ceased, and she is able to get up and walk around. Yes, another day or two and she can be released we all thought. Day Four, still there. Day Five, still there. Day Six, still there. I am losing my mind, what is the deal?

On seventh day, I went to visit my friend who is a doctor and told him the whole story.

He listened attentively and then replied, "You have to bribe the Doctor."

"What?" I replied incredulously.

"Tom, here is how it works here. That doctor knows you are an American and you must have some money. He works in an overcrowded hospital for low wages, he just wants you to give him some cash to help him out and he will help you out."

A bribe, if that's what it was going to take, oh well, all part of the grand adventure.

Into a dull grey envelope I stuffed $100 US and headed to the hospital. The doctor and I made chit-chat for a minute or two and then I told him that I would very much like to take my wife home today and how much I appreciated his hard work on her behalf then I slid the envelope across the desk, adding "Here is a small token of my appreciation."

He went silent, looked in the envelope, locked it in his desk and arose. "I think we can get this taken care of this afternoon. I will get to work on the paperwork."

Ninety minutes later, Halina was on her way home with me and we had learned a lot about socialized medicine. We would leave Poland in a few months to have the baby in America, quite certain I wouldn't have to bribe the doctor to get her and the baby out of the hospital given the costs in a free-market healthcare system.

### Stateside with my Bride (August 1990)

With Halina pregnant and my two-year volunteer stint almost up, we had a choice to make. We could remain in Poland and have the baby there, or hightail it over the pond and have it in the States. Since my job prospects in Poland would require a work visa, not an easy task at the time, we decided to head Stateside where I knew I could get employment that would at least keep us afloat. Thus, after Halina got her green card from the US Embassy in Warsaw, we booked our flight for early August.

Now Halina had never been on a plane before and here she was about to be whisked away to a foreign land with a foreign language and have a child. It all was a bit overwhelming for her. I must say that I knew we would be okay because jobs are plentiful to those willing to work hard in the States.

Off we flew, Warsaw to Chicago, Chicago to Minneapolis. Halina was wearing one of my oversized, old dress shirts and khakis. She never looked lovelier. As we exited the plane, about twenty-five of our friends and family were awaiting. Halina was presented with her first McDonald's experience, hugs, and kisses. Instantly, all had fallen in love with her, as I knew they would. The same remains true to this day, Halina is the glue in this family and the better half. I am fortunate indeed.

Our initial plans were to live with my father and Joan, a challenging proposition for sure. From Minneapolis - St. Paul International Airport, we headed to the western suburbs but the caravan didn't go to Dad's. Bob said he had to grab something at his home in Long Lake first and then we would be off to Dad's. When we got close to Bob's place, he pulled into an apartment complex and we all followed him in. He, my brother Bill, our friends, my dad, had all gotten together and rented a $400 per month small one-bedroom apartment. It was fully furnished with items that people had donated; Rick's King size mattress, the Miller's patio furniture, somebody's old TV, towels, mismatched pots and pans, glassware, etc. In short, it was an instant garage sale apartment and it was perfect because it was OURS!!!!!!!! It was the greatest surprise I have ever been witness to and the kindest thing that any group of people has ever done for me and my family. We had our own place, a little kitchenette off the living room, a big bay window and privacy. Many tears of joy were shed, my deepest love to everyone who helped out. It was our humble beginning but we were blissfully happy.

### That's my Boy Luke! (January 1st, 1991)

Halina was as big as she could get. I had never seen such a slight person have such a large belly. The baby was due any day and inducement was being discussed as an option within the week. On New Year's Eve, Halina woke up early, about 6 a.m. and felt nauseous. She didn't think much of it as it had become common in the mornings. About 7:30 a.m., she went into the little bathroom in our apartment and whoosh - liquid all over the floor. Her water had broken. It was game on. At the time, we didn't have insurance. However, Minnesota, being a progressive state, had a program for pregnant women funded by cigarette taxes: healthy babies, healthy mamas - healthy future for Minnesota. The caveat was that we had to get Halina to downtown Minneapolis ASAP and Hennepin County Medical Center since this was a government program.

I called the doctor, and they said to get her there on the double. We grabbed our pre-packed bags, piled into my "new" used $3000 Toyota Corolla and sped like hell down Highway

12. I have never in my life wanted to see a police car as much as I did that morning but it wasn't meant to be. Halina was sitting uncomfortably on towels and in need of medical help. Nobody said this was going to be so stressful. We hit the ER doors and in about twenty minutes, Halina was admitted. I went to park the car in the outdoor parking ramp, temperatures outside a balmy -20!

From here it gets chaotic, dull, hurry up, wait and then launch time. During the day, Halina is stabilized and is not adequately dilated, hence we bide our time. I am doing the ice chip thing and all the "Husbandy" things they taught us to do in birthing class. Halina is miserable, and I am not much use other than translating what is going on. Early evening, the doctors are worried that the baby is not getting enough oxygen and may be running a fever. Halina goes on an epidural. Machines that go "bing" start appearing. More doctors and nurses are coming in. About midnight, Halina is dilated fully. Contractions are strong. The epidural is wearing off and the concern for the baby's health is growing. We are moved to the Operating Room for mothers and infants.

Now it is all gowns, masks, gloves, medical staff, Halina and me. She is exhausted. I just want this to end, and more important to have a healthy wife and baby. As we roll past 3 a.m., we are close. They keep attaching this suction cup to the baby's head, trying to pull it out, no go. Finally, they use forceps and pull the baby out. A nurse lifts the baby, and I see two grape nuts as HE is whisked over to the intensive baby care station. We have a boy! Luke David Hickey! Within a few minutes he checks out well, healthy and strong. I am bouncing between the baby table and Halina, who was torn up good when they used the forceps. A surgeon was stitching Halina back up which would take almost an hour and an extended recuperation period would be needed for my hero.

At 7 a.m. on New Year's Day, I am starving. Halina is sleeping and Luke is sleeping or feeding. I decide to go get some fresh air (only 15 below today!). I find the only open place for miles, kind of a French cafe and bistro. I order eggs benedict and ask the kindly, elderly waitress if they might have champagne or beer, I am a first time Dad. "I'm sorry, but we don't have alcohol here" she replied. So onto the paper I go, glass of juice and hot coffee. About ten minutes later, the kitchen doors open and the staff comes out with my breakfast; a muffin with a candle in it and a bottle of champagne they had scrounged up somewhere. The fifteen diners on hand all joined in with the staff and they sang "Happy Birthday to my son - Luke!" Tears rolled down my cheeks and everyone toasted to our new family. My heart goes out to everyone who was there that morning. You made a new Dad's universe!

## Bull Elk Bugling to the Unbroken Circle (September 1993)

Life was pretty idyllic for us. We were renting a small cabin way out in the mountains of Wyoming, a half mile from the school for troubled boys that I taught at. The cabin had two tiny bedrooms, a big loft, kitchen and the smallest living room I had ever seen with a view that was grander than most mansions. It was rustic, simple, a wood stove as the primary heat source, and a charm that just simply said, welcome!

6:30 a.m. MST September 1, 1993: Our phone rings. It rings a couple of times more, and I stumble towards the phone knowing that no good news ever comes at this time of day.

"Hello," I croak.

"Hey Tom, Bill here (my brother), sorry to have to tell you but Joan called me a little while ago and Dad didn't wake up this morning. When she woke up, he was in an awkward position, cold and not moving." Of course, all these facts pointed only to one thing, but Joan was probably in shock and not processing things all that well. Bill continued, "I told her to call for an ambulance and that I would be right over."

Dad had died peacefully in his sleep, either from a heart attack or stroke. He had left explicit instructions, do not resuscitate or perform an autopsy if he died of natural causes. Balls started to roll into motion, and I suddenly had to figure out a lot in a little time.

I needed air, space, morning sun and to be away for an hour to figure stuff out. Halina was overdue with our second child and was scheduled to be induced at the end of the week if she hadn't delivered by then. I stumbled, walked, hiked whatever you want to call it done Fall Creek Road beyond where the county maintenance ended, meaning I was in a rutted old logging road that required four-wheel drive to be passable. My head was spinning. Dad is dead. Mom is dead. I don't have parents anymore. An unsettling sensation, yet in the next few days I would be a father for the second time. The morning sun was now above the pine trees, to my right were some stunning creeks, full of trout. Not a soul anyway near me, and then it started...

In all my years in the mountains, I had never heard it before. A bull elk started to bugle for a mate. The hair on my neck stood up. It was close. It was loud and it was so beautiful. Obviously, this bull was seeking a companion, but to me it was a lone trumpeter letting loose a lament of sorrow and a herald of good things to come. For minutes I did not move. I stood in place, the sun basking me in one of nature's most beautiful locales. It was as if the bull was just telling the truth, the good, the bad, and just the way it is. I walked on. The bull kept bugling. I felt that somehow that things would be okay. Dad had achieved a lot in his life and soon his bloodline would flow anew.

Back to the cabin I hiked and reentered the realm of "Gringo runs the World." I called our physician, Dr. Sugden, who was to deliver our child. He wasn't in. I relayed our situation and his office said they would get a hold of him. I called work and said that I wouldn't be into work this week, regardless of how this all played out. They couldn't have been more understanding. Relatives and friends were called and then uncertainty set in. About 1 p.m. Dr. Sugden called, he was in-flight from Denver to Jackson Hole and said that he would see us in the morning at 7 a.m. at the hospital to induce Halina.

I thanked him profusely and said, "Doc, the only chance I have of attending my father's wake and funeral is that I catch a flight tomorrow afternoon to Minneapolis."

Graciously, he replied "I will do everything I can to make that possible."

"Thanks Doc!"

The next morning, we reported to St. John's Hospital, Luke would be staying with our friends Bob and Jean Carruth. I had a suitcase packed for Halina and one for myself in case I could catch my 1:30 flight, important, but not - I am going to be a Dad again, a repeat of the greatest thing that ever happened to me.

Forgive me but the pace is all about to pickup, and I just have to retell what I can. Halina was induced about 8:00 a.m. We were on a VIP expressway at the hospital (I assume thanks to Dr. Sugden), as everyone was working to assist and accommodate us. Unlike with Luke, Halina had a natural birth this time. The room was setup as a launching pad, clean, with some really bad wallpaper. There was a midwife on hand plus two nurses - THEY WERE AWESOME! When your life is off the rails, incredible people appear and that was the nursing staff that day. I was a wreck, stress, anxiety. God, I wish somebody would have handed me a pill. Instead Halina and Jean Carruth kicked me out of the hospital to get some fresh air. I bought a Foster's 24-ounce oil can and drove down the Elk Refuge Road never getting farther than 1 mile from the hospital but the fresh air, morning sun and soaring Tetons were a welcome respite.

Back to the hospital I go, about 10:30 a.m. and things are going into launch mode: nurses here, doctors there, Halina in the middle and me in the corner as usual, the useless appendage - stick to what your good at Tommy boy. As natural as this birth was, it was intense. Halina, bless her heart, doing everything she could, the nurses and doctor the same. The only one without something to do was me as I just tried to be supportive yet knowing I couldn't do anything else to help than stand there and be a witness. Somewhere about 11:30 a.m. it happened, our beautiful, screaming little girl, Gina Marie Hickey entered the world. There just aren't feelings to express my joy, a boy, a girl and our family was made. Gina was sound, strong, and cranky, definitely my girl. Halina was fine, exhausted, but physically okay. Luke came in and met his little sister for the first time. Luke was soon to-be two year old but destined to be a friend and a hell of a great older brother. I felt my life was magical at that moment with the price I had paid for it being the willingness to seek adventure in life.

Warp speed now, kiss, kiss, hug, hug, thank yous aplenty. Love you guys and off I sped to the Jackson Hole Airport. Flight to Denver connecting on to Minneapolis. Five hours later I am in the parking lot of St. Therese in Deephaven, MN where I went to grade school and served admirably as an altar boy (no, I never got touched by the priests but I may have taken a pull or two from the unblessed wine after mass).

In the parking lot were assembled about twenty of my oldest and dearest friends. I think Mills had the presence of mind to have brought a case or two of beer in his trunk and we stood there in the late afternoon sun, sipping a cold one, talking about my new baby Gina. The beer cold, the friends great, of course a sad occasion, yet I felt a strange balance inside. Thirty minutes later, halftime was over, time to attend to Dad, the wake, relatives, family, friends, etc. Into St. Therese I headed, into the outer area of the church where Dad laid. What struck me in viewing him was his hands, those long fingers now interlocked into a final state. They had done so much in a lifetime, football, two years in Tokyo after WWII, held, swatted me, once hit me and now their work was done. You were not an easy man, Dad, but you were a damn good one, honorable, determined and I think you would think best of all, a good provider.

The next morning was the funeral mass, simple, Catholic Mass, just as Dad wanted it. I held it together throughout the service but just as with Mom, when they rolled him up the aisle the final time I broke down like a three-year-old. Gonna miss you Dad - no more cocktail cribbage matches.

The blur continues, off to the cemetery and burial. I requested Dad's flag off the coffin and have it to this day. Back to the St. Therese gym for I have to say a really bad post funeral meal. The mood lightened as everyone needed to breathe. Kids ran and played, adults talked about the Vikings upcoming season, the Twins, who else had died, etc. That evening the immediate family gathered at Bill's house for a bonfire in the backyard, stories in the kitchen and cocktails a plenty. There was one strange thing about it that I remember. No one was getting loaded, not a proper Irish Wake as I had hoped for. I sure as hell was trying, but rowing a boat with one oar is an exercise in futility.

Next day, flights headed west back to Wyoming, my expanded family awaiting with Halina cycling on postpartum depression that would rule our lives for a few months to come. Gina so cute, so cantankerous, so small, so ours.

Just a few days, but enough emotion to last a lifetime.

### "V" is for Vasectomy (December 1993)

WARNING: Graphic, disturbing, humorous, humiliating (for me). If you are squeamish, skip this section! You have been warned!

We had officially procreated two healthy children, Luke and Gina, a boy and a girl and my wife was 100% adamant that: A) we were done having children; and, B) that I was going under the knife to get a vasectomy. I couldn't argue. In Poland two kids is a lot, and we had a wonderful young family. It was my turn for some pain down under.

I scheduled an appointment with Dr. Sugden who had delivered Gina a few months prior. The appointment was set,

I showed up on time expecting to undergo the procedure and get this over. Instead Dr. Sugden refused to perform the procedure that day due to: at twenty-eight years old I was too young to become sterile, what if God forbid my wife passed away? What if we divorced? What if we changed our minds in time, etc. etc. etc. My respect for Doc Sugden was way too high to argue. He did say that if I rescheduled the appointment and I come back in, he will know that my wife and I are serious and he will perform the procedure, no questions asked. He is a wise man, and I knew he was right to make us think about this a little longer.

After talking it over with Halina, the result was the same, snip-snip. I was going down. My appointment was rescheduled for two weeks later. I arrived at Doc Sugden's at the appointed time and was ushered into the mini-surgery room. There was a premed student from Stanford who was observing Dr. Sugden's case load. Up on the table I went, devoid of all pride as I was stripped from the belly button down, legs spread in stirrups and my ample Irish unit and scrotum for all to see. It was showtime!

Anesthesia was administered, and after about ten minutes, Houston you are cleared for launch. Now I am going to have to get a bit technical and graphic here, each nut has a small pasta noodle called the vas deferens which deliver the sperm from the nutsack to the large Irish unit. Thus, an incision is made into the nutsack and a small piece of each vas deferen is snipped out (maybe a quarter of an inch tops). Once the little piece of spaghetti is cut out, the real fun begins. Starting with the left nut, they cauterize the ends of the vas deferens. I am telling you, you haven't lived until you look down and see smoke rising from your gonads and the horrible stench of burning spaghetti - which is yours!

I survive the left nut, now it's time for the right-side billiard ball.

Doc Sugden said to the med student, "Do you want to do this one?"

"Sure" replies the med student and he steps up with the branding iron to scorch my right-side. The cauterizing tool is put in place and as he touches me with the cauterizer, I come 6" inches off the table. It feels as if someone hit me with 1000 volts running from nuts to my brain. I almost kicked the poor bastard over it hurt so bad.

"Did you feel that?" asks Doctor Sugden.

"What do you think Doc?" I reply less than pleasantly. "Guess we didn't get that side properly numbed."

A little more anesthesia and ten minutes time, and it was time to wrap this show up.

Now, how I wish this story ended here but that was not to be my luck.

The next night was my work's Christmas party just across the street from our cabin. I attended in sweat pants, sitting on a bag of ice all night and for the first time in my life. I was treated like royalty by every woman in the room. "Tom, can I get you another beer? Do you need anything from the buffet?" and so on. I might have even got a neck rub or two, a nice reward for taking one for the team.

About five days later we were to fly to Phoenix for the holidays at my brother Bob's. I wasn't supposed to lift anything. I wasn't to exert myself, blah, blah, blah. Now you tell me how do you transport two small kids, luggage, etc. from Jackson Hole to Phoenix without exerting yourself? Not gonna happen. So, by the time we arrive in Phoenix, my nuts are now the size of oranges. I cannot walk and I feel like shyte.

We were staying at a Super 8 that had a small pool, about 50 degrees since it was winter in Phoenix. I am reduced to getting into the cold arse pool up to five times a day. I must say, it worked miraculously because in two to three days I was back to normal.

Boy, I wish this story ended here.

To prove that a vasectomy has worked, it is necessary to give a sample of your man juice to see if sperm are still present.

An individual has seven minutes to provide the "juice" to the hospital laboratory for testing. I lived fifty minutes from the hospital, shyte, what am I going to do now? Being the ever-resourceful chap that I am, I procure a "gentlemen's" magazine at the Mini-Mart. I am then off to the Amoco Station on North Cache, two minutes from the hospital, where I avail myself of the 1950's men's tile bathroom and get to work. Pretty romantic huh, sorry no candles.

Now walking into a hospital with a cup of man juice is really pretty damn humbling. Here Nurse, here's my procreative juices for your analysis. To top it all off, I would have to repeat this procedure two more times to get the "sperm free" call from the laboratory.

Crazy life sometimes.

### Bile in the Compost Pile (April 1994)

Before moving back to Poland, Doc Sugden ran a physical on me, it seemed like a good idea and so we did labs, blood work, etc. When I went back for the results in a week's time Doc had a bit of a concerned look on his face. "Tom, everything came back okay except for your liver results. I don't know how much you are drinking daily, or what you drink but your lab tests show that you had better cut back or quit, you are too young at twenty-nine to have this become an issue." Now of course, he was right. I was drinking Vodka Polish style and massive quantities of beer. I assured the Doc that I would cut back or quit,

A few months later, I am back in Poland with the family and it is Gina's baptism on April 12. From the church back to the house we go for a massive, Polish feast which Babcia had prepared for weeks in advance. Relatives and friends on hand, we must have been north of forty people, crammed into a three-room house. Not a three-bedroom house, a three-room house. All furniture had been removed and replaced with tables and chairs. Vodka was flowing like water and people's faces were turning bright red from the heat, the ties, the booze and the bodies jammed in tight. As the father of the baptismal child, I did my best to be a gracious host, toasting with all comers.

The next morning - Oh my God. My head hurt so bad it defies explanation. I knew I was going to hurl, likely many times that day so I headed out behind the outhouse where a compost pile existed and chickens were known to roam. I have no idea how many times I barfed that day, but a dozen would be my guess. Nothing but bile was coming out. Dziadek was in similar shape and was availing himself of the outhouse and chain smoking in between retching sessions. The chickens were watching us, and I believe they were angry about us soiling up their stomping ground.

As the afternoon rolled on and I blew chow again, and again, I had a Eureka moment, "I just can't do this anymore" I need to stop and I need to stop now. The only English speaking Alcoholics Anonymous meeting was ninety minutes away in Warsaw by slow train, located in an old hospital across from the Stalin monolith and they met once a week on Wednesday evenings. Tough shyte for me, I started commuting to Warsaw weekly, attending a sixty-minute meeting with other expatriates with a thirst for the drink. A five plus hour ordeal to get to a sixty-minute meeting each week. I'll be damned if I am going to not be there to raise my kids. They are my diamonds in the rough.

I read the Big Book on the train, ninety minutes one way, ninety minutes back. Even though I didn't agree with most of the big book, it didn't matter. I had to stop drinking and now. The funny, thing is, I did, that was the start of a seven-and-a-half-year hiatus from booze that brought me back to health, marathons and a good Father to our kids. I have no idea how I stayed sober as I attended meetings infrequently through those years. But I did somehow.

## A Decade of Family Life (The 1990's)

The 90's were great years for our young family. We spent 1991 in Chicago where I was selling cold rolled steel on the Southside. In 1991-1992, we lived in Jackson Hole, and I worked at Red Top Meadows, an amazing place, beautiful and remote, trying to help troubled young boys to make positive changes. In 1993-1994 we returned to Poland where I taught at a new private American Elementary School. We had a wonderful three-room apartment on the 11th floor and our children were a blast to play with, smart and very dedicated to each other's welfare. Finally, in the spring of 1994, we returned to the States and bought our first home in Driggs, Idaho, a small three-bedroom log cabin that was charming, warm, stunning views of the mountains, brand new on an acre and a half.

Our lives would revolve around the kids, sports, skiing, playing outside on the acre and half we owned. I wasn't drinking at the time, but I was nuts, completely obsessive-compulsive. You could eat off the floor in the garage it was so clean. I ran and ran, served on Boards and Committees and whatever else came down the pike. In short, I was a maniac but a damn productive one. Looking back, it is hard to say that I was "happy", but my family certainly made me feel proud, contented and as always, driven to succeed. Halina's family would visit from Poland, Art taking care of the house and Basia taking care of the kids. We were making good money and everything seemed poised for a smooth ride into the future, or so I thought at the time.

# ACT VI

## This is Adulthood?

### Run Forrest Run! (1983, 1996-2002)

What follows are brief recaps of the marathons that I ran between 1996-2002 (including the first marathon I ran in 1983). I was now married, had two kids, and a homeowner. And let's be frank, I did not drink from 1993-2002 while my kids were growing up. However, I still was as manic as ever. Where the hell was I going to channel all this energy, intensity, and time? Might as well go back to what I loved in high school: training and running. Never afraid to jump into the deep end of the pool, in I went!

**Grandma's Marathon - Take I -** June 1983. Grandma's Marathon began in 1977 in Duluth Minnesota when a group of local runners planned a scenic road race from Two Harbors to Duluth. The first Grandma's had 150 runners; now more than 10,000 run the race every year. In its sixth year, my brother Bob was signed up to run Grandma's Marathon and was planning to run upon his return from Notre Dame. A week before the race, he decided not to run it. Who decided to take his place? Yours truly, his idiot young brother Tom. Actually, I was going to run half the race and then hit the post-race parties with my neighbor Ted Freese. Northbound we headed, me not having done any more training than running five miles.

On your mark, set, go! Off I trotted, no clue what the hell

I was doing. I ran 13 miles and felt okay, might as well go on I told Ted. Mile 18, kind of okay, screw it, I'm going for it. Mile 20 - wheels are off! Everything I have no longer works. Somehow, I gimped my way to the end. It would take <u>months</u> for my body to recover, massages, breaking up calcium deposits, etc. I'll never do that again my brain screamed.

**Jackson Hole Marathon** - June 1996. A total train wreck. I ran a solid 17 miles and then burst into my flames. My right knee stopped working, both nipples were streaming crimson blood down my white tank top, and I was just too stupid and stubborn to quit. The last five miles down Teton Village Road I trudged, passing cars and tourists pointing at me and wondering which active battlefield I had just escaped from. I finished the damn race, but it was way too painful.

**Grandma's Marathon - Take II** - June 1997 Duluth, MN. Ate way too much the night before, including ice cream. Ran and felt like shyte. Dumb-arse.

**Big Sur Marathon** - April 1998. Sleeping in the Malibu Junior High gym the night before the race was quite the experience. Farts, grunts, snores and little sleep on leftover military cots. The race itself was as beautiful as you would imagine, with the seaside homes, manors, bungalows, etc. Proof positive that money can buy you stunning vistas.

**Crater Lake Marathon** - August 1998. It was the most beautiful race course in the world. Hardly a spectator on hand and the gorgeous scenery made it easy to mosey along. I can still picture the lake, so stunning, and the sky was so blue as a backdrop for everything from wildflowers, trees, and mountains. The only incredibly stupid thing was the last few miles, all up-trail on soft quicksand. It really took the luster off of the day.

**Chicago Marathon** - October 1998. My perfect race, my perfect day. 3:36:28 coming in 3,101 out of 17,289 finishers. I was light. I was fast. I was hungry. I knew the course and the biggest hill was an off ramp. At mile 19, I felt great but needed real food, not a banana, Goo, or other road fare, thus I grabbed a $5 bill out of my hidden pocket and bought a cheeseburger from some guy by the side of the road. On I sped, proteins hitting my body. I finished with a kick into Grant Park leaving nothing behind me.

**New York City Marathon** - November 1998. I got in through the lottery and was in shape from training for Chicago, so I decided to just go and experience the Big Apple. I stayed with one of my old Polish teaching comrades on Staten Island. It was a really cool apartment overlooking the water, and I loved the ferry. I had zero interest in my time. I just wanted to enjoy the day and see the five Burroughs. Not a bad time and had a great post-race dinner in Little Italy with an old high school friend. Thank you, NYC.

**Wyoming Marathon** - May 1999. Bad race day for me, but fun camping with my friend Mike Bredal at Veedavoo near Laramie, WY. Didn't run well, didn't care. The only highlight of the day was that I walked the last three miles with a beautiful woman in a purple sports bra and shorts, chatting away about our lives and families. It was worth the entry fee!

**Governor's Cup** - June 2000 Helena, MT. A family trip, not a great race, not a bad race. A beautiful course, decent time and Halina and the kids had fun.

**Twin Cities Marathon** - October 2000. Returning to my hometown to run a victory lap, shoot for a personal best and celebrate with friends and family. However, it was colder than a witch's tit! I had dressed for a beautiful autumn day, light and fast. Instead I was in a garbage bag at the starting line, shivering and freezing my arse off. Off I dashed - feck it - I'm going for it. 8:00 minute miles for 16 miles, way too fast for a dope like me. Mile 17, BAM, a two by four to the forehead and finished well over four hours.

**Post Marathons Tommy** - Soon, foot pain. And then there was a complete knee blowout skiing in Vail. Next reconstructive surgery of my knee. Then significant weight gain, and finally Doc Butcher strenuously suggesting I find another means of channeling my manic focus.

What the hell! Might as well start drinking again, I'm a success now.

### Empty Place Settings (March 21st, 1997)

In the mid-nineties, life was good. I was making good money managing the Jackson Hole Domino's Pizza and Halina had a successful childcare business in our home. Luke was six and Gina four. It was a time of promise, friends and family. Everything seemed to be coming together for us and others. The economy in the area was turning white hot.

We invited the Dunn's, Ken and Janet for dinner that evening. For dinner we had splurged as we had the greatest respect for Ken and Janet. Ken runs a large Angus ranch here in the Valley. His Father is way up there with the University of Utah, head of orthopedics. Janet was a warm, compassionate person who made all those around her feel at ease and lit the room with her smile. She was also eight months pregnant and headed home from Salt Lake to start her maternity leave. It was our hope that we would become fast friends and that our kids would hang out together and for years to come our lives would be intertwined.

6:00 p.m. - The dinner is ready; shrimp, cheeses, and crab dip ready for appetizers. Chicken and fish in the oven for dinner and beer & wine chilled. In short, the feast is ready, the table set and we are ready.

6:30 p.m. - No word and nobody on-hand. Halina and I aren't worried. We figure that Janet was held up on her return from Salt Lake.

7:15 p.m. - Still no word and now we are getting nervous, why no call? Just doesn't make sense. Ken is way too on top of things for this to happen. Let's give it thirty more minutes, and we will shut it down.

7:45 p.m. - We eat our dinner in silence. The kids are put to bed and there is just a horrible dread in the air. It is palpable.

10:00 p.m. - No word, time for bed. The fear of the unknown is immense. Why? What? When will we know something? That night was a restless night for Halina and I, tossing, turning and worry.

9:00 a.m., March 22nd - The phone rings and it is a relative of Ken who is struggling to keep it together. Janet and the baby were killed in Malad, Idaho in a single car accident. Details were scarce but evidently Janet drifted off the road, jerked the wheel to get back onto the road and the car rolled numerous times. They tried to save the child, Sabrina, but it just was not possible.

Now I have been to sad funerals before; Bubs Lowery, my Mother, classmates, etc. Nothing comes even close to how tragic and sad this one was. It felt like there was no fresh air - that oppression was pushing everyone down. Ken got through it somehow, but it would be years before the grief would subside a bit for him.

Today, in the most beautiful of mountain cemeteries with a grand view of the Teton Range rests Janet Schmitt Dunn (2/8/64 - 3/21/97) and Sabrina Dianne Dunn (3/21/97). I stop by there often, spending some time alone. It is quiet, beautiful, and I ponder what is and what could have been.

### Teton Youth & Family Services (2000 – 2003)

In 1996 I was an up and coming commodity in Jackson Hole. I was Store Manager of Domino's Pizza, making more money than I ever had before. I also was sought after by non-profits and the Jackson Hole Noon Rotary Club to serve on their respective Board of Directors. It was an honor to serve. More important, I was a young man with a future who could contribute to at-risk children's lives by dedicating my time to raising critical funding. It was right in my wheel house.

Now the other side of the equation was, how was I going to justify my seat on these nonprofit boards? Board members on the Teton Youth and Family Services Board included; a retired Air Force General who was in charge of the annual Air Force budget; the Chief of Police; retired CEO's; business owners; and me. How am I going to make a go of this? A signature fundraising event, a golf tournament, that's what I'll do! Jackson Hole Golf and Tennis agreed to host the first tournament, now how to draw people in? I love baseball. We'll call it the "Big League Benefit" and I will bring in ex-major league baseball players to play golf and host a banquet. In year one, Hall of Famer - Brooks Robinson, Coach Bobby Winkles and Bill Buckner attended, all super people who cared deeply about the kids we serve. In future years, Hall of Famer Fergie Jenkins, Don Larson, Keith Moreland, Dave Kingman and many more baseball greats would join us with Jackson Hole being an easy sell.

Sponsors were solicited, airfare obtained, accommodations, etc. In coming years, the tournament would grow in size, stature and revenue generation, the golf tournament continues to this day with broad support from the philanthropic, golf and business community. So, for six years I had my justification to take a seat on the Board, furthering the mission and providing badly needed funding, it all felt good, I was proud of myself for volunteering effectively. I thought it would end there. Oh no, there were many more upcoming projects which would start knocking at my door and I would be free to pick and choose as I saw fit.

**A Capital Campaign** - In 2000, the board decided that it was time for a capital campaign to address critical structural needs of the agency. The total campaign budget was $1,560,000 and a Development Director was needed to oversee the campaign. The Board Chair, Kip MacMillan asked me to lunch, and I assumed he wanted to pick my brain over potential candidates. Instead, he offered me the job. I was dumbfounded. I had no experience in this field other than volunteering throughout my life. "I and the Board don't care about that Tom, we know you can do it, you are the right guy for the job. We will support you with whatever you need to get it done." At the time I was getting tired of getting home every night from Domino's Pizza between 2:00-3:00 a.m. The final kicker was when Kip said, "You can do this job with complete autonomy. If you do it in 10 minutes or 60 hours a week, it doesn't matter to me as long as you produce results." After a few days of contemplation and waffling, I put my hands above my head and dove into the deep end of the pool. I was a professional fundraiser.

**The Ordway School at Red Top Meadows** - The first of the three projects to be funded was a new school building at Red Top Meadows. I had taught in the decrepit one room schoolhouse in 1991-1993. It was literally rotting on the foundation. There were major drafts blowing through cracks in the logs. The wiring was outdated and couldn't handle the classroom electrical load. The roof leaked, and so on and so on. In short, it was like teaching in a schoolhouse from the turn of the last century. After attending a grant writing course, I wrote a $250,000 Wyoming Community Development grant which received 100% funding. I was off! Next, a local philanthropist, Mr. Ordway, visited Red Top and saw firsthand the dire need. We received a check that day for $100,000 and thus the Ordway School at Red Top Meadows was fully funded.

**The Hirschfield Center for Children** - The next greatest need was a child advocacy center, a specifically designed facility that would be used for the investigation of possible child abuse cases in the community. It was designed to minimize the trauma to children during the interview process while allowing all involved community entities; police, medical, educators, health care professionals, etc. to be involved in the interview process (all behind a one-way mirror working with a licensed therapist conducting the interview). It was a very noble cause and between grants, donations, and a large donation from a local family, project number two was funded. In two plus years I had earned my keep and a substantial raise. The end of the campaign was in sight.

**The Trailblazer Wilderness Building at Red Top** - This last structure was to serve as base camp for the Red Top Wilderness programs, where gear would be stored, offices to coordinate trips, bunk rooms for the campers for intake and end of trip processing. In short, it was a small Outward Bound facility that would help at-risk youth from around the country to experience the magnificent wilderness of the Grand Teton and surrounding terrain. The key turning point in funding this facility was a meeting at a local bank with a group of philanthropists. Myself, and Peter Lee - the brilliant volunteer capital campaign chairperson made a pitch about the campaign and that we had come to the end of our ropes as to where to seek funding next and we had exhausted all sources we were aware of. The philanthropists met for a few minutes privately and then told us, "We had come in here planning to give you $100,000 but after hearing about your efforts and what you are doing, we would like to give you a $200,000 challenge match. For every $1 you raise from now on, we will match it $1 for $1." Bingo! Home-run for Pete, me and the kids who would benefit from this campaign.

**A 500 Mile Walk to end the Campaign** - As the campaign neared completion, it started to stall out. We still needed $159,000 to fund everything without adding any organizational debt. I kept pestering the Board to come up with an idea to finish it, otherwise I would. Stagnation set in and my contract would soon be up. Time for me to step it up, literally. I decided to walk twenty miles a day, for five weeks, five days a week pushing a converted baby jogger with a sign, a bell, donation can, and basic literature. My plan was to walk every road in Teton County, WY. Wow! Did I ever underestimate the physical toll that walking that much would take. I walked in every kind of weather; snow, sleet, sunshine, rain, wind and whatever else the Wyoming weather gods would throw at me. The local radio stations let me do numerous daily updates from the road and the public support was amazing. Daily I received honks, waves, thumbs up and donations from the public; one girl at a gas station gave me $3.23 which was her lunch $ for the day, one gentleman stopped and handed me a check for $10,000. Board Members walked with me and called their friends, soliciting pledges/donations. Finally, it came down to the last few hours and we were $12,000 from ending the campaign. I was sick. I was tired. And I had no clue who else to ask. I was tapped out. I went into McDonald's to warm up and eat when my phone rang. My dear friend Clare at the Community Foundation called with the news that we had a $15,000 pledge! We had done it! An hour later we celebrated the end of the walk at Town Square - I was 1 for 1 as a professional fundraiser. Exhausted but thrilled, I went home for some well-deserved rest.

## 9/11

I was chairing the 7 a.m. Jackson Hole Rotary Club Board Meeting that morning. We were about seventy five percent done with the agenda when a board member came in with the news that two planes had flown into the World Trade Center. We quickly finished our business and adjourned. In the lobby of the hotel, a TV on a cart was on with live coverage. Everyone gathered around. No logical explanation apparent, not a good sign. Some retired military friends had most concerning looks on their faces. Their reaction was all I needed to know that this was a worst-case scenario. Off to our offices we headed, mine just a few blocks away. Shortly thereafter, black objects started falling from the buildings. Quickly it became apparent, these were people. For a while the media showed the "objects" falling before someone finally caught on that it might not be quite suitable for live TV. The first tower collapsed, the dust plume engulfing Manhattan, roiling like an angry, gross, grey death intent on its path, objects in the way be damned. Down came the second tower, incredulity abounded, another plume of grey death swallowing New York City, our City. Clarity as to what was unfolding before my eyes had crystalized. War was upon us. Thousands, if not tens of thousands of Americans had been killed. Something on the scale of Pearl Harbor had happened, this time in Manhattan. I felt like I was going to throw up.

Later that morning at the group home for troubled teens, I was watching TV with the kids and staff. Understandably, the kids couldn't comprehend what they were seeing. I could. It was time for me to leave. The noon Rotary lunch meeting became a very brief prayer meeting for those who did show up. After that I went home, I wanted to be with my own family: to hold my kids, to be with my wife. Too much TV was a bad thing, yet turning it off was almost impossible.

For the first "real" time in my life, I was glad we lived where we lived. We were at the foot of the Rocky Mountains. Regardless of what 9/11 portended, we were in the safest place possible, a family of four, secure, nestled in a small log cabin. In the coming days, information would be pieced together as to who, what, how, etc. The wars would come. The outpouring of support and love for New York City was immense; the victims, the families, the first responders, all of it made America what it can always be - Great.

There is one other word from those days - pain. The cowards had had inflicted maximum pain. If causing pain is a success, they had won in the short-term. For me, all I felt was dull numbness. That dull numbness hung over our valley, the mountains, and the people. It was all just wrong, sick, twisted, and a poke to the sleeping giant who was awakening.

## El Hogar - The Home of Love and Hope

**Tegucigalpa, Honduras April 2002 & 2003** - As the Jackson Hole Rotary Club President in 2001-2002, one of the goals of Rotary for the year was an international community service project. It was to become my cornerstone goal to personally lead a group of local Rotarians and High School students to aid children in need. Additionally, and equally important in my opinion, was to change the lives of the gringos who went along. Where to go? A dear friend, Dr. Bob Volz, a retired orthopedic surgeon was on the board of El Hogar - a children's orphanage he had visited numerous times in the capital city of Tegucigalpa. We had our target now. We just had to get there and get it done!

As an FYI, I led two trips to El Hogar: one in April 2002 and one in 2003. Each group had twelve to fourteen participants, composed of half Jackson Hole High School students and half Rotarians/parents. Our route was to drive to Salt Lake City, fly to Houston, overnight there, and the next morning a direct flight to Tegucigalpa. At informational meetings, I did my very best to lay out a very clear picture of what the trip entailed; safety, hygiene, dangers, crime, basic rules and expectations. My worst fear was a whiny American teen in Honduras pissing and moaning about bathrooms, food, rules, etc. Fortunately, both years we had great groups. The kids were awesome and the adults had great attitudes with serious good humor. Travel on a "Tom Tour" and you had better have a warped sense of humor and be ready to laugh.

**Into Tegucigalpa** - Preface, I am not making this up! The full-sized jumbo jet was on descent into the capital which is in a horseshoe canyon, ringed on three sides by steep mountain walls and large hills. As we approached we flew right by a massive statue of Jesus with his arms outstretched, in retrospect I see now why he was there.

My seat was on the right-side of the plane, a window seat overlooking the wing. The plane started to bank to the left. My wing started to lift and outside the window, mountains and people were getting perilously close, what the? Shanties, lean-tos built by poor squatters were now within thirty yards of the tip of the wing, I could see women doing laundry and kids playing. The plane continued to bank steeply left, I had no idea a jumbo jet could maneuver like this. Was this normal? Passengers were now screaming, praying, crying, including several members of our group, as we just kept steeply banking to the left. Oh well, damn great place and way to go I thought. The plane then straightened out and began to drop like a rock, within seconds we hit the runway hard and the pilot went full throttle reverse and stopped so quickly that it was hard to believe it was over. Out the window, I could see car traffic stopped on both sides of the runway. I later learned that pilots specifically trained for this airport and that the runway was too short which is why car traffic was stopped in case we couldn't stop in time, very comforting.

We taxied in to the bland concrete terminal and came to a halt, everyone exhaled for the first time in minutes. Dr. Bob stood up with a huge smirk on his face, looked at me and said, "I didn't tell you about that landing on purpose. I knew you wouldn't come!"

**El Hogar, the Kids and the Hood** - El Hogar, the House of Love and Hope, is in a rough section of Tegucigalpa. It is surrounded by a fifteen-foot wall with barbed-wire fence and armed guards twenty-four-seven. The neighborhood is low-income residential to downright shacks within blocks. During the day, the streets are safe for foot traffic, shopping, etc. After dark it is another story. One Saturday night we and some of the adults were sitting in the garden area talking when gunfire erupted in the neighborhood. Such nightlife was a routine occurrence. That said once our group was in the walled compound, we were completely safe. With the high walls and armed guards, we were free to be with the two hundred fifty stars of the show, the children of El Hogar.

El Hogar was restricted to boys only until 2007, but has since started accepting girls into the four various programs and locations. There is the main campus for elementary students, a vocational site were students learn carpentry and mechanics, a rural farm were older students learn about agriculture and the high school student location. Our group was with the elementary students. There were about one hundred and eighty children so it was a hub-bub of activity. We played, held, laughed, cried, sang and danced with those kids every free moment. What made me most proud was the Jackson Hole students opened up their hearts and passion to those kids. In return they were extremely well compensated: hugs, kisses, high fives, laughter and unbridled joy. Both trips were a complete success, and we hadn't even started work yet.

**Projects, Our Team and the First Lady** - The first year our team covered all of our own expenses and brought $5,000 from our Rotary Club to expand a parking/play area for the kids. An anonymous donor gave $10,000 to buy a school bus from the States and had it driven down to El Hogar. For five straight days the gringos mixed cement by hand with shovels and a wheelbarrow expanding the front basketball/soccer/parking area. At 7:30 a.m. was breakfast: warm milk, tea, some form of warm cereal, oatmeal, cream of wheat, etc. Lunch was tortillas, rice, beans, perhaps chicken which was not the U.S. version of a gigantic six-pound piece of breast meat, this was a leg, a wing or a thigh that had been used in a hard scrabble life. In short, it was great. Our group got fed just like the kids. In the evenings, we did make sandwiches in our main housing apartment with provisions that I and a few other adults shopped for: bread, PB&J, lunchmeat, fruits, cookies, etc. No one could leave the compound period but being team leader, I of course headed to a tiny cantina around the corner for happy hour cervezas each day. It literally was a walk-up window and I would usually sit on a broken picnic table, eating and feeding pretzels to a scroungy mongrel I named Paco. The cerveza was cold and that was refreshing after a day of mixing cement.

The second year, we brought $6000 and spent the week adding onto the volunteer housing apartments. This project was adjacent to the quarters where the females in our party stayed while the men were in one communal room above some classrooms. In year two, the First Lady of Honduras visited El Hogar while we were working away. After visiting the staff and children, she came to see the gringos working away and to thank us. So, there I am, team leader, not a small man, with a large straw hat on, leather gloves, sweating and smelling like a goat. Yet she wants to meet me and get her picture taken with me. I grab my great friend, Toni Reno, former Ms. Michigan (now an amazing woman/mother in her 50's with a smile to brighten any day). So, two stinky Americans with the Honduran First Lady dressed to the nines in a golden dress, fully coiffed. Toni and I couldn't stop laughing. However, I must say the First Lady was incredibly genuine, personable, and her compassion for the children of Honduras was evident.

**Touring Day and the Banquet -** The last day of each trip was our sightseeing and banquet celebration. We went up into the mountains and visited an artists' market that had all local made products: carvings, clothing, jewelry, knick-knack paddy-whacks etc. It was lovely to be out in the fresh air, everyone strolling about in safety. I took this time each year to spend with Julio Villalta and his wife Carmen as a way of saying thanks for all their efforts in coordinating our trip and transportation. This also meant that Julio, myself and another

Rotarian or two would slip over to the "Cantina" for some Tequila and Cerveza on me. The laughter was infectious and there is that moment when you realize you are with great people - Julio and Carmen truly were.

That evening we either went to a Rotarian's home for a BBQ, or the second year, to an amazing Honduran restaurant. Julio and Carmen always joined us and it always struck me how the students' lives were deeply imprinted by the trip. They had grown up in one of the wealthiest counties in America and by the end of the trip, they were living on rice and beans, worried about orphan children living in one of the poorest, most dangerous places on Earth. Can't put a price tag on that.

**The eyes of a Specter** - One evening we went to a local Rotary Club dinner: Dr. Bob, Julio and Carmen and myself. The dinner was exquisite and the Honduran Rotarians were incredibly gracious. Post dinner cocktails made everyone feel warm, hopeful, and willing to help make positive changes as best we could.

Into Julio's sedan for the drive back into town and we are glowing with the warmth and friendship of a wonderful evening. As we entered into the city limits of Tegucigalpa, my world was about to be rocked forever. Stepping in front of our car was a girl of maybe twelve, walking onto the road directly in front of us, forcing us to brake hard to avoid hitting her. Fully illuminated in our headlights, she was stunningly beautiful despite the obvious poverty of her situation: matted hair, a dirty T-shirt and cheap flip-flops. The exception to her stunning appearance was her eyes. They were silver, opaque, glass, devoid of humanity.

I asked Julio and Carmen, "Why is she out here by herself?"

Julio replied, "Down the hill to the right is a dump where kids and adults go, usually to huff gas or have sex in trade for gas, drugs or money."

The vacant eyes seemed to stare inside me. A disquieting

feeling of the reality of how hard life is on this globe consumed me. I sat in silence, trying to process all this. To this day, I can still see that girl in the road. I think about how cheap human life sadly has become and what it felt like when those eyes peered inside me.

## Down Goes Frazier - Down Goes Frazier! (August 2002)

As the summer of 2002 progressed, my intensity, focus, irritability and acuity went through the roof. As that side of the teeter-totter tilted up, my weight, sleep, appetite and appearance crashed down. My hands were always clammy, I was sweating profusely, and agitated twenty-four-seven. My weight was down to one hundred sixty pounds. I attributed all of these symptoms and changes to all the marathons I had run over the last several years and my general daily intensity.

In my small cabin of an office, I was in the midst of a capital campaign meeting with a few key board and committee members. The ottoman in the middle of the room was being used as a table to review the architectural plans for the new school at Red Top Meadows. I stood to point out a detail on the schematics and I leaned over the ottoman, but I never came back up. Straight over the ottoman I went, landing in a heap on the other side, not sure how long as I was out for or why. As I came to, my nervous friends were debating whether to call an ambulance or not. At least the cold towel on my face and head felt good. A couple of friends helped me up and the Board President, Kip MacMillan, fired up his Suburban. I was assisted injured football player style to the backseat, I could not even sit.

We raced down the road a mile to St. John's Medical Center where I was put on a gurney and rushed into the ER. The next few hours were simply a blur: doctors, sleep, nurses, sleep, beeps, sleep, worried wife, sleep, friend dropping by, sleep. It must have been about four hours before I began to regain my bearings as the IV's pumped in fluids. I asked Halina what was wrong with me. "They don't know yet," she responded with her voice trembling. By now I was so cold that I simply could not warm up despite the warm blankets they brought me every five to ten minutes.

Around 5 p.m. the lead doctor came in and delivered his initial ideas on my downturn in health: "It could possibly be a heart problem, and we will be doing tests in the morning to determine if that is case. Or there may be some kind of small tumor somewhere near my kidney or something. If this was the case I would have surgery. Or finally it could be Graves' Disease - a thyroid disorder. We are just awaiting a few more results and by tomorrow we should have a direction," added the doctor.

Boy, those choices all made me feel very special. The first to get ruled out the next day was a heart defect, Yeah. I am down to possible cancer or Gravedigger's disease, whatever the feck that is! A few more hours and the verdict came in, NO tumor, so I have Graves' Disease - gee thanks Doc - what the hell is it?

Graves' disease is a disorder of the thyroid, the butterfly thingy on the front of our neck. It is the carburetor for the entire body. If it runs too hot, like mine had for a longtime, weight loss, all the symptoms I described above. A hundred years ago it was considered a death sentence until a Dr. Graves, a good Irish doctor, put the pieces together after seeing hundreds of patients wither away like I was and organs failed, resulting in a dance with Mr. Reaper. The other side of the coin from Graves' Disease is hypothyroidism where metabolism slows way down, major weight gain, lethargy, exhaustion, etcetera. Lucky me! How the hell do we treat this thing was my first question of my new doctor, Dr. Dennis Butcher, an internist in Jackson Hole, a rapacious fisherman and now I am happy to report, a very dear friend of mine. Yet I digress, back to the cure/treatment.

They had to slow down or obliterate my thyroid before

it put me six feet under. The only place in the entire body where Iodine goes in any traceable amount is the thyroid, so Ol'Tommy boy, here is what we are going to do. Radiation and Iodine were put into a pill that would be served to me by a nurse in a Three Mile Island radiation suit in a specially lead lined hospital room. I would ingest the pill. Over the next few days the iodine would end up in my thyroid, nice parting gifts backstage for my thyroid and I am no longer running hot. Pretty simple, huh? A little bit more data for your consideration. For three days I had to sleep alone, and I was radioactive. If I threw up I was to call the EPA as it would be considered a toxic waste site. No work and stay away from family and friends. It was like being a bit like a leper.

Well, to bring this all around, it is now seventeen years later, and I ain't dead yet. I get my blood tested two to four times a year and get my synthetic thyroid medication adjusted accordingly. Fifty pounds has found its way back on to my frame. Sometimes I run slow, sometimes hot, but let's look on the bright side, without Dr. Gravedigger and Dr. Butcher I'd be six feet under without a chance to see the Cubs win another World Series.

## Jackson Hole Community Counseling Center (2004-2007)

My second major capital campaign was to fund and build a new nine thousand square foot mental health facility in Jackson. The current operations were based in an old family home converted into an office space. Tiny rooms, crazy corridors, white noise machines trying to maintain privacy. Therapists and myself included, shared offices. Often, I would work in up to three different spaces throughout the day, about as highly inefficient as possible.

Not knowing a lot about mental health, I quickly immersed myself into the subject, reading books, websites and talking with my fellow professional coworkers. The one stat that always stuck with me was that one in three people in their lifetimes will have a diagnosable mental illness. This taboo subject hits every family in some way across the country.

The campaign goal was $3.2 million with the Board of Directors determining that $1.8 million was needed before they would begin construction. I had my challenge and even though no one wanted to talk about mental health, I would have to find a way forward.

Off I went on my grant writing, securing a $350,000 grant from the Wyoming Business Council and a $500,000 grant from a local foundation. I will never forget that phone call as long as I live. It was December and I was standing outside an architect's door in the cold when my phone rang, "Tom, Anthony Nelson here. Linda and I are wondering if you would accept a $500,000 gift from our Foundation to help build the new Mental Health Center." In the cold, the tears ran down my cheeks as I accepted their generous gift. Maybe I was nuts (yeah, I'm nuts) but to be asked to accept such a gift while working on such a challenging project that made people uncomfortable, was a validation that I was in the midst of doing something that really mattered.

Over the next few years the campaign progressed in fits-n-starts. We hit the $1.8 million mark and plans, design and construction began in earnest. Once the modular pieces were brought on site and assembled, donations went into a tail spin. High oil prices and a sharp downturn in the housing market had the economy edgy. Donors were hedging bets with a feeling setting in that we had gotten as much as we were going to get for now.

I came up with my second fundraising stunt to involve the public and raise awareness. The town ski hill is Snow King, a beautiful mountain looming on the south-side of the valley. All locals love it because it is the perfect place to hike, walk your dog and be done in an hour or less. The thought came to me, if everybody loves this Mountain, let's use it! Ergo, "Climb the King for the Counseling Center" was conceived and continues to this day. I climbed that mountain one hundred fifty-nine times in the summer of 2006, the equivalent of going up Mount Everest like seventeen times. On average, I climbed the King three to four times per day, riding the chair lift down for free (my knees could never take the walk down).

My last successful project in Jackson would be the next year when I helped to raise more than $300,000 for a small bouldering park at the bottom of Snow King. With each additional project, donors were tiring of Hickey coming towards them with a hand out. I knew my fundraising days as a full-time career were coming to an end, yet I am proud that I had raised over $5 million for human service non-profits. I can live with that as my legacy.

### Take Me Out to the Ballgame (August 2007)

Harry Caray, the famous Cubs broadcaster had been dead a few years and the Cubs decided to hold a contest for fans to be the first ever to "Sing Take Me Out to the Ballgame." It was a ludicrous long-shot, a waste of badly needed money and yet I knew I had to be there, come Hell or high water. Hence, I bought a ticket from Salt Lake to Chicago and back all within a 48-hour timeframe. Off I headed in our 1994 Toyota Land Cruiser (my favorite vehicle of all time) driving more than four hours south to Salt Lake. I arrived at 1 a.m. and slept in the back of the Cruiser to be ready for my 6 a.m. flight.

Bleary-eyed, off I winged to Chicago for my audition. Well rested certainly did not apply to me. Once in Chicago, I caught the train from O'Hare to Union Station, transferred and took the red line out to Wrigley Field. With ninety minutes before my audition time, I did what all Irishman would do, I headed to Murphy's Bleacher Bar just outside centerfield and continued to do my vocal exercises with brown libations as a vocal cord easer. I hooted and a hollered with several other idiots who would be competing for this most prestigious opportunity.

Off I rolled with my carry-on bag in tow, my oldest and luckiest Cub cap on my noggin, a Cubs T-Shirt and my license plate from Idaho "A CUB FAN" dangling from my neck. There were 14,000 other brilliant people/idiots out in the competition. I was directed to the first-aid room directly underneath home plate in the bowels of the stadium, most apropos.

I sat on a bench with twelve other wanna-bees and awaited my turn. This is the stupidest, most brilliant thing I have ever done in my life kept running through my head. Hickey, Tom was called and in I went with my carry-on bag in tow. I sang to the best of my ability, which isn't much. I dedicated my performance to my Mother, started laughing three quarters of the way through as the insanity of it all hit me. At the end, I started to say, "Oh, my God..." which is on the video at https://www.youtube.com/watch?v=b_bFHS6Uw3E. Obviously, I was starting to say, this is the dumbest thing I have ever done.

Interested now, the judges asked me about my journey, my love for the Cubs, my Mother, etcetera. Out of 14,000 fellow knuckleheads, I made the final fifty contestants. I promptly rolled my bag back to Murphy's Bleacher and celebrated with my fellow dreamers.

### Poster Child for the Great Recession (2006-2008)

In 2006, with my fundraising contract to expire the next year, it was time to figure out what's next. How can we make some money to secure our future and pay for the kids' colleges? The only real money I had made was off of our homes, buying our first home for $135,000 and selling it with improvements twelve years later for $342,000. Also, our current home which had cost us $295,000 to build, had recently appraised at $595,000 providing me with $300,000 worth of equity and capital to invest.

After talking with a few close friends in Jackson Hole whom I had been fortunate to meet by way of the nonprofit sector, a plan began to form. Buy two pieces of dirt in Teton

Valley with grand vistas of the Tetons and using my general contractor friend, Steve, build two beautiful log homes with high-end finishes and full landscaping. In addition, I would get my realtor's license and be the agent on both properties. If this simple plan worked, we would: A) have $100,000 for each kid's college education; and, B) own our family home free and clear, ensuring Halina and I had a healthy nest egg for the future. In addition, I would work on the crew with my son Luke as paid laborers to generate additional income and learn the housebuilding trade. Finally, I created LLC's for each property that would serve as a de-facto ownership trust for the investors, my friends from Jackson would own 50% of each project. The goal was to build for under $300,000 and sell for $400,000+. Got it? A solid simple, plan!

So, with all our ducks in a row, we started building in the spring of 2007. Our crew consisted of five guys. Steve was the lead dog with two salty old hands who were skilled in the process and the new meat, Luke and me. In truth, just like my father, I was a horrible construction worker, lucky to hit the right end of the nail. My role was quickly reduced to common laborer, lift that log, screw it in place, do it again. Luke was much more skilled than I, an intuitive worker who just had a feel for the building process. Regardless, that Summer and Fall, we built two beautiful homes on budget, on time, with first-class finishes. Time to stick the real estate signs in the yard and wait for the buyers and their money to roll in. So, we waited, and we waited and we waited. The hottest real estate market ever in the Valley was slowing down to a trickle. It was early winter 2007 when I finally realized that holy shyte, this might not work and we could lose everything.

## Happiest Place on Earth - Open Arms Home for Children, Konga, RSA (January, 2008)

**January 2008 - Komga, South Africa:** At the start of 2008, I knew I had to generate as much income as possible to slow the black hole that was appearing in our finances. I took a consulting contract with my brother's nonprofit in South Africa for the first six months of 2008. My brother, Bob Solis, has always been the genius/driven/purpose minded member of the family. A magna cum laude graduate of Notre Dame with a double major in Theology and Political Science, he was a Rhodes Scholar finalist and simply the most caring, giving individual I have ever known. There were times when his own kids were small, Bob would have families who were victims of domestic violence living on their couches in their tiny rented house. In short, he and Sallie's lives were mayhem in motion. There was only one thing that was certain, Bob was destined to make a difference in people's lives.

Now being brilliant, Bob also knew that he would need money if he was to give it away. With zero experience he was selected as a candidate to be a stock broker in the Phoenix area, 98 out of 100 candidates would flush out, yeah, you are right, Bob was one of the two who made it. I was most proud to hear how he would stand in grocery store parking lots, introducing himself, handing out flyers and creating relationships that have lasted until this day. So, the foundation is laid for "Bobo's Miracle" (the kids at Open Arms can't say Bob, so he thus became Bobo).

In the early 2000's, Bob and his family vacationed in South Africa, not to sightsee, not to vacation but to volunteer at an HIV/AIDS orphanage in Johannesburg aka Jo-Berg. Bob was so deeply moved that by the time he was stateside again, he was hashing out a plan. Bob and Sallie's lifetime savings were $250,000 at the time. Pushing all their chips to the middle, they would use all of it to buy a property in South Africa and begin a nonprofit to provide a home and a childhood to children whose parents had died of HIV/AIDS or were infected themselves. A daunting undertaking when you are thirty hours away by airplane. But what the hell, if they could win one for the Gipper, Bob could win one for the kids.

A property was located: a seventy-acre property that was

the estate of the region's doctor who had a small plane to get around to see his patients. It was on top of a hillside with stunning views, located about fifty kilometers from East London, the largest city nearby and located on the Eastern Cape. Once the property was secured, a nonprofit was created, "Open Arms Home for Children", based out of Phoenix, AZ. The Board of Directors consisted of Bob's friends, clients, and supporters. The main house, the doctor's personal home, was converted to nurseries, staff housing, etc. The garage was re-engineered into a classroom and an old livestock shed became Bob & Sallie's quarters.

Flash forward five years to 2008 and Open Arms is flourishing. It has maxed out at about thirty-one kids and without additional housing, they will have to turn kids away. Now after hearing about and following Bob's project, I am chomping at the bit to get involved, to be a conduit to the philanthropists, millionaires, CEO's and amazing people I have met in Jackson Hole over the last decade, I know this is something that will be a perfect fit for all involved. So, I finagled a six-month consulting contract from the Open Arms Board of Directors to raise $250,000 to build additional "Rondeval's", cement structures with thatched roofs that are the norm in the region. A possible six units could be built from the money I raised thus providing housing for up to 42 additional children.

**Enter Tommy Boy:** A day late, I am winging my way from Jackson Hole to Atlanta, about a five-hour flight and then onto a plane that will be my home for the next twenty-four hours. From Atlanta, it is nine hours to Dakar, Senegal where upon landing, you stay for three hours on the same plane while a new crew comes on board. The cabin is cleaned, customs agents check your documents, and I simply pace in the foodservice causeway. Damn it, my sleeping pills are in my luggage below, and I haven't slept in over twenty-four hours. I am wired, manic and incapable of sitting still. The poor girl in the seat next to me, a Peace Corps volunteer teacher in

Mozambique has to put up with my endless fidgeting. A few hours later we are airborne again, nine-hour hours to Jo-Burg. In my life, I have counted down days, hours and minutes. Here for the next nine hours I am counting down seconds, this is excruciating, is this some kind of sadistic torture? More than two hundred fifty people jammed into a tube for a day? Sick bastard who ever came up with it.

Ten hours later I arrive in Jo-Burg, delirious but just glad to escape that damn plane. No one is there. They all thought I was coming in yesterday. I call Africa Sky, the Guesthouse B&B where I am to stay, with the help of a kind local woman. They will be there in thirty minutes the kind girl on the other end informs me. I find a lukewarm Carlsberg beer and wait. I have never been this tired nor up this long before. Fortunately, African Sky is quaint, comfortable, kind and has good food to augment the fridge full of cold beer. I eat my dinner, grab a few beers for the room and off I go, amazing - I still can't sleep. I watch rugby on the telly and doze as best I can for six hours before having to get back to the airport to catch my next flight. I board South African Airlines and I am pleasantly surprised, the plane is immaculately clean, half-full and exceptional service from finely coiffed flight attendants. I haven't experienced such a delightful flight since I was a kid, when air travel was special, not a greyhound bus experience. Yet I digress.

I am in and over Africa, this is amazing! I, Tom Hickey, son of a bunch of Mick's has made it to Africa. Taking in every view of life below that I can, so damn beautiful out there. Down below is the Indian Ocean and now we bank and begin our descent, almost there Tommy Boy! We hit the tarmac, I roll off the plane with my bag and no Bob. Par for the course this trip. Another kind local lets me use their cellphone, I call Bob, "Thought you were coming in yesterday" he says, "I will be there in about an hour." Thank God most airports sell booze, I find the pub and bunker down for Bob to arrive and start mingling with the locals. They are shocked that I know about and played rugby, within minutes I had a bunch of new mates.

**A Change of Perspective:** Bob arrives, we hug, relishing in being together having come from the same roots and to be doing something noble, yet no words need to be exchanged. We run all over East London. Bob getting paint here, clothes there, a dash into the grocer and we have all the home's needs for the day. East London looks and feels like a very crowded old western town, except everybody is not white. The opposite is true. Cars, chaos, commerce all surround us as Bob winds in and out, knowing the place like the back of his hand. The Indian Ocean is so close I can smell the brine. Bob shows me where the beach was divided during Apartheid - if you were white, you got to use the sand beach, if you were black, you got to use the black rocks. Hard to fathom that this only ended a few years ago.

Open Arms and Komga we are bound, bouncing in the van jabbering about things like my travel screw-ups, issues at the home and then all of a sudden, I look out the window, (WHAT?!) "Bob, those are God Damn Giraffes!" There were more of them. There were elephants, a rhino, zebras, and they are just wandering around in a vast refuge. My tired brain just not able to comprehend that the Jungle Book is outside my window. Bob just gets a huge grin on his face and we motor on. Colors here are somehow different: reds are more orange, greens are lighter but more vibrant, and so on. Being so close to the sea the air is fresh and clean.

On we roll, turning off the main autostrada and headed on a side road to Komga, a small village originally for the Dutch Afrikaans settlers and farmers. As Bob had foretold me, the Afrikaans are the largest people on the planet with the largest damn heads I have ever seen. Think massive watermelon and slap a face on, that is a typical Afrikaans. One guys hands were so damn huge I couldn't even imagine what he could do if he got mad. We roll through the quiet village and make the turn up the old rutted road towards Open Arms Home for Children.

Until now, you have only heard me whine and snivel about my personal travel hardships. It is time to forget about me. I don't count for anything from here on out. We are about to meet the stars of the show, and I shall gladly bow out so they may shine.

**The Happiest Place on Earth:** Disney always claims to be the "Happiest Place on Earth". They have never been to Open Arms Home for Children. At the crest of the hill, they hear us coming and soon twenty older children are sprinting at us, chanting "Bobo, Bobo" obviously ecstatic to see Bobo and perhaps he may have brought a toy or candy or both. More importantly, because this crazy gringo of a brother of mine has made their lives, safe, secure, loved and cared for. As I looked at my brother, the guy who used to beat the shyte out of me at everything we ever played, I knew I was seeing the wealthiest guy on the planet.

Hands, arms, smiles all envelop us as the kids welcome me. There was Tandazwa, Asanda, Asehkona, Peliz, and other names I would never be able remember. I was ushered to my quarters, a clean, Spartan space, a room converted from a garage. It was VIP treatment all the way. Open Arms itself, sits on top of the very crest of a hill overlooking a breathtaking vista of the valley below and coffee plantations on the other side. Again, colors here are distorted, but they feel more real.

The grand tour is given to me. It feels like a wealthy doctor's home in Africa but now it has been repurposed. I am led into the nursery, a converted living room where about ten babies' beds are, several asleep with their rumps in the air like I used to sleep. There are a few nurses bottle feeding babies and one little child with black eyes the size of quarters staring at me, plug in her mouth, wondering who is this large Mick invading her space. Her hands extend up to me, the nicest offer I have ever had in my life. I whisk her up. She is so light, so frail and so beautiful. Uncle Tom regresses to bouncing like I did with my children, and she is asleep in my arms in minutes. This is all unbelievable.

After lunch I try to help out by cutting the grass, instead I put the wrong gas in the mower and oops, gonna have to get that fixed. I am bleary eyed, disoriented and never prouder to be somewhere in my life with important work to do. Off to my room I shuffle and get a restful ninety-minute nap.

Dinner is called for and the children all politely enter the room and at the beckoning of the Housemistress they all start to sing "Thank you Jesus..." followed by a prayer. Now, by now you know that I ain't much of a religious guy but I had tears rolling down my cheeks. They all sat down at these little plastic play tables and chairs and sang a song in Xhosa, their native language known as the clicking language (and Nelson Mandela's native tongue). Dinner was a small plastic bowl of seasoned rice and either a chicken leg or thigh. No one complained about their portion. They were happy to just have it. I never saw a plate that wasn't absolutely clean of all food when the kids were done. The drink was a fruit punch again in little plastic cups that would get used in the States for doll parties. I, being the VIP gringo, was served one leg and a thigh with a double portion of rice! I humbly ate knowing that this was the most wonderful feast I would ever attend, and if I ever complain about being hungry that I should hang my head in shame.

When dinner was done, the kids all helped to clean up and headed out to play in the yard, play area, etc. Here on a hilltop about as far away from Idaho as I could get, I was surrounded by more than thirty angels. These children were found in boxes, by the side of the road or simply taken in because all their relatives had died due to HIV/AIDS. Without prompting, they danced, sang, laughed and ran circles around Uncle Bobo's brother. Bob had made me an important person, and I sure as hell felt like it. It was movie night, so we all gathered in the TV Room (originally a dining room I think) and watched some donated extremely bad cartoon VCR tape from a church group back home. Lastly, Bob and Sallie and I retired to the former tennis court, now a bike/play area overlooking the majestic valley below. We broke the rules as Bob and Sallie had a glass or two of wine and Bob had gratefully smuggled a six pack of Tuborg beer on campus for me. Truly, a day like no other I have ever experienced.

**Schools, Clinic, Townships and Bobo's Dinner:** The next few days were a whirlwind of activity. Bob and I shuttled kids to school, to medical clinics, to market and scenes so incredible they almost don't seem real today. At the schoolyard, all the children were lined up in neat straight rows, all dressed in their immaculate school uniforms. To attend school, you must have a uniform. If you can't afford a uniform, no school for you. Many of the Open Arms Children had never been able to attend school as their families didn't have the scratch for a uniform. Enter Bob and Open Arms. I remember a story Bob had told me about a boy named Luthando. The night before the first day of school Luthando marveled at his uniform and wouldn't go to bed. He wanted to polish his new black shoes and make sure they were clean and ready for the first day because this was the most important and proudest day of his life.

At the schoolyard with hundreds of happy, nervous, and excited students watching, Bob was introduced as a VIP by the principal, which of course he was. I myself, hung in the back, declining an introduction, it just felt wrong to me deep inside, these students, these people had spent their lives being introduced to important white people. Of course, Bob deserved it, and it was warranted. But deep inside me, I knew that I was not comfortable. As I had said at El Hogar in Tegucigalpa years before, "My country has many of the same problems as yours: crime, poverty, inequality and social injustice. No one is better, no one is worse, we are all the same. We are all brothers, all sisters, we are all part of 'un Gran Familia'". I have never been prouder of what I said, and I was never prouder to be Bob's brother than that day.

Off we jetted to a medical clinic. Not wanting to get into politics here, but it would not be fair of me to fail to point out what a pleasant and heartwarming moment when the nurses and doctor informed me that any person in the region could come in and get free HIV/AIDS medications courtesy of the United States of America and yes, President George W. Bush. Chalk one up for W.

As we rolled about, Bob would zip me in and out of townships so that I could see the living conditions of where the children came from. Now, for those of you who may not know, townships are where the blacks were forced to settle during the time of Apartheid. The easiest way to explain it is, 90% of the population (all people of color) were allowed to have 10% of the land to live on. The other 10% of people (gringos) kept 90% of the land. Oh, and by the way, we are going to take your males away to work the mines, the fields, etc. This of course resulted in an inequality that is mind numbing to see firsthand given it destroyed the family structure for more than four generations. My favorite story in the Komga township was when Bob showed me a blackened foundation and I asked what happened to that house. "That's where the township Mayor used to live and people found out he was stealing money from the township, so one night they torched his house" came Bob's reply. Democracy in action, could we do that here for our corrupt politicians I wonder?!

Now, this next section is a tough task to tackle, how do you describe slums? ghetto's? shanties? etc. Most white people in South Africa have never set foot in a township (how about whites in America on the South side of Chicago? The garbage dumps of Honduras? The vast ramshackle slums's of Mexico City? The squalor and despair of the Wind River Reservation in Wyoming?) I have seen them all and in lumping them en masse, here is what I have found to be consistent among them all.

They smell, often of urine and fecal matter. Sickness abounds, if no one cares for you, you are in deep trouble.

Kids laugh, kids play, kids are everywhere. They fill the environment with unending battery power. Women work endlessly cooking, cleaning, and worrying. Many males despair and turn to drugs, crime, and alcohol. There is always garbage everywhere, garbage used, abandoned, floating. There are always scores of birds around, not nice birds, but birds that want to eat garbage and when they compete with people for it, they squawk and threaten. Adults do have fun, they do laugh, they want the best for their kids. Evenings are the nicest part of the day, nights are the most dangerous. People will do anything for money: prostitution, child exploitation, mining human organs, stealing, etc. On Sundays, there is always loud upbeat church music, singing, preaching, sleeping. It can be hot, cold or anywhere between. It is a bug's world, a rat's world, a spider's world. However, people are ingenious and they will use anything and everything to build shelter.

From all these places I've been, seen, experienced and tried to make a difference, the common thread is that: A) human life is the cheapest commodity of all; and, B) hope never dies as long as children abound. Yet, per usual, I digress.

Bob rumbles me around the townships, all that is listed above is on display. It can either make you sad or like Mother Teresa, give you hope because you have work to do. I think of Dr. Bob Volz in Honduras in his late 70's diagnosing child after child with sprains, temperatures, even a broken arm. Those children, those patients gave Dr. Bob a purpose, something to do, something he was damn good at, and even in his retirement, made him forget himself in helping others.

**Gazelle Fat Anyone?** - Back we bounce to Open Arms for a feast in Bob and Sallie's honor as they depart the next day, I shall be off the day after. I love this story and must preface it by saying that Bob is the most finicky, picky eater that has ever lived! I am in the kitchen watching the African women cook for the big feast. It appears to be some kind of gazelle ribs or some gamey, famished animal cooking in the big black kettle, there will also be something like barley, a fruit medley and a big cake for Bob and Sallie - in short, a true feast. So, there I sit watching the women cook and I have to tell you the only thing on those ribs is fat, gristle and an occasional strand of a nonfat brown substance - Bob's worst nightmare. So, I watch the women prepare Bob and I's heaping plates, drizzling liquid fat over the ribs onto the barley. Everyone is seated, Bob comes to the table, takes one look and just tells the cooks, thank you but he will just eat barley, stomach is upset. I chew on the bones for a bit, excuse myself and find the dogs to take care of the ribs I smuggled out in my napkin. Three hours later on the tennis court for our final African cocktail gathering, Bob is going on and on about how good the barley was. I start to laugh and tell him that it was because of all the gazelle fat slathered on top of his barley. He literally looks pale and is ready to gag! Score one for the little guy!

**Ending with an Angel – Asehko:** The next morning I am helping to wash the dishes in the kitchen when the phone rings, it is a call from a local family services worker. A three-year-old boy has been abandoned by the side of the road and there are no known relatives to care for him. His name is Asehko, he is badly malnourished and in need of quality care. Open Arms is close to capacity so Bob has to get legal authority to take in Asehko. I am standing there, washing dishes and this kid's life, his future is on the line. This is a day like no other. Bob works the phone lines and gets a legal opinion from their attorney and a local judge, that yes, they can take this boy in. This just can't be real, raced through my coconut!

Three hours later a station wagon rattles up the road and I am looking at a three-year-old boy, Asehko who is scared, disoriented, beautiful, and tired. The caregivers, saints on earth, clean him up, give him a bowl of beans and rice and shortly thereafter he is asleep on the living room floor. My heart hurts. My joy at being a witness to this miracle was unbounded. My esteem for Bob and Sallie was bottomless. The next day, Asehko was playing with the other kids on the swing set, running, laughing, smiling and being what he should be, just a kid. My favorite photo of all time is of Asehko and me, sitting together in the yard. Funny how life happens sometimes.

### Historic Times Part I: Market Crash (September 2008)

We were running out of chances. The two spec homes hadn't sold, and I knew that without some infusion of cash we would run out of cash in the first half of 2009. Bankruptcy would follow with loss of our family home and in short, a complete collapse of the Hickey Empire (at least it was an empire to me).

Hence, I started interviewing with non-profits across the country and internationally. I was invited to Chicago to interview for a development position with a nonprofit helping children with HIV/AIDS to go to summer camp. It sounds much nobler that it was, it was an inefficient organization that spent seventy percent of their budget on "Extravaganzas" with major corporate ties and glitzy Hollywood connections. It was run by a tyrant who ruled by fear, intimidation and sheer meanness. I am happy to report that the organization is now defunct and Susie the Hun was forced out prior to the demise.

Thus, there I am in downtown Chicago in September finishing up another day in the salt mines and ready to head home. I exit the building and was distracted, and ended up turning in the wrong direction. As I approach the next block, I see cop cars everywhere, fire trucks and an ambulance. I amble up to see what is going on and a woman says to me "Wow, did you see that?" "See what" I reply. "Some guy jumped off the roof of that building over there, pointing up, he cleared the sidewalk and landed on that Honda Accord there."

The Accord was quite simply pancaked, the center of the vehicle was now lower than the tires. The man had landed spread eagle with his back down on the roof of the car. There was blood splayed about and it was obvious the ambulance crew was trying to figure out how to scrape this guy up. I had seen enough and headed the other way to catch the El home.

The next day I was to learn that the man was an investor who had lost everything in the market and decided to end it with a swan dive.

## Historic Times Part II: Grant Park, Chicago (November 4, 2008)

I am a centrist. I cannot stomach the twenty percent on the far left, nor the twenty percent on the far right. America was built by the middle sixty percent and should this experiment in democracy endure, it will take a refocusing on the common person in the middle. That said, I was a witness to history in 2008 a black man, (African American) was elected to be President of the United Sates (not a Kenyan, not an Islamist, just a damn smart guy who despite a wee bit of political inexperience would serve all of us well in very trying times).

Hence, I take the El train down to Grant Park to watch this momentous occasion, something I never imagined would happen in my lifetime, having grown up seeing discrimination firsthand in the South. It was a cool night, well-orchestrated by security. Once through the entry screening process and security there were huge fenced off areas with jumbo screens throughout the park to follow the proceedings on the main stage. I went to the least populated area, towards Lakeshore Boulevard and Lake Michigan. From there I could see the trolley vehicles load up with VIP's: Oprah, Brad and Angelina, politicians and so on. This was to be like no other night in American history.

As the event progressed, the people around me who were African American and the vast majority, grew in anticipation and excitement. The results were announced and Barack Hussein Obama was to be the next President of the United States. To me, this was something to be proud of, this country founded in slavery had elected a Black man as President, not something I imagined I'd see in my lifetime. Perhaps there was hope after all.

The night progressed, the Obamas took the stage and I was struck by one thought: how lucky is this country to be represented by such a beautiful family? Much like the Kennedy's, this was a modern-day story of hope and the American Dream. All was again possible.

As the evening turned cold, my bowels screamed for a Loo and perhaps a nightcap or two, I exited the park and headed for a nearby watering hole. Bodily functions properly addressed, I headed up to the bar to watch the rest of the event. My seat was next to an amicable Scot and one row back from the bar. At the bar, sat the most discontented election result fan in history. He was drunk, obnoxious and racist. The racial and political slurs he hurled were appalling and distasteful. To the credit of those in attendance, he was quickly drowned out with cries to be quiet or head over to the Republican non-victory party. Little did I know that this lout's sentiments run broad and deep across this country and was a prognostication of the pending paralysis of the functioning of the government.

Regardless of politics, I was there and proud to see history made in America!

### Historic Times Part III: The End is Near (November, December 2008)

That fall, I knew I was living in historic times. The stock market was in free fall, losing close to a thousand points daily. I remember being so depressed that I called out sick from work to watch the DOW drop to 6,500 (the bottom?). The housing market was shot, the economy was on life support and yours truly was now sitting behind the dead stick in the cockpit, watching the mountain get closer and closer.

When the Chicago nonprofit froze the budget and all hiring on December 4th, 2008, I knew our hopes were scuttled.

I couldn't afford to stay on in Chicago without a raise, and I was needed back home for the inevitable ending. I recall I cried my eyes out on the flight from LA back to Chicago, the best of dreams and intentions cruelly wiped off the blackboard. Historic times indeed.

# ACT VII

## THE SHYTE SHOW (2009-2019)

### "ABBY NORMAL"

As we head into the final act, I wish I could give you sugar plum fairies, unicorns and the like but that is not how addiction and mental illness play out in real life. The story heads into dark corners, into scary places; jails, institutions, active addiction and loss. Thus far, I have had the courage to tell you the truth, I shan't stop now. Perhaps in time, my life will change to the point that I can give you that happy ending that is so craved by American culture; it just won't be today. Touched, obsessive, depressed, bipolar, addict, personality disorder, cyclothymic, a few cards short of a full deck, Abby Normal, and on and on it went. These were the diagnosis I have received from two "brilliant" psychiatrists, a licensed nurse psychiatric practitioner plus the half dozen therapists who have tried to work with me. Yeah, I know I ain't got my mind right, but do they? I am mentally ill, obsessive is true, addict is true, cyclical is accurate and on it goes.

What am I guilty of? Feeling too much, caring too much, having a brain that runs anywhere from fifty percent to two hundred fifty percent of normal depending on the day. Thinking too much, ruminating too much, loving things, people and life too much. What am I afraid of, being boring, dull and wasting the very short-time that has been allocated to me on this sphere. Those are sins I can live with regardless if "society" approves.

My life has always had a cyclical pattern; intense periods of massive outbursts of energy, lasting two to three weeks followed by several days of rest, inactivity, and recharging of the batteries. This pattern is what made me successful in school, in work, in travel and in life. For me it was just normal, it was my way, focusing with a laser on fundraising was how I was able to raise over five million to build important projects for at-risk children. It was how I coasted through school with B's, applying myself at the moment-of-truth to create great papers, exams, and whatever was needed to keep moving forward. It was also how I was able to drink, travel, chase women and live like a hound from Hell. Isn't this how everybody lives?

This is also how I became addicted to the written word, to stories, to textures, to ideas, to mind-numbing explorations of the mind. Some of my best friends include: F. W. Dixon, Milne, Rey, Hemingway, Tolkien, Homer, Dickens, Tolstoy, Dostoevsky, Mandela, Marx, Faulkner, Mailer, Kerouac, Hugo, McCourt, Dante, Uris, Salinger, Orwell, Melville, Kearns Goodwin, Conrad, Steinbeck, Solzhenitsyn, McCullough, Kandinsky, Lao Tzu, Harrison, Kesey, Vonnegut and many, many more. Having been to three continents, over forty states and more than forty countries, my companion has and always will be great books, ideas, stories, histories and at its core, life. I am the luckiest guy in this sense and if I spent the rest of my life living in a library, I would consider myself wealthy beyond measure! Yet, again I digress...

As the property investments in 2007 started to head south, my stress level, anxiety and tension all started to skyrocket accordingly. My net worth of $300,000 was on the line, my unrealized net worth of $600,000 was in the deepest of peril. Much like many others, I did a great job of handling it like shyte. Soon, I was drinking almost around the clock and hoping for a miraculous turnaround that wasn't meant to be.

The first real indication that I was "really off" was my 2008 trip to South Africa. I sat in the Jackson Hole Real Estate Office in Driggs, ID when my brother called me and couldn't figure why I wasn't en route. I was befuddled. What the hell was he thinking? The next day, I knew I was I was scheduled to go Jackson Hole - Atlanta - Dakar - Johannesburg - overnight, and then to East London, South Africa. My brother is a genius but not so hot with details, or so I thought.

The next day I showed up at the Jackson Hole Airport only to be informed that my ticket was for the day before. What the hell? They did honor my ticket, with a $200 change fee that I gladly paid. I am great with details, so how did this happen? Once en route, I was manic, I didn't sleep for two days. My brain raced at infinite speeds. In short, my brain was at Mach speed and the next five days in South Africa were harried, frenetic, brilliant, muddled and a grey zone. Something is wrong, what the feck is it?

Upon my return to the States, my symptoms only increased: depression, days of sloth, periods of hyper activity, increased need to self-medicate with booze. My work was either brilliant or deplorable. Irritability with family and friends grew. I chalked it all up to stress, defeat, the economy and on and on. I once heard David Feherty, the golf analyst, talk about how watching the evening news was the "most interactive depressing activity" of the day - that was me. There was no leaving anything behind, everything was personal, painful and cause for self-medication or twenty-four or forty-eight hours in bed. Having no other medications to go to at the time, beer was my go to. My family could plainly see that Dad was rearranging the deck chairs on the Titanic.

### Margin Call and Chapter 7 (2009)

D-Day for us was June 14, 2009 - the day when all of our reserves and money would be gone. After that date, it would be impossible to pay our mortgage, our bills, and for the investment properties. In anticipation of this looming date, I sold my interest in the LLC's so as to not negatively impact my partners, my friends. Vehicle payments would cease, college applications would show that we were destitute. Food and heat would become the priority.

In September we set up the appointment with an attorney in Idaho Falls. We would file for Chapter 7 bankruptcy. Our 3200-square-foot family home, appraised at $595,000, sold at a short-sale for $221,000, a real deal if you had money left. Both spec homes sold in the mid $200,000 range, a loss that would sadly be eaten by our partners. I paced, I cursed, and I pounded on the wall as we met with the attorney in Idaho Falls. The attorney commented that I looked like, "a tiger in a cage, willing to do anything to escape." He had no clue how prescient those words were.

A couple of months later, off we trotted to bankruptcy court. The huge courtroom was packed with other folks just like us. The common trait amongst us all was a glassy stare that looked as if we had all been hit in the back of the head with a two by four. How the hell did this happen was all that kept running through my mind? Quickly it was over, debts erased, good luck out there folks and don't be too hard on yourself - BUT that is what I am really good at!

### The Funnel

Imagine a large unbreakable glass funnel, filled with a beautiful aquamarine color on the top, dark blue color in the middle of the funnel and a burnt orange discomforting color at the bottom. It is not filled with liquids, just color so that breathing is possible. At the bottom of the funnel is the narrow outtake neck which has been securely sealed shut with cork and steel. With me so far, gotta use your imagination to envision this scenario.

Now, on the aquamarine level is everything you and everyone you know floating about, everyday life. Friends, family, society norms, rational thought, etc. Each is like a small bobber floating on the top of the aquamarine layer. Sometimes a bobber starts to drift this way or that way, being bounced about by storms, challenges, etc. It is simply everyday life and each bobber is able to stay in the game. There seems to be uniformity to life in relation to everything else.

One day, my bobber starts to get heavy. There is a tiny pin prick of depression, and my bobber starts to sink just a wee bit. Still seeing everything and everyone I care about, I try as hard as I can to stay afloat with everyone else. I do for several years. It's taxing. I don't even know what is going on, but I stay above water. Odd behaviors begin to occur; sleeping on a cot in the master-bedroom closet for months on end (I did sleep great in there). Paranoia begins to rear its vicious head. I'm afraid of illogical things. I feel as if I am always under scrutiny by something or someone or both.

My bobber starts to sink lower. I can still see everyone above me but despite all my efforts, I cannot get my bobber to rise back up. At this point in the equation, my stress level is getting the best of me. I know who I am. I also know what I am capable of. Despite this, I am incapable of rising. I cannot stop my descent. My bobber sinks. The dark blue is starting to envelop me. Those above me are still visible but unclear in form. I am going down. It's just a question of when.

As I sink deeper into the blue, everything above me starts to disappear. I can no longer see any bobbers above me. I have thoughts of them, however those thoughts are becoming infrequent. My anxiety, paranoia, depression and fear are now in control and pushing me down. There is only one respite: booze. When drinking, I am not scared. I feel comforted and that things will be okay again.

But in the morning, that feeling has dissipated. My demons are back stronger than ever.

My descent into the orange begins.

There is no longer awareness of anything above me, no bobbers, no blue water. I am now alone and must ride this journey solo. The color of the orange is dark, foreboding and lonely. Once going into the orange, there is only one place to go. I descend down into the neck of the funnel.

There are cries of despair, fear, hopelessness, but no sounds exist here in the orange. It is as if the dark, burnt orange is so heavy it will not allow noise to exist. There is no longer any awareness of anything. I am alone with zero thought about my loved ones. The descent has erased all thoughts of what lies above.

Finally, I sink into the neck of the funnel and stand upon the sealed bottom of the funnel. There is no possibility of going up, there is no possibility of getting out down. I am now in the worst place imaginable, devoid of all hope. There is only one option to avail myself: check out of the hotel. Nothingness is better than this fucking orange place.

Where's the razor?

## Checking Out of the Hotel: Part 1 (January 25, 2011)

Things had been spiraling downward into a black hole for months: paranoia, depression, stress, lack of sleep, booze and avid use of sleeping pills. In short, the wheels were off and I had no idea it was happening. I came home from work with beers en route. Upon my arrival, I went to sleep for a few hours then woke up about 9:30 p.m.

The next thing I recall was being in the master bathroom, dismantling my razor so that I would have a tool to end my misery. Not wanting to make a mess for people, I went into the shower stall and sat down on the cool, travertine tile. The light was honey colored from the mustard colored walls and the travertine. Without any thought of consequence, I went to work.

I knew at some level that if I were to be successful, I would need to cut long, straight lines parallel to my arm. I made about eight to ten cuts on the right wrist, bringing blood to the surface of the skin but never striking a vein. I was too clueless to realize that the tiny razor blade strip I was using was unlikely to achieve my objective. Sitting now in my own blood, right arm bleeding but not in peril, it was time to try again.

I switched wrists. I now went after the left wrist with a purpose and a vengeance. I slashed sideways, diagonal, up, down and in any way that I could. There was a solid flow from my wrist, but again a major vein refused to burst, leaving my arm looking like a horror movie gone awry. Gashes, slashes, blood and pure ugliness. It was apparent that I was failing miserably in my efforts and that I was to live another day.

Being the tidy, nut job that I am, I decided I had best clean up my mess. I started to run the water in the shower, washing the blood down the drain. It looked like someone had dumped a pitcher of cherry Kool-Aid down the drain as the water diluted my blood. In the midst of cleaning, Halina came into the bathroom. The jig was up. She took one look at my wrists, saw the blood and the dissembled razor and chaos ensued.

I don't recall everything about the rest of that evening, but here is what I do remember. Halina's friends, Todd and Dani came over to be with us. Halina worked the phone, getting a hold of those who would need to know as well as medical personnel who would have to deal with me. From 2004-2007, I had helped to raise $1.9 million to build the Jackson Hole Community Counseling Center, a new nine thousand square foot mental health center. At that time, I had worked closely with Deb Sprague, the Executive Director who is a saint. Little did I know that someday I would become a regular client at the center. But first, we reached out to Deb.

I was to meet Deb at St. John's Medical Center at 6:30 a.m. where I would be expected to commit myself for seventy-two hours of observation under the law for being a threat to yourself or others. With that being the plan, and given my confidence and love for Deb, I relaxed. Throughout the night, I drank a few beers, as much as they would allow me to, talked, and oddly enough, relaxed. The storm had come, and I had weathered it. I wasn't alone anymore, and hopefully I would get some help.

The night passed, my poor wife weathered it all, grateful for her friends and worried about her very sick husband.

At 5:30 a.m., we were off for St. John's Medical Center in Jackson Hole. Upon our arrival we met Deb who had laid all the ground work for my entry into one of the two "observation" rooms aka nut-job rooms for criminals, drug addicts, suicidal patients and now me. Deb explained all the ramifications of what I was to sign. For seventy-two hours, I would be foregoing my rights and would be the responsibility of the State of Wyoming, Teton County, WY and a consortium of medical professionals. I was under no obligation of any kind to sign. But that if I did sign, I would have to comply. My hand shook as I signed the document. But I did sign.

### Into the Hamster Cage

So, with bandaged wrists, a hospital gown, boxers, and Crocs, I was wheeled into my new accommodations to be observed. The room was completely devoid of furnishings other than the bed and the TV mounted behind plexiglass in the corner of the room. The bathroom had to have been furnished with prison furnishings, stainless steel, a tiny toothbrush and toothpaste, a small plastic cup and a small towel. No shower curtain and nowhere to hide.

Mounted in the hospital room and the bathroom were cameras that had a 360-degree view of all spaces. I was officially on "Suicide Watch". I would be watched twenty-four hours a day until that door opened. There was no handle or way to open the door and no window to see out into the hospital corridor. There was a decent sized window looking out into a courtyard in the room, and I could see that my room was about half underground and half out of the ground.

They were medicating the shyte out of me now so my acuity was intermittent at best. I recall Halina visiting daily, sitting on the bed looking at what had been her bulletproof husband, who had just taken several direct hits to the chest.

I could sense it was depressing for her just to come into this room and our talks were low volume, subdued, and tense. No idea if the room was wired for listening devices, but I have to assume it was.

A well-known Jackson Hole psychiatrist visited. She did her assessments, wrote multiple prescriptions and whirled out the door (after a few months, I would change my psychiatric care to another provider as I was sick of being an ongoing brain chemistry experiment).

On day number two, I had to take an alcohol-drug assessment from the Curran Seeley Foundation, administered by a big, goofy, red-headed great guy named Steve. It was overseen by the Program Director - Ed Wigg, a man I would do battle with in the months to come. My failure of the assessment was a foregone conclusion. Telling the truth in such situations means you get the label "Alcoholic" with treatment as the only recommendation even if you don't share all their beliefs.

During the three days in the hamster cage, the Arab Spring was raging on the TV. CNN and all the major networks covered it twenty-four-seven. To me, a depressed, suicidal student of history, it looked like that World War III was beginning. All hell breaking loose, Hosni Mubarak ousted, chaos and fighting in the streets, etc. Without any filter to what I was seeing (no newspapers, no internet, no contact with people other than nurses and Halina), I struggled with perspective with even headline news.

The bright stars of my stay were the nurses who took care of me, brought my meals, kept me comfortable and were beyond kind. I am certain that they must have received special training to work with patients like me. The nurses worked very long shifts, and for me, they were lifelines of humanity, compassionate, kind and gentle. My sincere thanks to all who have chosen such a challenging profession and serve us all at the toughest moments of our lives.

I could not leave early, but the one-way door would soon swing open. When it did, I would walk back into society, regaining my rights and responsibilities. My future was certainly an open-ended question. How would I heal? What would my support team look like? How would my professional life look like as a fund-raising professional? All, yet to be determined.

Halina helped me out of my gown. I dressed in civilian clothes again and the door to the room swung open. Shaky, nervous, scared, withdrawn and relieved, I walked through the door and headed for home with the challenge of how to find my way forward. This all sure as hell wasn't in my life script!

## Twenty-Nine Days in the Box (April/May 2011)

With one suicide attempt behind me and with my landing gear up on approach, the quest to figure out what the hell is wrong with me was priority number one. Having been a quaffer of mass quantities of beer since age seventeen, the target seemed to indicate alcoholism, a logical conclusion but no fun for an Irishman. That said, how could I object? I was obviously all feck'd up and things were not getting any better. Guess it's time to drink the Kool-Aid and give myself over to a higher power that I no longer believed in.

My brother Bob, Angel on Earth that he is, came up to Idaho to be with me and help to work towards a treatment plan that might work. I recall that I was completely out of it. Everything was a joke to me at the time, and I didn't care what the hell happened. My physical and mental systems were firing on just a few cylinders. The plane was going down and the control stick had shyte the bed. I ended up being "accepted" at a facility in Cody, Wyoming which would have an open bed in four days. "Accepted" denotes that I had insurance and said insurance would cover 80% of my tab at the spa.

Bob returned to Phoenix and with two days to go. I was completely useless. I knew I couldn't as much drive to the mini-mart as drive to Cody. I called one of my best friends,

Matt, who valiantly drove ten hours to my place, then six hours to Cody and another ten hours back home. Upon our arrival in Cody, I was too sick to be admitted. I was running a fever of 101, dehydrated, and completely lethargic. Now it takes some real talent to be too sick to go into rehab, I guess I just was "extra special." Matt hooked me up in a Holiday Inn Express and hit the road. I promptly went to the liquor store and picked up a six pack. If I am going down, might as well do it with a beer in hand.

I was admitted to St. Joe's a most unwilling candidate and thus I only know that I hated every minute of it. It was like a fake log structure next to the hospital. All the bedrooms in the log facility were on the first floor and all the therapy rooms, classrooms, etc. in the basement. I survived the intake by having no illegal contraband on my person. Next, off to my room, which was a cheesy blue affair with inspiring mottos on the wall, two hospital beds, and permanently sealed windows. Depressing is a compliment to the ambiance of the room. Once settled, it was time to go downstairs and meet my fellow campers.

Into Hades I descend. Not a single window to be found in the basement. This is truly a bunker. There are screaming florescent lights blaring down on me and no fresh air to be found. The stairs lead me into the common room that has a TV with DVD player and exceptionally uncomfortable institutional chairs. Adjoining the common rooms are long tables that will serve as our work space. To the left, two bunker classrooms where we will spend six plus hours a day trying to figure out why we are all fucked up. Beyond the classrooms are the therapist's offices where I will do my best to agitate the woman assigned to my case and in return she will do the same.

My fellow pals are just like me. Everyone enters this place because life isn't going so swell. Tracy was there because she had become hooked on meth and fallen so far that she was give two choices, prison or treatment, she choose the latter. Joe, the most narcissistic human I ever met, was here to shave some time off his jail sentence. Joe had no concept of what remorse is, and of course was an upstanding guy in his own eyes. He also was the most dangerous piece of shyte I ever met. Ben was an old guy, about seventy-two, whose second wife had given him the ultimatum: treatment or divorce. After I met his wife, I seriously came to believe that deep down Ben regretted his choice. Another Joe, my roommate, was a cool guy who had baked a few too many brain cells in a small town in Wyoming. He was harmless, but it was obvious to see that Joe all feck'd up on drugs was a disaster waiting to happen. Christina was very rough around the edges, but a sweetheart at her core. She had been a meth addict and became pregnant. And now Christina had spent a year clean, working at a nursing home and just wanted to have her kid back. Twenty-eight days was what she had to do in order for that to happen, and she was determined it would happen. As tough and rough as she was, I liked her and respected her determination to be with her daughter and emerge from here a self-sustaining and independent person.

Now, why did I hate it so bad? It was as if I was five years old again. I have already mentioned the bunker spaces, the sealed rooms and minimum access to fresh air. There also was a rule against sunbathing on the micro-patio we had access to (I broke that rule every time I could, including the liberal use of sunscreen). Breakfast, lunch and dinner, you line-up, single file, staff in front, staff in back, then walk the block to the hospital cafeteria. Going to the recreation center for exercise, same routine line-up, single file, staff front, staff back, etc. Going to AA, same routine, line-up, single file, etc. Going to Narcotics Anonymous, same routine, line-up, etc. It was stifling, humiliating, and embarrassing. Trust was not in these people's vocabulary. You were guilty until they proved you were guilty.

The entire treatment program was predicated on the twelve steps of AA. Now as an agnostic with severe mental illness, I don't quite fit the mold. I have attended AA off and on for 33 years, I keep hoping for that the promised "psychic change" or "spiritual awakening" will miraculously occur. I guess I'm just defective, because God sure as hell hasn't banged on my tambourine yet. Thus, my time in Cody was a $20,000 experiment in futility.

Once in a therapy session with my counselor I muttered the sacrilege words aloud, "God, I love to drink."

She about jumped out of her seat.

"You can't say that!" was her declarative.

I thought, 'Why not? It's the truth, guess I'll have to kiss your arse to get out of here.' Or not.

After twenty-five days in the spa, they wanted to keep me an extra week to finish up my treatment. Not gunna do it! I asked for a meeting with the Executive Director, and we were joined by my counselor, Ms. Sunshine. I explained that I had given a month of my life to this, and that I was a voluntary admission. Given that, whether they liked it or not, it was time for me to go home, back to work, and support my family who were making sacrifices every day throughout this process. I added that I'd like to leave here having completed the program but if that wasn't possible, I was walking out the door on Saturday afternoon.

My wife picked me up on Saturday. I completed the program and now it was time to go home. More adventures awaiting.

## Checking out of the Hotel #2 (July 2011)

In retrospect, my second attempt at ending my life was in many ways scarier than the first, primarily because I don't remember much of it. My electrolytes and potassium levels were near nonexistent. My thyroid was functioning six to seven times slower than a normal person, an almost near-death level. I was beyond depressed and drinking heavily to self-medicate as my grip on reality slowly slid away.

Here is what I do remember. I went once or twice to Dave's Pubb in Tetonia, Idaho, a short drive on country dirt roads so as to not risk a DUI or other vehicles. I got smashed, buying drinks for the bar and seriously ramping up into a non-coherent state. I drove my 2001 VW Bug home with zero clearance and ran off the road into the ditch, trashing the bottom of the car before I was able to drive it out of there. I didn't go to work. I didn't call work. I drank. I slept. Repeat process. This went on for at least three days, but I know I was spiraling downward for several weeks.

At some point, I did research online to see if taking a bottle of sleeping pills would kill me. I can't remember what the results were, but the idea was now in my head. Late one night I ended up in the half bathroom near the family room where I swallowed a bottle of sleeping pills. At some point shortly thereafter, I crumpled to the floor and was incoherent and comatose. The next thing I recall was coming to in a hospital room somewhere (Eastern Idaho Regional Medical Center) and a huge guy who looked like Gene Shalit was sitting next to me. I faded in and out of consciousness, but I was able to deduce why Gene Shalit was there. I was on suicide watch again. The next day, many different doctors came into see me, one of whom talked really fast. My off the chart lab results were coming in and the immediate concern was fluids, electrolytes, thyroid medicine and whatever else they dreamed up. I was a hurting Cowboy.

Later that day, I agreed to and was transferred to the Behavioral Institute across the parking lot. It was where the severely messed up, like me, were sent for full medical exams including psychological assessments. I had made the nuthouse. What a proud day. I slept most of that day and night as the pills dissipated from my system. Of course, my poor wife was beside herself with worry and just wanted me to get whatever help I needed. I am still not sure how she kept her chin up in the midst of all the chaos.

In the morning, I attended a meeting with my fellow campers where we introduced ourselves, and if possible, explained why we were at the Institute. Here are some stories of my fellow campers; Irene was about seventy years old and could hear voices coming from the soles of her shoes which had been wired by aliens. Also, drug traffickers were tunneling into her basement to manufacture meth. She was fine and didn't need to be here, but she just needed the police to stop the drug traffickers. Laura was a sullen, dour heavyset eighteen-year-old girl who did not wish to speak or participate. Her wrists had fresh stitches that were meticulously sewn. Laura never spoke more than a few words. Larry was a forty-year-old man who had decided to drink himself to death. He grabbed two large jugs of Vodka and went to a local reservoir to get it done. Larry passed out, no shirt on, in the sun for five hours before being found. I don't know skin burn levels, but Larry was so severely sunburned that it was likely he would need skin grafts. Larry smelled so bad of alcohol oozing out of every pore that I couldn't be anywhere near him. Lisa was detoxing, and for the first thirty-six hours all she did was wail, cry and see hallucinations as she went through the DT's. And so on, and so on...

Throughout the day, I had numerous medical appointments and conversations. One thing that became abundantly clear was that I slept very little, not getting anywhere near enough rest. The doctor ordered sleep tests for me when I got home with the suspicion that I had severe chronic sleep apnea. Also, we had to get my blood levels back in range and try to keep me off the sauce.

My final night in the institute was unlike anything I have or will ever experience. At 8 p.m., they brought in a seventy-eight-year-old man, Ernie, who had irritable bowel syndrome and an open hole in his abdomen from a recent cancer surgery. Ernie was a methane time bomb, a howitzer of flatulence. It wasn't his fault, but he erupted every thirty seconds like clockwork. The stench was so bad that at one point I wrapped my head in towels and pillows, all to no avail. At 2 a.m., I went to the common room and curled up on a micro chair where I could still hear Ernie firing away but I was no longer subject to the mustard gas assault.

The next day I was discharged and was monitored weekly until my blood levels returned to the safe range. It all was a blur of chaos, mayhem, and characters that will remain with me to my last breath.

## A Decade without Sleep (Fall 2011)

Under the recommendation of the Eastern Idaho Medical Center and my Internist, Dr. Butcher, the time had come for my sleep study at the Sleep Institute at St. John's Hospital. At 7 p.m., I checked into the sleep institute and began the hour-long paperwork process and then almost two hours of hooking up wires, sensors, computers. By ten o'clock, I looked like a wired Rastafarian and thought there is no way I can sleep with all these wires hooked up. This night a baseline of my sleep pattern would be determined without a mechanical sleep aid - CPAP. The technician, Jerry, was a decent enough guy but lacked any zest, probably because he spent four to five nights a week monitoring meatheads like me.

Into my hospital bed I curled, a bit cold as the blankets were too thin. Jerry found me a few heated blankets, and the test was back on. To say I slept restfully would be a total lie - I did my usual tossing, turning, spasms, snorts that re-awoke me, etc. About 4 a.m., I was so exhausted that I got a few hours of restful sleep. At 7 a.m., Jerry woke me up and the test was over. All the wires and machines were unhooked. After getting dressed, it was time for the preliminary results.

Jerry took out the test strip results and said, "It looks like you have severe, chronic sleep apnea. Sixty-three times per hour on average, you stop breathing anywhere between four and twenty-three seconds. Each time that happens, your brain goes into self-defense mode and sends out signals, wake up! breathe! The only REM sleep you achieved was in the 7th and 8th hour of the test. I would guess you haven't had a good night's sleep in ten years based on these results."

All of these results were confirmed by the sleep doctor

from Casper, WY. A prescription was written for a CPAP machine, and I did another night at the sleep institute this time trying out differing CPAP machines and masks. Same procedure, Jerry attached a zillion wires to my head. And then a miracle, I SLEPT! I mean I actually slept.

Now seven years on, I sleep like a king who slightly resembles Darth Vader. I can sleep on my back, something I had not done in twenty-five years. Naps are my friend again, put on my mask, sleep sixty to ninety minutes and awaken refreshed, sharp and alert. Despite all my other medical issues and challenges, solving this one issue has been the most important day-to-day improvement to my health. ZZZzzzzzz....

**We've Evolved (March 2012)**

By the spring of 2012, I was an active chemistry lab, seeking the correct medications to effectively control my runaway mind. I was put on a medication called "Geodon" which I knew nothing about. Shortly after starting Geodon, I began to hallucinate with mind-altering experiences, much like the effects of LSD.

One night I awoke about 4 a.m. and the TV was on (my wife likes to sleep with background noise) the show was some South American fishing trip. I remember that the TV looked different, the chop of the waves looked 3D. The colors were altered and the fish that were being caught looked truly spectacular, shimmering and way too real. In short, I was seriously tripping.

When I awoke a few hours later, everything, including myself was in slow motion. I looked out at the Tetons and was mesmerized. I was one hundred percent positive that I had evolved. The rising sun streamed into the master bedroom as my wife started to stir. I looked at her, relieved and said, "Awesome, you made it too! We have evolved." My daughter came in to get a brush out of the master bathroom,

I was ecstatic, she had made it too! I was one hundred percent certain that I thought we had really evolved into another, peaceful, brilliant realm. Everything was beautiful, food tasted exquisite, my libido screamed and I must say, I felt damn happy. By late afternoon the effects were diminishing and only then did I comprehend it had been a chemical reaction in the brain that caused this euphoria, not evolution into a new paradigm.

## Father Knute - Dancing with the Broom (May 2012)

What I am about to share with you is perhaps the hardest thing I have ever done. It was brilliant and beyond difficult. Somehow, someway, I survived the event and kept a tiny grasp on reality until I successfully got through it.

I had promised myself that there would be no more hospitals, no more locked doors. Nobody was going to get me to voluntarily go away, come hell or high water.

As previously mentioned, one of the new medicines that the psychiatric brain trust suggested was Geodon. So here I was at home, with my wife and my daughter in the house, and I am ramping up to a complete psycho level. My voice is rising. My paranoia is climbing. And I begin to realize that I am in the fight of my life - I will not go quietly into that good night.

I tell Gina and Halina to leave immediately. I know what is coming down the pike. This is going to take all my focus to avoid succumbing to the insanity. Halina and Gina both leave, worried as hell yet knowing that I was moving out beyond the bend. I told Halina to call Lou Parri, a brilliant man, a therapist in the valley. Lou is someone I trust completely.

Now I descended into full-on protective, paranoia mode. I wouldn't put my head into windows because the snipers would pick me off. The SWAT teams were out there. They'd be coming in soon. The safest place in the end was for me to be in the garage with the windows covered. From there, I could hear anyone who might be trying to get in.

About thirty minutes later, Lou showed up to find me wired, pacing, frantic and quite simply way out around the bend. For my brain, it was beyond intense and yet satisfying to know that I could travel out so far without snapping. Lou pulled up a seat in the garage on a milk crate while I prepared for the imminent onslaught. As we talked, I ramped up even further and started dancing with the broom.

At my high school, we had a priest who spoke seven languages, had an IQ north of 160, but snapped. He memorized the student directory, scaring the shyte out of the girls when he knew their home address and phone numbers. He would talk to himself in foreign languages and reply in another language. Father Knute was completely harmless, but he was "touched" at the time. The final straw came when Father Arnold, the President of the school, caught Father Knute dancing with a broom in the gym. Time for a much-needed rest for Father Knute.

With Father Knute and a "Brilliant Mind" as my inspiration the time had come for "Hickey's Last Stand." I would make it so they couldn't take me away - Feck'em!

Back to the garage, where now I was in a super manic state exacerbated by the psych meds. I had a broom in hand and was dancing around the garage roaring that I was dancing with the broom and I was with Father Knute. My goal was to let those who knew and loved me that I was fighting as hard as I could to not lose it completely, that despite the current madness, I was still here on this side of things, barely.

In the history of the world no one was more caring or patient than Lou. He asked me questions and tried to reel me in. Most importantly, he NEVER said anything to challenge me. He knew I was dancing in a ballroom far away, and yet he patiently tried to bring me down while I danced around the garage.

As time ticked away I realized that this was going to get

really bad. That someone was going to try to take me away. It was time to prepare. I cut my driver's license in half, foregoing my right to operate a motor vehicle. Grabbing my backpack, I started stuffing all my camping gear inside. I grabbed my passport and tied it on. It's gonna be a long night. Once I had prepared myself, as I had when I lived in Europe, it was time to set off. Lou was doing everything he could to keep me in place. It wasn't meant to be.

Off I tramped, using every legal ploy I had ever learned plus logic to avoid detainment. Our house was in a very rural area, five miles from town, so I knew I could get some distance without interference. The sane part of my mind also knew that I had to stay off private property or I could be detained if the owner so wished. Heading north, I made my way along the public thoroughfare which was simply a dirt road.

Ten minutes out, Lou was behind me in his Toyota Sequoia all the while imploring me to just go home. That was not an option for me at this point. Behind me, a blue and red glow appeared. It was the local fire department and an ambulance with EMTs. They drove by me and parked on the side of the road, waiting for me to catch up to them. Holding my passport high, I approached them.

They inquired, "Where you headed?" "How was I doing?" and "Could they help me?"

I jubilantly said, "Thanks, I'm fine, it's a beautiful night for a walk and that I am headed to California to raise money for mental health awareness."

I don't think they liked my answer much. I would later learn that they wanted to bum rush me, take me down, and bring me in. Remember, at this point I am still fighting with everything I have got to stay away from locked doors, yet still I am intelligent enough to understand how the system works.

Down the dirt road we go, me with my passport held high, fire truck and ambulance in tow. Damn I'm special!

After about twenty minutes, the local sheriff's deputy

shows up and the officer, a friend of mine, pulls forward to talk to me. I know now that this is the moment of truth.

"How's it going Tom?"

"Great, officer," I reply. "Here is my U.S. passport identifying who I am. I'm just out on a walk to California to raise awareness of mental illness. I have never felt better in my life to be walking public thoroughfares and not disturbing anyone's peace."

Check and mate. The officer knew the law. Given that I posed no threat to anyone, myself included, he peeled away and told the fire department and ambulance to leave.

Now I am just out for a lovely stroll in the countryside. After about ten minutes, Lou pulls up and offers me a ride. I agree but say that I am making camp at my friend's house in Tetonia. By now I am starting to cycle off the Geodon and come back to reality.

At Jeff's place, I set up my tent in the dark as a light snow flurry descends. By the time I have the damn thing setup, I am close to being back on the good side of things. Lou asks if I really want to sleep in the tent (it's after midnight now) or sleep at home with my wife and children. Tough choice: cold and snow or comfortable mattress with heat. I take the deal and head home.

Until tomorrow...

## Speaking in Tongues (April 2012)

The next day, the Geodon was again sending me into orbit. This would be the last day that I took Geodon. I was ramping up and definitely in a manic state. My mind began to transform. Halina called the doctor. He prescribed a sedative. However, it was Sunday, so she would have to go Jackson Hole to pick up the prescription. That left me at home and freaking out again. God bless him, Lou came over to be with me for three hours.

Now what follows is the farthest out my mind has ever

gone out around the bend. I striated into numerous languages and dialects depending who was with me. If Halina was in the room, I spoke Polish, if our dog Cozmo came into the room - I started talking to him in my Cozmo voice. If I thought about real estate, I conversed as a licensed real estate agent, if I thought about the law, I went into my best legal mind. If Lou came in to talk with me I had two choices: A) talk to him as my friend; or, B) give him a penny, thus establishing a therapist-client relationship and voila, he was my therapist. I could not have two beings in the room with me at one time as it was too painful and confusing trying to converse with more than one being. It finally got to the point where I posted a note on the bedroom door as to who I wanted to talk with next.

After three exhausting hours, Halina finally came home. I took my knockout pills, and I was down for the count. To this day, I always keep a supply of knockout pills on hand just in case.

## Two Days, Two Lives
### (September 2012 & July 31, 2015)

Despite my previous chapters, I was still a functioning adult in life most of the time. I was and am still a father and a contributing member of society. In other words, despite my troubles, I have always had to work to pay the bills.

In September 2012, I was working with the boys of Cabin 7 when over the radio a call came in "Backup in Cabin 6, please hurry, Backup in Cabin 6." Being that I was near the front door and Cabin 6 was fifteen feet away, I took off to help with an eerie feeling based on the urgency in the radio call. Within twenty seconds I was in the girls' bathroom where CPR was being performed on a fifteen-year-old student, named Ellie.

Ellie had had her wisdom teeth removed that morning and was in the bathroom face down in the tub, the water overflowing the tub walls. I got the water turned off and assumed a position at Ellie's left shoulder, ready to assist with CPR, which we all staff were certified in. Ellie was Native American and her normal skin color was a dark bronze. Now it was grey, opaque, not good and she wasn't breathing. Within a minute, I took over doing the chest compressions, another staff was doing the mouth to mouth with a protective cover and in time another staff member would alter chest compressions with me from Ellie's right-side.

The scene was chaotic; screaming, crying, people cheering for Ellie to stay with us. The staff administering CPR remained focused and efficient, we were going to do what we were trained to do. At one point, a rust colored fluid emerged from her nostrils. Everyone took it as a positive sign. I knew at some level that she was gone, and she wasn't coming back.

We kept the CPR up for about eight minutes when paramedics, police and EMT's arrived on the scene. They took over for us and used the cardiac paddles to try to get Ellie back in the world of the living. It was all a strange, sad situation. Every one of us did exactly what we were supposed to do. We did it the right way. And it was to no avail. Ellie would be pronounced dead that night after being life-flighted to a hospital in Idaho Falls. An official cause of death was never revealed but reports were that Ellie had a history of seizures and black outs and that she most likely went unconscious at the tub's rim and went in head first.

I was offered numerous opportunities for counseling to talk with people about it, but I just didn't feel the need. I had done everything the right way and as we were taught. I am still certain she was gone before I ever entered that room. As my first experience with a death that close up, it has stuck with me to this day, guess it probably always will.

Fast forward three years to July 31, 2015, and I have a fifteen-hour day with a head cold working in the school and cottage with really messed up kids. Time to go home, get some serious rest, recharge the batteries and be ready for Monday.

As I climbed Teton Pass, on the right side of the road were numerous vehicles and very obviously, a fresh accident scene. *Damn*, I thought, *I don't want to deal with this, especially right now*. However, I am trained in first aid, and I made a commitment to help whenever possible. My Subaru did a U turn, I parked, and headed to the accident scene.

Lying in the gravel was a seriously messed up biker. He had black leathers, no helmet and a hell of a lot of blood covering him. In time, the accident story filtered out. He had hit the car in front of him, bounced back off the guard rail and was now in a world of hurt. His head had major trauma with so much blood oozing out that it was difficult to assess where it was coming from. The right nostril was literally half torn away, an eerie bloody flesh sticking out perpendicular to his face. He was rasping and gasping for breath, leaving his head down risked him choking on his own blood.

It was time to get to work.

There was an off-duty nurse on hand who was monitoring his vitals, primarily his pulse. Lights everywhere, changing, leaving, coming, with no rhyme or reason. I took a position above his head and trying to keep his breathing passageway clear. I elevated his head and upper torso, cradling his head on my forearms and supporting his shoulder blades with my hands. His breathing was labored, snotty and borderline, but improved when elevated. Two or three times, his pulse became very faint and his breathing seemed to cease.

At one point, I barked out to the people assembled using their cell phones to tell 911 that this guy didn't have long. Having done this dance before and losing Ellie, I was determined to not have that happen again. We held on, probably ten to twelve minutes, doing all we could for this guy. It seemed like forever. At one point, there was a very obviously Christian woman who had placed her hand on his forehead and was praying. For some reason, one I will never know, she looked at me and asked if I was religious man. It was a startling question given the situation, I promptly replied, "Not me, I am trained in First Aid and CPR and just stopped to help."

With his life in the balance, a few more minutes passed and people began to cheer that emergency vehicles were en route, lights, and sirens on full throttle. Suddenly, there were Sheriff's officers, EMT's and an ambulance on scene. Since I was in a strategic position with regard to his head and neck, I would keep cradling the man's head onto the flat-board gurney, carry him to the ambulance and put him on the stretcher. As we began to move him, his eyes opened - a great sign. At last, he was in the ambulance, alive as they pulled away headed for St. John's Medical Center.

Exhaustion just isn't the word for my feelings. A look down at my arms, hands and clothes, I looked like a MASH surgeon, blood from armpits, elbows, the tips of my fingers, belly and thighs. There were some kind women on scene who gave me some water to rinse off with. They were startled by my gory, crimson appearance. Knowing I had done my best, I headed to the Subaru. At home I was rewarded with a long, hot shower and twelve hours of peaceful sleep. A week later I called the hospital to see if there was any news on the guy. A nurse in the Intensive Care Unit said that yes, he had made it and was getting better. She couldn't tell me more, but that was more than enough for me.

Two days. Two lives. Three years apart.

## The Gauntlet Ends - Johnny Law
## (November 11, 2015)

It was a glorious Veteran's Day, and I had the day off. Sunny, warm and the day all to myself. Wanting to escape Teton Valley, I decided to head to Bone, Idaho, some twenty miles outside of Idaho Falls. Bone is literally a bar and micro store with a population of two (yes, "2") according to the 2006 census. Years ago, I ran a relay race there, "To Bone and Back" twenty miles uphill from Idaho Falls and twenty miles downhill to the start/finish line. I ran the twenty-mile uphill portion, and my friend Adam ran the twenty miles downhill section. We did well, had a great time, and enjoyed the rolling foothills of Southeast Idaho.

In 2001, I hosted a party at the Bone Store with a dozen plus idiots, I mean friends, from all over the country coming in for January 1st, 2001, thus 1/1/1 at 11:11:11 p.m. (notice a pattern here - Bones!). We rented the place out, huge ribeye steaks, plentiful cold libations and cocktails. T-shirts and the original digital flip clock that Dusty has read 11:11 for all eternity. Ah, but yet again, I digress.

Back to 2015, I grabbed a twelve pack of Bud, put it behind the passenger seat, and nursed a few cold ones en route to Bone. Once there, I made a video for my friends of the improvements at the Bone Store & Bar-Grill, the patrons, the management, etc. I had one shot of whiskey and a few beers along with a delicious prime rib sandwich. Hitting it off with a few folks, we swapped stories and laughs for a while. Full from the sandwich, I headed down the hill into Idaho Falls and did a few errands: Target, Staples, etc. Time to make the seventy-five-minute drive home.

I took the Pine Creek Pass route, as it is more scenic than the North route and a more pleasurable drive. A few beers were quaffed en route, but I was most definitely not impaired, yet. Into Teton Valley I descended, noting that it was just after 3:30 p.m., I decided to stop at the Westside Yard in Victor, Idaho for a beer or two. I planned to be home safe and sound before 5 p.m. to cook dinner. A pleasant day all around.

Seated at the bar, I ordered a Bud draft from Joe the bartender, a friend of mine. A few minutes in, Ernie came in, also a friend of mine and a Vietnam vet. My Father had spent two years in the Army serving in Tokyo at the end of WWII and Veteran's Day was always an important day in my family. I waved Joe over and told him to buy Ernie a beer and a shot on me. Ernie chose Jameson's Irish whiskey and asked me to join him. I was happy to do so and honor his service. Down went the shot and we shot the shit for a bit, basic small talk. I was getting ready to leave when another veteran came in and sat down next to me, repeat the same steps again. I pop for a beer and a shot and I asked Joe for my tab. I gotta get out of here and get home, off the road was my thought process. Thus, in forty minutes I had two Jameson's whiskey and two Bud pints on top of the beers I had had earlier in the day. I settled up with Joe, thanked the guys for their service, and out the door I went.

Heading north on Highway 33, I am feeling no pain and gonna get home early. I pass the Spud Drive-In, and what the feck! At 4:35 p.m., cherries are on behind me and an Idaho State Trooper is on my arse - I'm fucked now. State Trooper Kelly had me dead to rights. To top it off, I got pulled over right in front of my wife's work place. I was going 65 in a 55-mile zone, "Have you been drinking?" asks Officer Kelly as he squats down to smell the booze on my breath. My eyes are bloodshot. There is beer and empties in plain sight in the backseat. Game-set-match. After thirty-five years of running the gauntlet, my goose is cooked.

The field sobriety test is administered. I fail honorably, yet I fail nonetheless. The eyeball flashlight test is administered, and my eyes must have been pinballs in hyperdrive. Time to cuff the big Mick and put me in the backseat. One problem, my Irish barrel chest is so damn big that one set of handcuffs isn't enough. So, Officer Kelly links two cuffs together, and now I am guided into the backseat. The breath analyzer is administered, Trooper Kelly is doing everything by the book so that there will be no legal loopholes for a prying lawyer to find. I myself am being most honest and agreeable. My come-uppance is here - kind of knew it had to at some point. I am just grateful that I didn't hurt or kill anyone else. I fecked up big time and now the piper wants to be paid.

Trooper Kelly is being extremely kind. I think because I am being polite and respectful as well. He has a job to do, a tough one, and he is a good man. I don't need to cause him any additional consternation. He calls my wife so that she can come get the car and thus avoid paying a $150 towing bill. She will be right down to get the car, and see the cuffed arsehole she married in the back of the state trooper's rig.

Dusk is upon us when my wife arrives with my son to pick up the car. I look out the left window to see my 24-year-old son looking in at his old man. This being about the lowest I have ever felt in my life. Our eyes lock, I can see that he loves me, that I love him but that this is an event that will always be seared into both our memories.

Off to the hoosegow we go (about 3/4 of a mile), and I am processed in, printed, etc. The double set of cuffs is removed, and I am placed in a small holding cell, door open. I pose no threat. Within thirty minutes, my wife posts the $500 bail and I am released. No night in the box. I spent more time in the squad car than I did in the cell. Once home again, conversations are low or nonexistent. There will be plenty of time tomorrow to discuss what a brilliant piece of shit I am, and what this will cost us.

## Checking Out of the Hotel #3 (February 2016)

I had gone five years without a suicide attempt, sadly my streak was about to end. Each January or February I have a major manic or depressive episode, most likely correlating to the short days, lack of sunshine, the initial diagnosis is Seasonal Affective Disorder (SAD). February of 2016 was no exception, the difference this time I was very melancholy, indifferent and in slow motion.

Massive quantities of booze had been ladled onto my daily doses of pharmaceuticals, continuing to see how the lab rat responds. For weeks I had been "off", really off. It was evening and with no zeal or passion. I went to the medicine cabinet, pulled down a bottle of migraine headache pills that I thought were just like Tylenol. To my bed I strode, counting out fifteen pills, 'that should do it' was my thought.

I was again at the bottom of the funnel. No way up. No way out. No thought of anybody. No one else existed.

Calmly, I swallowed the pills, three at a pop, washing them down with Budweiser. I distinctly remember laying down, putting my head on the pillow and looking at the ceiling. 'I won't be waking up' was my only thought. I was just fine with that. The level of fatigue I was experiencing was an oppressive weight. 'I have valiantly fought, there is no shame in this' was my final thought before fading into a dark, troubled sleep.

I did wake up though, the pills weren't as lethal as Tylenol, I had screwed this whole thing up again somehow. Trying to commit suicide isn't "normal", but after fucking up three attempts, it sure as hell was starting to feel that way.

Like a good patient, I reported the attempt to my therapist and doctor. Everything else about that month, that time, is just a grey haze. It is strange to forget days, weeks and even a month. Looking back, it just merely seems a foggy dream and I was just a bit player in a bad play.

Note: I now have a Seasonal Affective Disorder lamp and daily from November 1st - April 30th, I get thirty minutes of light that in 2017-2018 actually worked, I had no massive bout of depression in January and also of note, I was stone cold sober all winter.

### Oh, No, - From Bad to Worse (February 16, 2016)

How do you spell Shame? Stupidity? Drunkenness? Indecency? Depravity? Vulgarity? Foolishness? Warped humor? Crassness? Loutish behavior? etc. ...

You are correct - Tom Hickey.

Let me begin with how I got to the correct answer. I was scheduled in court to appear for my DUI sentencing in the morning. Not having a clue what to expect, I decided that I should get good and drunk that night as I thought I was about to be sentenced to two years of mandatory sobriety and this would be my last opportunity to enjoy libations for a long time to come.

I was working the evening shift at a gas station and convenience store, half a mile from our home. After the dinner rush subsided, I availed myself of liberal access to the beer cooler while I did my closing checklist. All good so far, no problems.

About 10:30 p.m., I had closed the store and gotten everything ready for the morning. A couple of beers more, time to go home, get up, go to court and start my new "sober" reality. Now about 11 p.m., I got home and hey, there is a party going on downstairs in Unit #35, a mini microbrew keg on the deck, I think it was four gallons. A couple of neighbors I knew were outside, drinking beer, taking some shots of Jaegermeister and some cinnamon fireball shit. Now, the last thing I needed on top of Budweiser was various coma inducing shots and numerous heavy microbrews. Yet, always being the cautious one (sarcasm), I jumped in with both hands over my head. Dumb feck'n arse.

Over the next ninety minutes, the party migrates inside from the cold to the warmth of the apartment. I head in to the much less inebriated, cerebral crowd. However now I am veering towards the dark side. I get louder, more argumentative and have serious bad juju going with a few of these cerebral millennials. Shockingly, I am asked to leave the party about midnight. (Me get the boot? Tis' never happened before).

Out to the deck I traipse, dark clouds swirling through my mottled brain. I finish my beer and decide that I will show them how it is done; I drop my pants and boxers, stuff my unit and nuts into a green solo cup and I enter their apartment from the deck door, making my way to the front door. 'What the feck is wrong with these people? They aren't laughing at this, they are offended instead? What the hell happened to make these folks miserable at twenty-five-years-old?'

Now, I am getting screamed at by a screeching woman who is going to press charges. Not having much fun at this point, I pull up my pants, argue for a bit, get a beer for the stairs and let loose a howling "FUCK YOU" as a I ascend to my abode. With a sense of dread this is about to get really ugly, I head into my room, lock the door and the deck door and await the inevitable siege to punish the crazy drunk old fecker.

As portended, statements are gathered, charges are pressed and a citation is served to our condo by an officer who is repelled from entry into my domain by the locked door. I am in bed, drunk, loud and obnoxious, and refusing to comply (at least I ain't no quitter!). After everything has quieted down, I pass out, the officer leaves the citation with my wife and calm is temporarily restored.

The next morning, I am up early and off to court. I reek of alcohol. My lawyer, a member of the Latter-Day Saints' faith is aghast at how I look and smell. On top of it all, we now have a new charge being levied against me, things just went from bad, to worse. Sean counsels me not to speak to anyone in uniform; the police, the bailiff, the prosecuting attorney, all of whom who could have me arrested for public intoxication. Our only option is to get a continuation on both charges to deal with this mess in two weeks, which is exactly what happened. Once the Judge approved the continuance, I high tailed it of the courthouse. Way to go dumbarse!

### Apology + Tears in the Courtroom
### (February/March 2016)

On February 25th, I received a copy of the police report detailing my actions on the night of February 16th and the statements of those present during my "solo cup incident". Reading the report was so shocking, humiliating, embarrassing and excruciating that I immediately sat down and wrote an apology to all individuals involved and delivered it the same day. On March 3rd, when I had my next court appearance, Judge Walker asked if I had anything to say in response to the charges, I read my apology letter to the court, voice cracking with the first word, tears streaming down throughout, all pride gone. I felt like I was back in green solo cup in front of all, but stone cold sober.

Here is what I wrote:

*February 25, 2016*

*To:     Individual #1 (Name withheld)*
*Individual #2 (Name withheld)*
*Individual #3 (Name withheld)*
*Individual #4 (Name withheld)*
*Individual #5 (Name withheld)*
*And anyone else present in Unit #-- on February 16th*

*Please accept my sincere apology and regrets for my behavior and actions on the night of February 16th. Only as of today, February 25th, have I been made fully aware of my actions that evening - I admit that I was inebriated at the time.*

*I am appalled at my behavior and fully understand why anyone was deeply offended by my actions. As the father of two adults in their early twenties, my embarrassment is immeasurable.*
*Should the legal case proceed, I shall not contest the case. I fully understand you may not accept my apology or forgive me, yet it would mean a lot to me if you could.*

*Humiliated, Embarrassed & Saddened.*

*Sincerely,*

*Thomas J. Hickey*

Once finished reading/crying, the bailiff handed me tissues. The courtroom was eerily silent. After a long pause, the judge continued, and I was put on probation for the DUI, Open

Container, and Indecent Exposure. As we exited the court room, my attorney whispered to me, "I CAN NOT believe you didn't get jail time." He of course was right. I just felt that being fully human despite my own stupidity had been my salvation.

### Dennis Will Robertson (Summer and Fall 2016)

On November 2, 2016 my friend, Dennis Robertson killed himself with a gun. It was a tragic ending for a troubled man. Yet, I shall always remember Dennis for his smile, his gentleness and his appreciation for the smallest act of kindness. Before I get ahead of myself, please let me go back in time to tell you how Dennis and I became friends.

Due to my bipolar swings from manic to depressed, I was working for a friend as a cashier at a gas station and convenience store in Driggs, Idaho. Almost every day, this guy came in with dreadlocks, rumpled in appearance, full beard and a faraway look in his eyes. Some days he would just enter the store, mutter something to himself, turn and head back out the door.

Who is this character kept running through my brain?

In early summer, a friend was in the store when Dennis made his entry to buy some cigarettes with crumpled his money. My friend told me Dennis' story. He was a severely schizophrenic, bipolar genius. Dennis lived close to the gas station. He would often go into local restaurants and ask patrons to buy him a cheeseburger, which would get him promptly eighty-sixed. There wasn't a mean bone in his body.

The next time Dennis came in, I hooked him up with a box of Swisher Sweets and introduced myself. He stuck out his hand and looked me in the eye. From that moment on I had a new, authentic friend. Going forward I would always buy him something: a bag of chips, a cup of coffee, a big can of beer, whatever I could. He was always most appreciative.

In July, the station was dead in the middle of the afternoon.

I was sitting outside the door on the curb getting some fresh air on such a glorious day. I am not sure how the conversation started, but I told Dennis about my own battles with depression, suicide attempts, and being bipolar. He listened attentively. When I was done, Dennis gave me a solid handshake, and with a piercing look in the eye and a half hug, he said, "Hang in there my friend, these folks out there don't have a fucking clue what it's like."

We had crossed a threshold of brotherhood.

The last time I saw Dennis, he was having a bad day and looking out of sorts. I pulled a $10 spot out of my pocket and handed it to him, "Get a good meal on me man."

Dennis stood up straight, looked me squarely in the eye and said, "Thanks Tom, you are a damn good guy."

"No sweat Dennis, we gotta look out for each other," I replied.

With that, I was on my way as was Dennis. I would never see him again, a shame as he battled so valiantly. Should you wish to, here is the link to Dennis' obituary: http://www.jhnewsandguide.com/valley/obituaries/robertson-ministered-despite-his-illness/article_3920a623-dfd8-552b-b807-7361ed8c6e90.html

It is beautifully written in the Wyoming way.

I miss my friend, but I am glad he has at last found peace.

### Cubs Win! Cubs Win! (October 2016)

It's happening, the Cubs are advancing through the playoffs, beating the Giants, then the Dodgers. Next up, the World Series!

The Chicago Cubs going to the World Series, and I am not dead yet. Lazarus has risen! In advance of this possibility I have booked a week-long stay at an International Hostel in Chicago about a mile from Wrigley Field, a classic old Hostel, great neighborhood, $60 a night for a private room for a week. It is an ideal setup and locale for my twenty-five-year-old son

Luke and I. As this cataclysmic event draws near there are a few minor obstacles that will need to be overcome.

First, I am flat broke, we don't have enough money to drive a hundred miles, much less 1423 miles to Chicago over twenty-one hours. Oh, it's just money, somehow, I WILL make it happen, always have, always will.

Second, I am on probation. I can only leave Idaho with the permission of my probation officer. If he won't sign off on the trip, I either: don't go; or, go at the risk of a probation violation and execution of sentence upon my return, a healthy stint in the Madison County Jail.

Feck it. The Cubs are going to the World Series. I promised my mom that I would be there if they ever made it. They made it. Time to tuck in my skirt and man up! This is going to really be a tremendously stupid thing to do. We will be in Chicago for a week for Games 4 through 7 and any potential parade. Time to get my arse in gear and make this happen.

What follows is a Go Fund Me posting I put up and distributed to any and all friends I could think of, Facebook, Email, etc.

> *A Promise to be Kept - Chicago Cubs*
>
> *My mother was a lifelong Cub fan whose dream was to see the Cubs play in a World Series. In 1984, she had World Series tickets and the Cubs failed to make it, two years later she was killed in a car accident on her way to give a talk to a church group about "How wonderful it is to be alive". At her funeral, my brother and I vowed to represent Mom if they ever got to the World Series. I will keep that promise along with my 25 year-old son Luke, somehow, someway. (We got wiped out by the Great Recession)*
>
> *What will the money go for:*
>
> *$500 for gas to drive our Suburban 25 hours from Idaho to Chicago and back. We will sleep in the back of the Suburban en route.*
>
> *$497.86 to stay at a hostel October 29th - November*

4th, two El stops from Wrigley Field for one week. (We would be in Chicago for games 4-7 of the Series and there for any potential parade)

$500 for food and drink for a week. (We will cook meals at the hostel) We have no delusions we will get tickets but we will be in Wrigleyville and watch the games in local establishments.

Please wait to donate until the Cubs win the National League Championship Series.

I am a 4th generation Cub fan, my son a 5th generation Cub fan. Keeping this promise in honor of my Mother means the World to me. It is very hard to ask for help but without it, I don't know how we can go otherwise.

If any funds are leftover, I would donate them to the local domestic violence shelter in our town, Family Safety Network - Driggs, Idaho.

I thank you in advance for your consideration and any support you may offer.

This one's for you Mom!
Go Cubs!

Tom H

If this was meant to be, it would happen. Without funding, we were watching the Series from home.

Would this work? Could this work? Am I completely nuts? (Yes to the last one...haven't you been paying attention to what you're reading). Within an hour of posting of our campaign, donations started to pour in, and within a few days we had enough to ensure we could get there. If we had to sleep in the truck, we slept in the truck. My probation officer signed off on us going, I would be subject to a urinalysis test immediately upon my return. In the end, friends and family donated $1705 total from 24 donations, our heartfelt eternal thanks to each and everyone of you. There was only one problem, the Series had started in Cleveland and the Cubs weren't doing well, down two games to one headed into Game 4 Sunday night. God, what if we do all this, make this incredibly stupid effort and they lose the Series in 5 games? Aw, feck it - that's thinking like a loser!

Friday night, my son comes down from Bozeman after work. We throw our sleeping bags, air mattresses, clothes, cooler, beer and food into our twenty-six-year-old Suburban AND we're off! We will take turns driving, one guy chewing up three to four hours at a time through Wyoming-Nebraska-Iowa and into Illinois. Our goal was to roll into Chicago late Saturday to catch Game 4 in the city, but we were both exhausted before we even left Idaho which put us in Iowa as game time loomed. Just east of Des Moines, in a small town called Altoona, we stopped to get gas, and I couldn't take it anymore. I didn't come this far to not watch the Cubs play Game 4. I asked the kid behind the counter for the nearest bar with TV's and he gave us directions to one of those stupid big box bars a mile or two away. I told Luke, keep your eyes peeled man, we need a dump bar. We need a place where "real" people will go, not "box" people. About half a mile away, my son comes through, spotting the neon glow from an ugly cinder block bar. I pull a U-turn, we circle back and we have hit pay dirt, a small bar three-quarters full of properly inebriated local Cub fans. (Nice job son!)

Now I need to interject here that I was nervous then, and I am nervous now just recalling this. The Cubs were in the God Damn World Series, and we were going to be there. We were excited, tense, happy, and stressfully hopeful. All our chips had been called in, cashed, and were on the table. These could be the greatest days of our lives or somewhat painful. Regardless, I was with my boy and headed to the City I love on the banks of Lake Michigan. Back to the bar and Game 4.

Our fellow fans and patrons are people who live within a block or two of the bar and have walked down for the game. Cubby Blue everywhere but these are long-term fans, with shirts, sweatshirts and caps like mine, worn, dirty, sweaty, no fresh tags here. Within a short time we are exchanging shots, toasts, moans and groans and hanging on every pitch. The Cubs need clutch hits, and they can't buy one. About the eighth inning Luke and I exchange comical glances, they are going to lose. They will be down three games to one. If they lose tomorrow's Game 5 and the Series, what do we do? Just go home? The absurdity of it all becomes comical, comical becomes hysterical and we are almost wetting our pants as they lose Game 4. Rather than get down, we pin our hopes on Game 5, have another round and then head to a truck stop to stop for the night. Nothing like two grown men sleeping in the back of an old Suburban. Damn, I live for this shit!

Now, a strange thing is about to happen. It is Sunday morning and we are going to cross the Mississippi River into Illinois. Everything is about to change, to become surreal, to become an anomaly. For the next seven days we are to reside in and interact in a fantasy reality, What to call it? Cubby World. Everyone, everything, every action by us or anyone else centers on the Cubs. People aren't just happy, they are elated, there is palpable electricity everywhere, there are no strangers, anything and everything Cubby goes. It was as if once over the Mississippi we were being pulled by a magnet to Wrigleyville, to the Windy City, to something karmic, to just somewhere we had and were supposed to be. Win or lose, everything that happened the next week was to happen exactly as it should, life was temporarily on hold, we were in an oddity in the seam of things. Wherever we went, that was where we were supposed to be.

Sunday afternoon we arrive at the hostel, awesome setup! We unload then find free street parking (a rare find!) a few blocks away from the hostel. We beach the Suburban there and become pedestrians or public transportation junkies for a week. No worries about drinking and driving.

Once settled into our third-floor room, Luke on the top twin size bunk, Dad scoring the full-sized bottom bunk with a gorgeous view of the quiet residential street below. We clean up and get ready. Game 5 starts in about ninety minutes. Down to the corner tavern we head to make sure we have a spot on the inside for the game. Every bar in the area packed to fire marshal capacity limits with bouncers counting folks with clickers as they entered. Once full, it is one out, one in. Luke and I park in front of one of the twenty TV's in this outdoor patio area now converted to a four-season space with a dark green canvas shell aluminum structure. It was perfect. Shots and beers ordered, we were now with several hundred fellow Cub followers hanging on every pitch. Game 5 was a nail biter, 3-2 Cubs win! Yes, there is a Santa Claus. Now fully committed to what may come and proud we made it, Father and Son strolled about the neighborhood hitting local watering holes. Everywhere Cubby blue and a current of anticipation. I knew then, my mom and Dad were happy and proud of us for making this effort. We were grateful to everyone who had helped to make it possible.

The next day was an off day, a travel day for the World Series, and it was Halloween. Being that I am an old fart, I chose more to consume libations during the day and evening. Being young and in a big city, Luke was more into late sleeping and late nights. We made it work just fine. I would get up in the mornings, grab a cup of Joe, Chicago Tribune, read about the Cubs and then walk the neighborhood, often heading down to Wrigley, a scene of mayhem even in the mornings. Off to Lake Michigan and then usually find a watering hole about lunch time for barley rehydration. Back to the hostel, Luke up and moving, time for lunch, good Chicago fare like Italian Combo's, peppers, au jus, pizza, burgers, etc. Back to the hostel for a break, then happy hour with the hodgepodge of young people at the hostel: France, Italy, Argentina, Russian, Japanese, etc. Every day was interesting, new, and, fun. On Halloween, I conked out early. I had to get some rest. That left Luke loose on the town for a costume party of epic proportions.

Tuesday, November 1st, Game 6. My oldest friend and the man my son is named after, Dave Lucke came in from the burbs to watch Game 6 with us. We would again return to the tavern on the corner with the hope in our hearts that the Cubs would force a Game 7. Just get us there Arrieta, may the chips fall where they may. In order to ensure we got in, we were at the bar ninety minutes early, pulling up at the short bar. Yes, we drank a lot. The Cubs rolled 9-3. We high-fived, hugged, hooted and celebrated with the mob. The Chicago Metropolitan area has 9.4 million people and it was estimated that 5 million more Cub fan idiots like ourselves had descended on the City, making 14 million people, for one team, for one game. Shyte!

Preface to Game 7. My friend Gil Hundley, a stalwart Red Sox fan, told me about what it was like for him when the Red Sox won the World Series for the first in 86 years - it nearly killed him. He was a nervous wreck and just drank like a fish because of the stress. He said that since winning was never expected, the joy he felt was overwhelmed by relief. So, there I am with 108 years of not winning, never once getting there in my 51 years of following the team.

TONIGHT is Game 7! I am here with my son and my best friend. I have honored my Mother, my father, my family and my team. To so many people who don't get it, this is just a silly narrative. To me, this is a Karmic moment in my life. I had gone above and beyond the call of logic and reason to get here, Silliness be damned. Today will be THE day for my team.

### World Series - Game 7

November 2nd, 2016. This is how it went down.

I was a wreck, nervous, tense and every other descriptor you could imagine. I started drinking early and wouldn't stop until it was over. There could be no relaxing. It was excruciating. Game 7 tonight. We got through the day somehow. Dave had stayed downtown overnight at his Mother-in-law's condo and would join us for Game 7 again (we are not going to mess with our mojo). Two hours to game time we are counted into the corner tavern, getting stools at the sidebar again (mojo preserved). People are buying shots and taking shots like it is their last night on Earth. Go Cubs Go! was sung countless times. You could do, say, scream whatever you wanted, it didn't matter. It was mania, and being Bipolar, I know all about manias. People on their feet. The bar is packed. No room to move. Bartenders taking shots, giving shots. It is truly unchartered waters.

Game time. I feel almost sick. This is too much! By the third inning I can't watch, my head is under the bar. The bartender wants it above the bar. Dave is telling him that I am just praying. Cubs are up, looking good, leading 6-3. Indians then score three in the 8th, and it's 6-6. Worry and stress surround me, but I am suddenly calm. IF the Cubs ever win the World Series, this is how they will do it: ugly, backwards, illogical. If they lose, it will be a collapse to remember forever. Regardless, for me, this it. I won't be back for next time. I have pushed all my chips onto the table, either win big or go home a LOSER. It was worth it all either way.

To the 10th we go, my complete and utter exhaustion coupled with massive quantities is most evident, but I am still soldiering on. Mama Hickey didn't raise no quitter. The Cubs score two in the top of the 10th, now up 8-6. The energy around us is indescribable, Cleveland scores one run, 8-7. Then came the play: short hopper to Kris Bryant at third, Bryant chargers the ball and throws to Rizzo.

CUBS WIN! CUBS WIN! CUBS WIN! CUBS WIN! CUBS WIN! CUBS WIN!

THE CHICAGO CUBS ARE WORLD SERIES CHAMPIONS!

I LITERALLY FALL OFF MY BAR STOOL BACKWARDS, CRASHING INTO PEOPLE AND TABLES BEHIND ME!

I AM 86'D FROM THE BAR BY THE BARTENDER!

DAVE, LUKE AND THE BOUNCERS ARE TRYING TO GET ME UP!

I BADLY TWIST MY KNEE, EVEN DRUNK THAT HURT LIKE SHIT!

I AM ESCORTED OUT OF THE BAR, A GAME 7 CASUALTY, WOUNDED IN THE LINE OF DUTY!

BACK TO THE HOSTEL I AM SHEPHERDED BY DAVE AND LUKE!

The next day I wake up and try to stand. God, that hurts. Then I tell Luke, "The Cubs won the fecking World Series."

It ended as it should have. Amen.

The next day and a half is spent in delirium in the City with great food, cocktails, high fives, bleary exhaustion. The parade was intense, an estimated five million people in attendance. Luke was spent, and he wisely went to check out the Art Museum. At one point I was on Michigan Avenue with an eighty-year-old woman who had died her hair Cubby red, Cubby blue sweatshirt and she was playing a trumpet like she was possessed by demons. Volumes, decibels, all at level ten. Cops, security and I even saw soldiers in full gear dispersed. I tried to watch the parade from the street but it was freaking me out with 50,000 people standing in front of me and 50,000 standing behind me. It was just a sea of Cubby humanity.

Was it easy - no! Was it worth it - YES! My deepest and sincere thanks: to everyone who donated through "Go Fund Me"; to Dave Lucke for being the best friend a guy could have; and, to my son Luke to putting up with all my shenanigans.

After fifty-one years of hoping, I was starting to lose hope. I loved the Cubs when they stunk. I loved'em when they win, and I will love them until the end. My love for the Cubs and Chicago is eternal. It is hard to express and often defies logic, yet it remains.

Father and son climb into an old Suburban, smelling not so rosy and drive twenty-one of the next twenty-four hours to get home. We did it, not easy, but we were there and that will always count in the scheme of things. I am happy, and I am proud.

Go Cubs!

## "I Feel Great - Think I'll drink today."
### Friday 2/17/2017

What follows is what I remember and recall from this most pivotal day.

Fecking Idiot!

Quick setup: for the preceding month I had not had a drink. I was going to AA meetings almost daily, working with my friend who has successfully navigated similar issues and has over six years of sobriety. I was seeing my therapist weekly and generally, things were improving. I was working in Jackson Hole with a snow shoveling crew of 5-7 Hispanics and "El Grande Blanco Gringo." We shoveled walkways, driveways and roofs and I was making $17 an hour. It was fun, great exercise, and I was outside. Solid hard work up to twelve hours at a pop.

6:31 a.m. - Alarm goes off. 'Damn, I feel great - Think I'll drink today.'

That was it. No other thought, no internal discussion. I have a plan. I like it. Go execute it. Into my snow gear I slid, gleefully thinking about how wonderful that first beer will taste. I raided my coin jar, got the $8.00 I would need in quarters to buy a six pack of 16-ounce Budweisers. At 7 a.m., I was at the gas station, "Mornin' Jenna, How goes it?"

"All right" came her standard response, but I could tell she was feeling upbeat like me. She had more energy than usual. I stacked my quarters on the counter, put the beers in my back pack and had one hour before work to enjoy my purchase. A glorious morning in the Tetons, probably a half day of work ahead of me. The women folk will be gone to Idaho Falls tonight, so I will be a bachelor. Enjoy Tommy Boy.

Ksshhtt! Number one, damn that's nice! Morning beers taste awesome. I am not impaired. Johnny Law isn't on the hunt, and I will work it off shoveling. Ksshhtt #2, and I start to climb Teton Pass. Not a cloud in the sky with the sun beaming off the snow and the valley floor coming to life. I pull over at the top, 8432 feet above sea level and survey the glorious view. I've got a few minutes to burn so I listen to the news on Wyoming Public Radio and gulp away. The descent begins, ksshhtt #3. This will be the last before work as I don't want to have an open container on the Valley floor in Wyoming because Johnny Law is everywhere and tough as nails in this tourist town. That being said, for all practical purposes I won't have time for number four before 8 a.m.

I get to the multimillion dollar property whose roof we will finish shoveling today. Gorgeous views. I actually really like this property. It's not too ostentatious, great layout, and looks comfortable rather than austere. Mi amigos are running late. They will be here in 20-30 minutes with the equipment - ksshhtt #4 - radio, sun, good buzz now, fuck this feels great. Amigos aqui, time to work. Morning is spent shoveling, sun warming us as time progresses. All is right with the world.

11 a.m. and it's time for a shyte. Off to the porta-poddy down the road. Ksshhtt #5 quickly quaffed. Shovel, break ice, shovel, 12:30 lunch time, didn't bring lunch, I dash off to Wilson Gas quick, ksshhtt #6 en route. Out of beer, screw lunch, better grab some fresh supplies (two Bud 24 oz. tall boys). Ksshhtt #7 on the way back to the job site, better slow down dude – you are pretty altered – forty-five minutes more shoveling and job's done. Load up the gear. It's payday and

gotta go get my check at the office. I get my check, head to the bank.

I could have gone home then, of course I didn't, dumb-fuck! All the other are guys done for the day. For some stupid reason I push to keep working.

Javier, the Supervisor and I end up at some housing units on the Eastside of town breaking up ice on sidewalks. I've had enough, I drive down to the Eastside Liquor Store and buy a six pack and a shot of Wild Turkey. As I leave the liquor store, the most beautiful extreme female athlete I know drives by in her white Nissan pickup. We used to work together for more than three years, Meg is a world class athlete, blonde, petite, stunning, and one of the most independent minded woman I have ever known. Off I follow her in my Suburban knowing that she lives a few blocks away in a rental with another friend. I roll up to her drive as she gets out looking amazing in athletic garb, probably having just finished a twenty mile run uphill and then an hour of skate skiing after already having been to the gym in the morning.

Meg strolls over to my truck, radiating health, fitness and a damn great friend. We catch up a bit but it all feels a bit off, could be that I haven't eaten today or that I'm just drunk (or both?). She is a tired, cold extreme athlete and there I am with a six pack now on the seat next to me. Meg doesn't drink, and I am sure she can smell and see that I sure as hell have had more than a few. Anyways, "Always great to see Meg, take care" as I pull away with a final glimpse at Meg, I sense she wasn't very happy to see me today.

Enough! Time to get home, pick-up a good dinner and chill out tonight. Back up Teton Pass I drive, happy and starting to chill a bit. I call a great friend, Mike an artist who totally gets the struggle part of the artist's equation with equanimity and is a huge support to me in my writing pursuits.

I simply was feeling great, nothing more, nothing less.

Down the Pass and into Victor, Idaho I drive. I stop by the Victor Valley Market and get a first-class dinner: some large shrimp, two jumbo crab legs, asparagus and a great local bread. Tom, don't forget the butter and the lemon. Quick glance at today's trivia board, no clue, some freakin' science question. Out to the truck I stroll, dinner in hand, sun shining, I glance left at a local watering hole. Aw, just a quick one and then get home.

DANGER WILL ROBINSON!!!!!!!!!

I put the food in the truck and wandered into the bar, a pleasant environ at happy hour time on a Friday afternoon. I stand, no sitting down, and I ordered one whiskey and one bud. I paid for it immediately as I wanted to get home, be off the roads and have a great night. I took my shot and drank my beer over the next 10-15 minutes, chatting with folks and friends. I was just about to leave when a good friend and a fellow baseball fanatic came in. I smugly reminded him that the Cubs won the World Series (he's a Tiger fan) to which he made some quality quips back and the verbal banter flows fast and furious. As I turn to leave he says, "Hold on" and he buys me a World Series celebratory shot of Jameson Irish Whiskey which is easily a double. I thanked him, I tilted it back, swallowed and headed for the door. I saw the Suburban in the bright afternoon sun down by the stop light...

...

...

...

...

... I am sitting on a stool in the Teton Valley Hospital Emergency Room with two uniformed police officers. They are preparing to take my blood, by force if necessary as I slowly regain my bearings. Oh Feck! Now I have done it. I start co-operating fully, blood is taken...

...

...

Now I am handcuffed in the back of a squad car, Officer Hale driving, and we are headed to Rexburg, Idaho and the Madison County Jail. I am glad the plexiglass is solid so that Officer Hale

doesn't have to smell my breath. Oddly, as my world is cratering, the darkness of the sky, the silhouettes of Mountains and the streetlights in the distant is stunningly beautiful...
...

I am standing at the booking desk at the Madison County Jail handcuffed to the counter, about as uncomfortable as anything I have ever experienced. A friendly, tall young officer is processing me in, fingerprinting me, taking my photos which for some reason the devil in me made me laugh and smile for. I was then led into a bathroom where I had to shower and delouse in front of the guard. I even got to hold up my nut sack to prove I didn't have any contraband with the family jewels.

Now in my orange and white horizontal stripes and matching orange crocs, looking as horrible as it sounds, I was led into Pod B and up to Cell B6 where my roommate was the ugliest acned, toothpick kid I have ever seen. Instead of arguing about bunks, I was supposed to be on the bottom since I am an old fart, I just climbed onto the top bunk, pulled the blanket over my head and slept.

### Five Days in the Box (February 18-22, 2017)

At 7 a.m. the next morning, I woke up to the screaming of the guards inside our cell block (Pod B) as well as to their shouting coming over the speaker in our cell. Pimple boy (over the five days, I never learned his name) told me to get up and stand by the door of our cell. Once all the inmates were seen and counted, we were released to go back to bed. However, the cell doors would remain open until 11 p.m., definitely a huge help with the claustrophobic feeling. And allowing for movement and space when I felt I had to be in motion would help too. My morning self-assessment was bleak. I was wearing the ugliest, tattered orange and white striped jail garb with "Madison County Jail" stamped in black across my back. On my feet were matching orange Croc's, thus making me look like a stocky Ronald McDonald with wide, thick stripes. Definitely not Fifth Avenue apparel, but at least I fit in with the rest of Pod B.

We ate three meals a day: 8 a.m., noon, and 6 p.m. All meals were served in two to three inch thick brown trays that had compartments for each of the five items on the menu. Each inmate was issued one "spork" (half spoon, half fork) and one small plastic coffee mug to be used for all drinks. Once a week, everyone turned in your spork and cup in order to get a clean one. I was amazed how efficient, territorial and compliant all the inmates were. But in reality, nobody wanted to lose any privileges. The Madison County Jail is known for having good food and jail grub. And it was very good. For example, on Sunday night we had pork roast, a baked potato, apple sauce, corn and a small chocolate muffin. The only thing I felt shorted on was liquids. We received a 10oz. cup of milk or fruit drink with each meal, that's it. I drink fluids all day long so I was guzzling water all day from our tiny, sink, water fountain in our cell.

I always stayed aware of where I was in relation to others. Hard to believe, but most of these guys didn't get in here for scoring high on IQ tests. We had one guy who looked like Curly Howard but the eyes and laugh of a seriously off kilter dude. His cellmate was a loud mouth who was the self-ordained King of the B Pod. To me, they were just Beavis and Butthead, comical because they didn't know they were funny, as they held court in the commons area and monopolized the lone TV remote for the pod. I did my very best to avoid extended interactions with these two cretins, because nothing good was go to come of it. Most of the inmates were young 18 to 25-year-olds who treated me well. I was viewed as the old guy, in for a second DUI and I kept to myself for the most part.

On my third morning in Pod B, an inmate was released. His name was Homer and his story absolutely blew me away (what follows is what Homer said, I have no idea if any of it was true). Homer had an outstanding arrest warrant from seven years ago and was living and working openly in the community. He made the mistake of sleeping with a cop's wife and that was when they decided to bring Homer in. When they went to get him, he was in his underwear, sleeping with the Cop's wife, and high on heroin. They dragged him in his skivvies and threw him into solitary where he would spend the next fourteen days coming down from the heroin, frequently shitting himself and seeing things that weren't there. Homer had eleven DUI's, one of which he got while working and driving a seventy-ton crane. Homer swore to me his drug and alcohol days were behind him as he headed out the door.

Jail, in reality, is a "void" where time passes but nothing changes. Every day is like the one before, and tomorrow will be the same. For one hour a day, each pod gets recreation time outside in a walled in space about forty feet high with fencing and razor wire covering the openings that let fresh air in. Sleeping and napping is essential to making time go away. Also, reading is critical to keeping sane. I read a five hundred page thriller in about twenty six hours. Made the time fly right on by. Your bunk becomes your refuge, a chance to lay down, read or nap. The bunks are solid steel frames with a green rubberized canvas mattress, maybe an inch thick at best. Shifting positions all night is a mandatory: my hips hurt, my back hurt, my shoulders hurt. If I could find a comfortable position for forty-five minutes, I was a happy camper.

Finally, you really can't trust anyone, not in what they say, their stories, their lives, etc. Everyone is innocent, everyone got screwed by the system and all cops are evil, out to get people. To me, the guards were extremely kind, answering my questions and treating me with respect after I had extended the same courtesy to them.

## A New Deal, Ominous Tones and a Long Path Ahead (April 5, 2017)

Much back and forth had occurred between the Prosecuting Attorney, the Public Defender and myself; hammering out a prospective plea bargain deal to present to the Judge. There was no satisfaction to be found by any party. It was a deal that no one felt good about given the gravity of my offenses. I just wanted it all to be over, to know what my punishment was and to get on with it. I really screwed the pooch this time, and leniency was unlikely.

Into the courtroom we filed. The atmosphere was austere, subdued, and grave. The Judge entered and court was in session. Cases were handled in an efficient yet fair manner. Is it just me or does this room feel heavy? Must be me.

After about forty-five minutes, the case of the *State of Idaho vs. Thomas Hickey* was called. Judge Walker asked the attorneys if a plea bargain was on the table? The attorneys responded in the affirmative and the Prosecutor was given the floor. The main thrust of her comments was that I had three major citations in the last 24 months, all involving large quantities of alcohol. She felt that the best option for the State and County was for me to participate in the Adult Drug Court program where I could be monitored, tested and supervised to ensure my full compliance and sobriety. In her tone, there was a sense of urgency, exasperation, and finality. It was clear when she concluded, if Mr. Hickey can't make changes to his life via this program, the next alternative would be a long stay in the Madison County Jail.

Next was my defense attorney, Feren, a hardworking and a promising young attorney. He highlighted my past accomplishments, languages spoken, travel and literary endeavors. Feren admitted that the Drug Court would be the best alternative for me and that we were willing to stipulate to such in a plea agreement.

Next was me, "Mr. Hickey, we are starting to see too much

of each other. Do you understand the charges against you? Do you have anything you wish to say?" added the Judge.

"Your honor I wish to address my comments towards my parents as I feel their disappointment and concern for me. In less than two years, I have had two DUI's while severely impaired, that is abhorrent and egregious to me. I could have killed people or severely injured them, that is not okay with me. I have surrendered my driver's license to the State of Idaho with no intention of driving again. I accept without reservation whatever your sentence for me will be."

With that, the Judge scolded me a bit and concurred with the attorneys on the plea deal with the exception being that I would serve six more days in jail, the next three weekends to meet the Idaho minimum sentencing guidelines, with fines and admission to the Drug Court program pending me failing two assessments to get in (oh yeah, I told the truth and failed those tests - I was in). Now the one kicker to this whole thing is that my new plea agreement replaced and incorporated the previous plea bargain agreement, thus if I successfully complete the drug court program and graduate, my DUI's would be withheld for ten years, not appear on my record and go away in a decade. I sure as hell don't deserve it, but I'd be a fool not to take that deal.

### Spa Session #1 - Oskar (April 7-9, 2017)

For the first of my three Spa weekends, I arrived at the Madison County Jail at 7:45 p.m., fifteen minutes before the appointed time. I went to the general public waiting room which also served as the Driver's License Center for the general public. The jail was backed up with ongoing chaos in the pods so the guard's voice over the speaker told me to hold tight, it would be awhile before they could get to me. Being tired, alone in the room, and resourceful, I curled up on the floor next to the wall with two folding chairs, used my coat as a pillow and *ZZZZzzzz...* About 10:30 p.m., a guard woke me, and with a huge smile on his face as he inquired as to how my rest had been. Off we went for intake processing, a full hour endeavor of mindless minutia.

Just before midnight I was escorted to my home for the weekend, a wing of the women's jail that was to be used by men due to the number of male inmates on hand (no, I never saw or heard any women that weekend). The wing was a completely self-contained unit with three bunkbeds and a small TV/dining room. The only upgrade from a men's cell was that we had a great bathroom, a real toilet, shower, sinks etc. Much nicer than the stainless-steel johns on the men's block. My two spa attendees for the weekend were jabbering away about meth, street stories and general manly braggadocio.

One the two guys was Wes, a big, solid guy, probably about 6'5" and 240 pounds. He was an affable, funny, hardworking guy. Wes's only fault was that he had a fondness for Meth and that had put him in deep doo-doo with the law. His options were dwindling with each new positive urine analysis test and a lengthy stint in the state penitentiary was looming on the horizon. For the most part, Wes just slept all weekend, day or night. And when he did stay awake, his body twitched like a fish on land. The effects of coming off the meth I am sure.

My other cellmate was someone I will never forget, Oskar. Half Cuban, half Mexican and all nuts. Oskar was about 5'7", fit but not stocky, shaved head, some kind of a Chinese looking beard with a rubber band under the chin, Tattoo's everywhere and eyes were full force, intense, almost like looking at a bird of prey's eyes. Oskar was thirty-one years old and had spent nineteen of those years incarcerated, either in juvenile, jail or prison. He was ADHD, wound way too tight, edgy and unpredictable. I would spend my weekend constantly keeping one eye on Oskar and do everything I could to not cross him.

Oskar had spent the previous twenty-nine days in solitary for fighting with guards. It was the second or third such offense for Oskar and this one resulted in a full riot team having to bust into his cell and take him down. Thus, after twenty-nine days alone, Oskar had me to talk with and Wes when he wasn't twitching in his bed. Over the weekend, I was regaled with stories of Oskar's life, exploits and adventures. His girlfriend, a really ugly tattooed woman, (he showed me pictures) was purportedly the Meth Queen of Southeastern Idaho. When Oskar wasn't in the box, he spent his time delivering product, collecting outstanding debts with whatever means necessary and trying to avoid the police at all costs. I'm not sure he was so good at that last one.

Being self-identified as ADHD, wound tighter than tight, Oskar slept about four hours a night. How do I know? Oskar's bunk was four feet from my bunk and all night long I would open one eye to see Oskar reading, drawing, swaying back and forth in a cross-legged position on his bunk. He looked like a mad Chinaman capable of anything and everything. To his credit, one morning when he was tired, we had a long talk. He told me that he also can't sleep because he has nightmares of the "bad things" he had done. He also admitted that he felt bad that his life had turned out like this but it felt as if he had been fucked from the get go, most likely a verifiable fact. It was humanizing for me to see his remorse and torment.

Come Sunday evening, I was released to my waiting wife. Weekend #1 in the books. Wonder what will come my way next weekend? (Note: I did hear subsequently that Oskar got transferred back to prison for the assaults on the guards).

### Spa Session #2 - Mr. Ohlson (April 14-16, 2017)

My second weekend in Club Med was a mighty strange one.

I did my processing, now an old hand at the squat and cough, and was ushered to my accommodations for the weekend. It was a very tiny pod with three cells, two inmates per cell. There was room for six, but the first cell had just one guy in it. The mirrored guard control room literally shared about a third of the tiny common space. I was put into cell #2 and being an old guy, I got the bottom bunk. My cell mate was less than pleased at having to relocate to the top bunk for the weekend but he did comply. How to describe this guy? His name was Scott, about 5'8" tall, fit, maybe thirty years old. On his lip was literally a little Hitler mustache. He had a scraggy beard underneath and he sure didn't talk much which was fine by me. Around his bed he had a ton of Christian books, pamphlets, etc. along with right-wing doctrine. I was left with undeniable impression from Scott, that he was a small, Christian, Nazi. The less he and I interacted the better. In the end, the time would go by without an incident with Holy Hitler.

In the next cell was a serial drunk driver. He was a skinny old guy around sixty-five-years-old named Dan and the recipient of nine DUI's over his lifespan. Dan was in jail until his sentence ran out, something like eleven months to go with eight already served. Sober, he was decent enough but it was clear that Dan was a professional drinker. Drink, drink and drink some more, get a DUI or public intoxication and then back into the box. Dan was well institutionalized to the whole thing. Dan's roommate was Ted, a young architect from Jackson Hole that I have become friends with and you will be hearing more about in a bit.

The lone guy with a private cell was Eric, a beanpole of a guy who had lived in Jackson Hole. Eric had been in the Madison County lockup for the last eight months. I could swear I had met this guy before, somewhere about The Valley. On Saturday, we really got to talking. Ted worked for a small family company in Jackson Hole that did sprinkler installations and maintenance. Ted, Eric and I spent a good chunk of Saturday talking about this or that, people we knew, etc. During our discourse, I felt that there was something odd about Eric, he seemed off. His replies took a few moments to collect, words trailing off at times. I also noticed a huge law book in his cell and asked him if he was studying law. "Something like that" he replied. The weekend passed without incident, little Hitler keeping his distance.

On Monday, I saw Ted at one of our mandatory alcohol awareness classes. At break, we stepped outside, Ted fired up a butt and chatted about the weekend.

"You do know who Eric is?" He asked me with a strange look on his face.

"No, but I swear I know him from somewhere."

Boy, did I. Here is what Mr. Ohlson is alleged to have done on July 5th, 2016. Living in Jackson Hole, he got extremely inebriated and made the forty-five minute drive to his ex-girlfriend's cabin arriving in a drunken stupor. She opened the door and Eric pointed his 45 caliber Glock at her and unloaded all eight rounds into her body, taking special aim to shoot the unborn child in the womb. With his work done, he drove away, throwing the gun out the window and into the ditch. Deciding that he wanted to die as well, he drove his truck into a utility pole where he would shortly be arrested for DUI and reckless driving. The next morning when the body was found and the Glock was found, the evidence indicated that Mr. Ohlson, who was sitting in the Madison County Jail, was the shooter. Later, he would be arraigned on two counts of first degree murder.

Ted and I looked at each other, the incredulousness hanging on our face. Perhaps neither of us was quite well suited to life in a correctional facility.

### Spa Session #3 - Silas (April 21-23, 2017)

It was my last weekend in the box. This whole jail thing was becoming routine, a routine I want to never be part of again. Out of my street clothes, into the orange and white striped ragged threads, orange crocks, etc. etc. I was put in C Pod for this last weekend. It was a bigger pod with twenty something of society's finest.

The weekend proceeded along. I was keeping a low profile as much as I could, lots of bunk time, naps, reading, etc. I wasn't here to make lifelong friends. I was there to learn that I didn't want to be there - mission accomplished.

I did make one mistake on Saturday at lunch time. I grabbed my lunch tray and sat down at the nearest open stool, little did I know that I had just sat down at another inmate's sacred spot. He was about 6'3" tall, extremely light-haired redhead, kind of a redhead albino with a long goatee and a most effeminate affect. My table mates quickly told me that I had sat in "Harley's seat". My bad, I apologized and shuffled away to another table where the Pit Boss, the obvious controller of the C-Pod pointed to a suitable place for me. I shoveled my food in and headed to the safety of my cell. Yes, I went to my cell for safety, other inmates are not allowed to enter any other cell.

Sunday morning rolls around and it is Cell #2's turn to clean the Pod. That meant Ted and myself. Sweep and mop the floors, replace the garbage bag, wipe down the tables, clean the shower, etc. Easy stuff, fifteen to twenty minutes of work. Ted and I get after it. He is sweeping and I am mopping. Then after about ten minutes, in Harley comes down to take a shower. I keep mopping the floor and as I turned towards the shower, over the half wall I can see Harley's, aka Silas from the DaVinci Code's, upper torso. Both nipples are streaming blood done. He had either cut himself or some event went on in his cell that I do NOT want to know about. Ted caught a full visual as well and just stared at Harley in disbelief. Thankfully, Harley cleaned the shower floor. I sure as hell wasn't going to!

Eight hours later I walked out of the Madison County Jail for the last time. Definitely a painful learning experience but one that I more than earned and deserved. In order to ensure time does not dull my memory as to self-disgust and penance, during my third spa session I wrote the following:

### *February 17th, 2017 Revisited*

*I drove 10 miles from Victor, Idaho to Driggs, Idaho while being blacked out due to alcohol.*

*I could have killed or seriously hurt someone, a family, kids, etc. That's not fucking okay with me!*
*I have NEVER driven while blacked out before.*
*I got a second DUI that day, I God Damn deserved it.*
*Here are my thoughts, actions and intentions regarding my incredible stupidity and negligence:*

*On February 28th, 2017, I surrendered my license to the State of Idaho, exchanging it for a State Photo ID. I have no intention of getting a license again, I don't deserve it and I don't want it. I have removed myself as a driver with my insurance company. I am not insured or licensed to operate a motor vehicle.*

*Had I hurt or killed anyone that day, it would have shattered my existence until the day I die, a burden I couldn't possibly endure.*

*I don't care what the Judicial System, the State of Idaho or the Federal Government decree as just punishment for my crime nor a potential willingness to reinstate my driving privileges. By my score, the only just punishment is for me to adjust to life with alternative transportation.*

*During my eleven-day sentence in the Madison County Jail, (not nearly enough time incarcerated in my opinion but that is the state minimum statute) I have met men with numerous DUI's, ranging from three to eleven. How the fuck does someone get a license after 11 DUI's - COME ON!*

*I believe in the European model: one DUI is a significant transgression with serious consequences and a second DUI - no more driving for you, end of discussion, you have proven you are a threat to society.*

*Currently, I am on probation for twenty-four months and enrolled in a State Alcohol and Drug Court Program. It is a huge time commitment and accountability is mandatory. I am subject* to random UA tests every day. I attend drug court bi-monthly before the judge and drug court team, take classes three times a week, meet with a counselor, a therapist and I must attend AA or other support groups for a total of seven documented meetings a week. I AM LUCKY to be in this program.

For transportation, I get rides from my wife, hitchhike ($2 Tommy, give me a ride - you get $2), bike, walk, take the bus, the local transportation van or a taxi. All doable and commensurate for having driven while seriously impaired twice!

I am hoping to save up to buy an all season electric bike that will get me where I need to be independently and efficiently.

Going forward, I will be a user and supporter of public transportation and non-motorized means of transportation.

I created this problem, I need to own it, to make sure it NEVER happens again and be cognizant and grateful that my stupidity didn't hurt/kill anyone else.

Please accept my heartfelt regrets for my actions. I seek no praise. I sure as hell don't deserve it. My atonement will be to adjust my reality to a life without driving.

## A Typical Tom Blowout (August 2017)

I was in the Drug Court program, and I was doing well: 88 days sober; passing the urine analysis tests several times a week; and, attending all the required classes and therapy. Thus, as is the case with me, it was time for one of my quarterly manic or depressive episodes. It is difficult to put into words what it is like to have darkness or insanity descend on me several times a year. It is so disheartening to be doing your very best one day and then brain chemistry goes awry flipping the switch to "I just don't give a fuck anymore." So, this brings me to August

2017. People were celebrating my sobriety, my progress, and I was two days away from the AA 90-day chip. (I can't stand AA chips - they either make me feel inept or overconfident, neither of which are good for me).

The time had come for me to turn my back on it all and do what I know best, drink. Which is exactly what I did. It felt so God Damn good. Such a relief. I know this feeling, it is my friend, and I love to drink. As you can imagine, my next UA comes back dirty. I am sent off to the Madison County Jail for several weeks while the drug court ponders what to do with this wayward lad. The decision is made to send me to the Walker Center, a drug and alcohol rehabilitation center in Gooding, Idaho. The funds for my stay will come from federal dollars channeled through the Idaho Supreme Court. I am put in a holding pattern in jail while I await an open bed at the Walker Center. Prior to going to the Walker Center, I had a phone call with my wife whose message was direct and austere, 'I was to go to this treatment center and try my best to get better.' I agreed and I did comply with my very best efforts at "getting" this sobriety thing.

## The Walker Center - Gooding, Idaho (September 2017)

Unlike my first round of rehab, my experience and time at the Walker Center was fantastic. The Walker Center is in south central Idaho, in the small town of Gooding. The facility is large, clean, comfortable and almost like staying in a nice Marriott property. Most of the staff are recovered alcoholics and or addicts, so they know the ropes and are exceptionally good at seeing through bullshit. The food was exceptional, full salad bar lunch and dinner. The goal was to rebuild meth heads and drunks and get us healthy in 28 days and teach us about our afflictions. The program was comprehensive, well-structured, and there was even a full wilderness course to challenge and teach us to change our thinking.

The amazing thing about the Walker Center were my fellow campers. I was rooming with Jim, a massive man in his early thirties. Jim had spent his twenties in a federal penitentiary after getting busted at age 18 for meth distribution. Jim was well acclimated to institutional living, doing 1000 pushups and burpees every morning plus perhaps a few steroids. We had little in common, but we got along great. Usually before going to sleep, I would read passages from Popeye. Jim was enthralled by all the travels and adventures. Other guys included, Taylor, a 25-year-old meth addict who had more social skills than most people I have ever met. Taylor was smart, funny and deadly serious about getting sober, because his family was about done with him. There was a professional golfer, Harry who I would have never guess was an addict. He looked like a smart country club guy, witty but scared to death of going back to using heroin. About 80% of the guys there all were addicts, while the other 20% were drunks like me. There was one guy named Matt who came in in rough shape, coming down of meth. Matt used a cane as he had been hit and run on a street when he was wasted out of his mind. With each passing day Matt's health returned, his humor started to show through. It was an incredible transformation to witness. Finally, there was a mountain of a man, Bridger, who had stolen prescriptions, money, and other valuables from his aging parents until they had to ban him from their property. At one point, Bridger was pronounced dead on a hospital table at 11 a.m., then with an injection of Naloxone straight into his heart, brought back to life. Three hours later he was back on the streets for his next fix.

There were females, but they had their own wing of the building. There would be no fraternization. The only time we saw the women was at lectures in the main auditorium. Regularly, we exercised at the YMCA, a very nice facility with a pool, bikes, racquet ball, hoops, volleyball, etc. We were trusted to be on our own at the YMCA which was a welcome freedom, and everyone toed the line. Nobody wanted to lose their privileges. Several nights a week, we loaded onto a bus and attended either Alcoholics Anonymous or Narcotics Anonymous. There were lots of unique characters; bikers, native Americans, gringos, and our troop of about twenty-five people.

The real strength of the program was your peers. A cornucopia of misfits if there ever was one. Every one of us was battling for our lives. We spent fourteen hours a day together. We had groups in the evening with no counselors present, just us fuck-ups trying to put our lives back together. In these private meetings, anyone could call bullshit on anybody else. At times there were tears, lots of joking and laughter. Yet for what an oddball group we were, there was lots of understanding and compassion. I was with my own kind, fellow addicts whose stories matched or superseded my own. I was lucky.

Now I really tried to make the most of my time there. I got uncomfortable. I shared openly. I wanted for this experience to be a success. After 28 days flew by, as is the custom, the group sang me out with "Na-Na-Na-Hey-Hey-Hey Goodbye" and ending with "Don't fucking come back". I had made it through with honors, now the challenge would be to live in the "real" world without drinking. My wife picked me up and with shaky legs I walked out of the Walker Center

## A YEAR OF PEEING IN THE CUP (AUGUST 2017 - AUGUST 2018)

With my successful stay at the Walker Center as a fresh start on life, I returned home to continue on in Drug Court, routine U/A's and mandated AA meetings to attend. I was able to get a good job at a lumber yard. I worked hard, was brutally honest about my issues and would become a valued member of the team. At home, everyone was pleased to have sober Dad/Husband back. I met all my obligations, I graduated from Phase I - Phase IV of Drug Court and was on track to graduate the program in early August. As always is the case with me, success may not always bring the desired result. In late July my daughter was married, family and friends travelled in and I was confident, way too confident that I would make it through without wanting to drink. (For years I had always envisioned a toast to my daughter and husband to be with a healthy shot of Whiskey, being Irish and all). I did just fine at the rehearsal dinner, at the wedding itself and then when the wedding ended, someone in the younger set busted out a case of Pacifico while people packed up all the wedding decorations, gifts, etc. It was as if someone turned on a magnet in me, I wanted one of those Pacifico's so bad that I could taste it. I stared at that case of beer, dreaming of poaching a few for the Father of the Bride, but I was able to overcome those intense cravings and keep it together for my daughter. The snake had once again raised its head though and I was skating on thin ice, well prepped for a fall.

On August 5th, I celebrated my one-year birthday of sobriety in AA. Everyone was kind, said encouraging words, and surprised that I had actually made it a year. I was given a one year coin with well wishes, hugs and hopes for better days. Meanwhile, at some level inside with coin in hand, I knew I was in deep shit, that the addiction was back, pressures of success were building, expectations were growing. I was feeling like shit on the inside. Perhaps a bout of Bipolar mania drawing nigh? I was sensing that I had all the skills necessary to fuck this up good. I left that AA meeting not upbeat, just the opposite, my demons were near, and I knew it.

And then...

## With Just Four Days Left of Drug Court Program... (August 2018)

On August 5th, 2018 my psychiatric doctor changed my psych med's, adding an extra dose of Zoloft in the evening to hopefully combat the dread with which I usually woke up. There were the typical warnings, potential adverse effects, etc. Since I was already on the damn thing, I thought that there was no risk involved. I assumed my body was already accustomed to it, and maybe I could wake up feeling like a "normal" person. Why the hell wouldn't I try it? Interestingly, I was four days away from graduating from the drug court program a success, sentences withheld, let's all clap for Tom and take his picture with the Judge.

In the next four days, I careened out of control: drinking beer, seeing everything in silver like the tin man from the Wizard of Oz, why am I the only one who spins into hallucinations on prescribed pharmaceuticals? Why am I so special? Trying to work this impaired was impossible, I was driving a fork lift and seeing shit that wasn't there. My co-workers quickly assessed that I was horribly off and sent me home for much needed rest.

Come August 9th, graduation day, I am not going to be patted on the back. Instead, I was going to be sent to jail for ten days. Even though I had two doctors avowing that my mania was a result of the medication change, the judge was not buying any of it. You may be mentally ill, Mr. Hickey but we are not going to treat you as such. I was incredulous; there would be no mercy, compassion or understanding. Thus, I was sentenced to six more months of drug court, sobriety being the only metric. Failure to meet that expectation would mean off to jail to serve out my time. To this day, I am firmly convinced that had I been granted some small token of mercy or kindness I would have made it, but it wasn't to be.

# S.O.S - Checking Out #4
## (November 25th, 2018)

"The Blob" slowly, silently oozed into my room all week, paralyzing me with fear as my addled brain began firing some synapses. Per usual, I awoke in fits and starts, drawing up the covers tight to ward off the usual dread of the day. Today there would be no defeating said dread, as I lay there a warrant for my arrest was probably being prepared on a probation violation for a dirty UA test I provided last Wednesday morning, November 21st. Unless I choose otherwise, within the next thirty-six hours I will be a guest of the Madison County Jail for a six month stay. I am guilty of: an unsuccessfully treated mental illness; and, my own inability to avoid self-medicating my brain with alcohol. I am guilty as charged, no need for any appeals, last minute lawyering or the like. "I yam what I yam!". I have battled as valiantly as I can, but the battle has led me once again to the Funnel, the Funnel shall lead to my end on this big blue ball and today is that preordained day. I shall not go meekly into that dark night. I shall take my final swings with gusto and then bow out. Ah, yes, I know - but I once again digress...

It was time for my "Plan B", procure libations, head to a suitable venue for the task at hand and above all, have a good attitude about it. Yes, that is correct, I was trying be as positive as possible about this unfolding scenario, neither assigning "good" nor "bad" to the unfolding events. I had maybe four hours left and all week I had been coaching myself on staying "positive" about my mission. Going out with a smile, enjoy the fact about how much shyte I didn't have to do anymore. Hell, I didn't have to floss my teeth this morning - Bonus Points! Silently I arose, slipping on comfort clothes most apropos for my journey that day that would feel right in the chaos, Callahan T-shirt, Carhartt's, steel toed boots, favorite stocking cap, etc. Doing my best to not wake my wife, I wrote out a post-it" note that said something like 'Went for a walk to town to get some fresh air, be gone awhile. Love, Tom' (numerous suicide notes to loved ones had been written and left in my armoire along with my last will and testament). Note penned, I silently slipped out the front door about 8 a.m. Sunday morning. The time for The End is Nigh.

I strolled the half mile to the convenience store where Jenna was at her post per usual, Jenna looked a little bit tired and worn down this morning. With my secret bounty of treasure ($150), I didn't need to worry about money today, I was a wealthy man this morning. The limitations of my backpack did dictate a limitation as to quantity, so I bought a 12-pack of Bud, one large bottle of Stella Artois, my final meal would be a small bag of Cheez-its. Provisions in hand, I sallied forth to pay up with Jenna and shoot the shyte about jobs, family, yada-yada. In need of a bracer, I took my purchase to the bathroom, quaffed two Budweisers in rapid succession and was on my way, about a mile walk to the town center where destiny awaited. The stroll down the bike path was filled with overwhelming sensations that alcohol recently consumed augments: warmth, glee, giddiness, relaxation, counter intuition and cultural feelings. In summation, I was happy, and the booze was doing its job oh so well.

My pace quickened. The early morning fog enshrouding me and all that lay about. The fog will burn off within an hour once the mountain sun has its way. Due South I tromped, stopping at several safe locations (other gas stations, back door commercial buildings, where I could imbibe in freedom and not draw the attention of Johnny Law). There was no hurry, I had about three hours left in my hourglass and once the beers were gone, I would have work to do. The most overwhelming feelings I had were: contentment with myself and utter weariness. The closest I can compare it to is that feeling after playing several rugby matches in a weekend tournament where everything hurts equally but the barley water is easing your pain, and your memories of playing the match are most satisfying and peaceful.

Somewhere about 9:30 a.m., I arrive at the town center where I headed to my destination, a public restroom in a visitor center that is open 24/7 and has one of those family bathrooms: baby changing table, toilet, sink and a recessed drain in the floor, ensuring that the crimson scene I was to create would be self-contained and easily cleaned up. Now safely ensconced in my final nesting spot, I drank my beers, staying as positive as I could. Surprisingly, I felt quite buoyant, knowing I was down to about ninety minutes to go.

Preparations complete, I emerged from the bathroom to a sleepy Sunday morning in a sleepy mountain town. I took in the glorious sun as it sliced through the fog and vanquished it for the day. A beer was enveloped in my right-hand, sunglasses on, and it seemed that this was all unfolding just as it should. As the count of my beer supply dwindled, (yes, I was drinking fast and furious here, if I am going to do this I sure as hell ain't getting cheated out of a few last libations) the eleven o'clock hour loomed, it was time to get to work.

In I went, locking myself into the "exit chamber." After all my vagabond nights in Europe, I knew how to best make myself comfy in a public bathroom. I used my coat as an underlayment and laid down with my head behind the door (the cleanest spot on the floor). This would give my blood a clear, down sloping flow to the drain. I removed my box cutter knife, a heavy, solid metal piece. I took one look at my left forearm and ripped the metal edge across my wrist. "Thar she blows!" with blood flowing out at an unhealthy pace. Second slash, second incision, floor turning red, kind of made a pattern like Alaska on the floor. Slash, bleed, rest...slash, assess, bleed...

Now, here is where memory becomes choppy as I am certain I lost consciousness quite a few times for very brief periods...I woke and looked at my wrist which was starting to coagulate, more cutting, seems like I am trying to cut bone or sinew at the base of my left-hand. What the hell is that?...Pry open the incisions with fingers to keep the blood flowing...Open my eyes and see that my blood on the floor is starting to setup into crimson Jell-O...It dawns on me that I haven't much time left. I am going to leave soon...I try to sit up and can barely do so...I lay back down, a thought is "IN" my mind. I didn't think it, the thought is just there, just now, 'Mom, if you exist out there, on any plain, in any spectrum you can see my situation for yourself'...I then did something very strange for an avowed agnostic, without a thought I said one Hail Mary and laid back down to die...Intermittent conversations began via phone with my old friend, Lou Parri, almost taking the form of hostage negotiations. Would I give myself up? How was I doing physically? Where are you? etc. And then, about as close to my demise as was possible, I did something I hadn't planned on at all, I gave myself up - I told them where I was. I was choosing to go back towards the living, the consequences, the mental illness. Is this what I am supposed to do? Is this what I truly want?

The bathroom itself now looks like a slaughterhouse, a MASH unit post-op. My attempt at being clean in this bloody endeavor completely rendered moot with the blood splattered on the nice white walls, floor, sinks, stool. Hard to lift up my head now.

Knocking now...strong knocking on the door...my name is being called and with the most black-blood left hand imaginable, I reached up, pulled back the dead bolt. The door swung inward and in came the living to keep me in their midst for a while...

## Erik Ohlson - Murder One

With the latest mauling of my wrists and post-depression binge, the State of Idaho decided it is was time for Tommy to spend more time in the hoosegow.

The timing of my incarceration just happened to line up with someone I met during my spa sessions back in April 2017, Erik Ohlson. In all, I would spend about four months as in inmate in the same pod as this murderer. He had been locked up since July 6, 2016 after he drove his truck into a utility pole and was subsequently arrested for DUI and reckless driving. Later, when the body of his ex-girlfriend and the Glock he murdered her with were found, murder one charges were added. He confessed, but that confession was thrown out because he was denied an attorney. During our second stay together in 2019, on Valentine's Day, Ohlson signed a plea agreement and confession that stipulated the death penalty be taken off the table and amended a second count of first-degree murder to involuntary manslaughter for the death of the unborn first semester baby.

I was the only inmate who knew who Erik Ohlson was and what he had done. It was beyond strange to contemplate how I would live with a man who confessed to a brutal, cold blooded murder. Having no choice, I made the best of it as I could, I treated Erik with decency and respect, he did the same to me. Each night we watched the news and Jeopardy. Erik was very good at Jeopardy, usually beating me in close competition. We talked a lot about history, politics and life in jail. About halfway through my time there, Erik asked me if I knew why he was there? Yes, I did, I answered.

In May 2019, Erik was sentenced to 25 years to life for murder of the ex-girlfriend and ten years for the involuntary manslaughter charge. It was the best deal he was going to get and could allow for his release in his mid-sixties. On several occasions, we openly talked about his case, his legal team, and all the efforts to avoid the death penalty which had drawn national attention to his case. He did admit to me that he had done the crimes. Speaking face to face to a murderer was beyond surreal, but having one admit his crimes to you was absolutely chilling.

Erik routinely said to me, "Hickey, what are you doing in here? You don't belong in here."

I concurred wholeheartedly.

## The Diddler (December 2018)

The creepiest man I met in jail (yeah, more than Erik Ohlson) was a man I called "the diddler." He was tall, 6'4" or so, bald as a billiard ball, mustache, glasses and a person who emitted the worst vibe I have ever encountered. He was 72 years old and had been a leader in the Church of Latter Days Saints (Mormons) primarily as a religious education teacher and summer camp leader. He also had a lifelong preoccupation with touching little kids. (Yes, my skin stills crawls). Anyway, here is an "upstanding" man who after a lifetime of perversions is finally caught, wearing stripes, and right where he belongs.

It was obvious that the Diddler was scared to death to be in jail. He only left his room for meals, rarely talked and was most apprehensive when taking a shower-always showering at times when the common area was empty. It was an interesting dichotomy to see this "upstanding" person now incarcerated for his "depravity". I had the hardest time having sympathy for the man, the thoughts of all the kids he diddled always got in the way of my thinking. I don't know what happened to the Diddler as I was transferred to another pod, but I hope he will be held accountable for what he did to all those children.

## Turtle Suit (January 2019)

The court's grand plan for me was that I transfer out of the Drug Court program into the Mental Health program. Thus, I am to be released from jail, go home and pack up my belongings and move into a group home in Idaho Falls. I will start over, having one more year of classes, U/A tests, counseling, medication management, and in general fun, fun, fun.

One hitch, a room is not available in Idaho Falls yet. So, for two nights they plop me in the Rexburg group home temporarily until a bed was ready in Idaho Falls. All sounds good huh? NOT! First, the group home in Rexburg was more disgusting than any college housing I ever experienced. The bathroom was a biological experiment of fungus and filth. The kitchen was overflowing with dry encrusted dishes that had been there since the Paleozoic period. My room was a subterranean dank closet devoid of anything resembling warmth. My probation officer left me at 8:30. At 8:35, I stood outside in the cold, soberly assessing my situation. There is no way that this is going to work. I'm fucked. Screw it, I make the conscience decisions to run away and drink, or drink and run away. Off to the Maverick I trot and procure a twelve-pack. I then buy a bus ticket for the next night to get to Salt Lake City and then somewhere far away after that. There is no way that Idaho will extradite me from a distant locale for two misdemeanor DUI's. Yes, I will be a wanted man, but it sure beats a year more of failing in a program and all the shitty feelings that will come with it.

The next day I go home, pack up my stuff and get a ride back to the group home. I am five hours away from my bus to Salt Lake City, to freedom and becoming just another face, no more demanding expectations from friends and family. FREEDOM! As I descend into my basement lair, I hear noise from my room, two officers are going through all my stuff, numerous empty and full cans of Budweiser are to be found. Instantly it became abundantly clear that I wasn't going to be on that bus tonight. The cops started to treat me most unpleasantly until I said the magic words, "I want to talk to my lawyer". Boom, cuffs go on, conversation ceases and up the stairs I go for the two-block drive back to jail. I just don't care. I chose this path, and now I shall walk it.

At the jail, my new probation officer Cassie shows up, and she is adamant about one thing, I am going in on "Suicide Watch." Thus, I will be in an isolation cell, monitored 24 hours by the guards, and live the lifestyle of a monastic monk. My clothes consisted of a Teenage Mutant Ninja suit. It was a green smock made of moving blanket material that provided zero warmth. I would also have two additional blankets of the same material, non-rip, heavy plastic fiber. I had a bunk and a steel toilet/sink. That was it. For eight days I lived devoid of knowing whether it was day or night, what time it was, etc. The only way I could tell time was by meals. The only time I left that cell was to take a shower in an adjacent bathroom. There was only one saving grace, books. I was given access to a book cart and would spend my time ripping through 500-page books in a day. Finally, after eight days the psych doctor made his rounds. I was evaluated and deemed to not be a danger to myself or others. The cell door swung open, and I was ushered off to general population.

My latest intransigence resulted in the Judge and the Prosecuting Attorney having had enough of the Tom Hickey fun show. I was to spend 65 more days in jails to serve out my sentence of 180 days total. After that, I would be "rehabilitated" in the eyes of society and walk out of jail a free man. After all I had been through, 65 days was a cakewalk to freedom. Strange how the things I feared the most - jail, etc. aren't what they I thought them to be. Experience sure impacts perspective.

A quick author's note: Technically, the isolation cell was attached to the women's jail, thus almost all my guards were women. They couldn't have been more kind, compassionate and helpful. They made those eight days bearable, and I will always be grateful for their understanding and care.

## Served in Stripes (February 2019)

I was sitting on my bunk in my stripes, making time go away, a popular activity in jail, when a Sheriff's officer entered. He trotted up the stairs to my cell and handed me a bunch of papers. After twenty-nine years, I was officially divorced. It was just simply awkward. So many years of a relationship, and now with these few legal documents it was over. I was once again single. I sat on my bunk, numb and unsure of what to feel. How the hell did this become my life? Is this just all a bad dream? I was at a loss to comprehend the enormity of what had just happened to me.

Before going any further, I must state that I in no way blame Halina for the divorce. Four suicide attempts, mental illness and active addiction to alcohol (and that is just the headline material). She endured more challenges from her husband than is imaginable. It's a wonder that she was able to put up with me so long. I love Halina, always have and always will. I want her to be happy. If I am no longer making her happy, I want her to seek joy in her life. I love her that much. That said, when I said I do in that little Polish village church on January 20, 1990, I meant it for life; thus, I will always consider Halina my life partner regardless of what the future holds for both of us.

Now I would be remiss if I didn't say that I am lonely now. I am. I miss being with the ones I love. One strength I have is to not look back and ruminate on the past. I have the strength to accept the current reality, to go forward and compartmentalize things for future consideration. Such is the situation I find myself in now. I move forward daily, a survivor's mentality towards what might one day be.

So, let's not pretend this doesn't hurt like hell, but I will find my way forward. Perhaps in time I will both find again peace, comfort, and companionship.

## Manuelito (March 2019)

Manuel entered my pod, a giant, jovial Mexican bear, perhaps a comparison to Winnie the Pooh is most apt. Manuelito, as I would come to call him (little Manny), had two DUI's, one which was a felony charge and then he had been arrested in his buddy's truck, drunk on beer, headed out fishing for the day and to top it off, he had his loaded pistol in his backpack. No one ever told him he couldn't have a gun as a felon so Manuelito was in deep shit when he fessed up to having a loaded gun in his backpack. Furthermore, he wasn't a US citizen, so he was looking at five years in jail and then a prompt deportation to Mexico, a place he hadn't lived since early childhood.

Now why am I telling you about Manuelito? I have never met a more joyous, curious, contented man than Manuelito. In the simplest of things - a spider's cobweb, a game of cards, a good meal, a racquet ball left in the yard - Manuelito would find divine happiness in the simplicity in everything. Each day, I marveled at how happy this man was. I once asked him what he would do if he got deported. Without a moment's notice he replied, "I'll start a new life I guess." In the month that we were together I simply marveled at Manuelito. We became friends, and I felt as if I was always in the presence of a living Buddha. If I could only adapt my warped mind to be like Manuelito's, to be childlike with curiosity with the dawn of each new day regardless of circumstance, I would be most contented.

## Stinky Feet (March 2019)

I was making time go away sitting on my bunk before dinner, solo in my cell, as was Manuelito in his cell. We were just down to us two in F Pod with short-timers coming and going every day. About 5 p.m., a guard showed up at my door ushering a young kid who would be staying for at least the night. Let's see if I can get this description right. He was one of the most homely, forlorn, ugly people I have ever seen, an almost albino with a hint of red in his hair. His stripes were at least a size too small, so he looked like an over-stuffed sausage with no muscle definition to speak of. He was eighteen and in jail for the first time. In he comes, we chit chat a bit and he climbs up onto the top bunk to rest before dinner. It was during his ascent to the top bunk that it hit me like a hammer, his feet stunk so bad it was horrific. Smelling like rancid vinegar, it was all I could do to not gag. Twenty-four hours with stinky feet, can I survive this I pondered? At this point, I was still trying to be civil and asked what he had done to get sent to jail. "Rape" came his first reply which was quickly amended to "child molestation" - which did little to make me feel better. The night before at 3 a.m. the police had raided his mother's house with a warrant for Stinky Feet who had missed some court appearances and hadn't paid anything towards his fines.

Off to dinner we go, with Stinky Feet permeating the common area as we tried to consume our dinners without hurling. Just after dinner, a miracle happened, Stinky Feet got moved to Manuelito's cell because he was subject to seizures and had to be on the bottom bunk. Since I am old and have to have my CPAP machine at night, poor Manuelito would have to endure the night with the feet. My regrets to Manny, but I felt like divine intervention had occurred with the cell to myself.

About 8 p.m., I was on my bunk when I heard sniffling at my door. There stood Stinky Feet silently, eerily staring at me and crying in my doorway, "I miss my Mom" "I want to go home" "I don't like it here" etc. It was odd and discomforting to hear an 18-year-old in such a state. Trying to show some level of compassion I got up talked with him about how to make time go away, 'watch TV for sixty minutes, take a long hot shower that'll take up thirty minutes (please wash your feet), read a book, play a game, etc. Stinky was happy to have a road map of what to do and he thanked me profusely.

Later that evening Manuelito and I would talk in my cell about Stinky Feet. Manny's first words were "He was crying in jail, there is no crying in jail!" Manny then went on to tell me more about Stinky Feet. He was borderline IQ. He lived with his mother and was already on permanent disability for both mental and physical disabilities. Whether he understood that what he had done with other children was wrong was debatable. The judge was still trying to figure that out and how accountable could they hold this simple kid?

Anyway, Stinky Feet was with us for a night before being bailed out the next day by his mother. As he exited F Pod, it was as if a fresh breeze had entered. We had survived the onslaught of Stinky Feet. In all honesty, it was hard not to feel some sympathy for the guy. He really had no more than the simplest of tools in his tool bag and was overwhelmed by every aspect of his life on a daily basis yet that had to be balanced with posing as a real threat to children he gets access to.

## A Grown Man Runs Away! Eugene, Oregon (May 2019)

Back in the Summer of 1987, I travelled out to Eugene, Oregon with friends to see Bob Dylan and the Grateful Dead at Autzen Stadium. Nothing too remarkable happens yet a seed is planted. Please let me elaborate with a bit of narrative. We are driving through a canyon about 4 a.m., Derek is driving, I'm in the passenger seat and the girls are passed out in the back. Bam! Something explodes in my face, it looks like someone threw a gallon of whole milk onto the windshield in front of me. It was a white owl that flew into our car, it portended only one thing - Bad Juju. We scraped off the windshield as best we could, owl feathers everywhere. All of us in the vehicle sensed this was not a positive development, yet on we pressed. That afternoon we are in the stadium on a perfect day, hippies everywhere, mind altering substances everywhere, counterculture everywhere. After some shrooms, I was handed a tab of acid and took it.

The rest of the day went down like this. Dylan takes the stage. He is either on heavy drugs or just plain flat. He would play a song, start another, no communication. I am now tripping my balls off, so I head to the top row of the stadium to check out the golden sun and fresh winds to be found. Bob wraps up, and the Dead take the stage. I descend from the upper rim and take up position in the far end zone away from the stage. This is where the seaweed dancers dance, the flaming juggler juggles, Moses swings some kind of baton, and some dude has a God Damn snake. This is somewhere over the rainbow. I listen to the Dead, watch the circus, and it all ends well. Eugene is about as abnormal of a place I have ever been. File this one away for future reference.

Flash forward thirty-two years. I am now: divorced, just out of jail, fired from my job for being drunk at work, alone, depressed, and broke. What's next Tommy Boy? Run away! If I am going to be destitute, homeless, miserable and penniless, where the hell should I go? I survey the possibilities and realize that Eugene is 739 miles away. Hell, I'll load up my bike, road trip, start over and make everything right. My brain crystallizes my Marshall Plan. This is perfect. Now to just execute.

The execution - here is where my good intentions run amok. Great ideas, but I have always had issues with execution. For days I worked on packing and loading up my recumbent bike with more than it could ever safely handle. If I can make 20 - 30 miles a day, I will be on the road about or a month or less. I am not telling anybody anything about my plans. This subterfuge was intentional. I am once again Master and Commander of my own destiny, and I shall not be defeated. At the appointed hour, I shove off, headed North to Tetonia, Idaho, optimism abounding - I'm back in charge. Yet, I pick a shitty route so as to not be seen, I am on a decrepit old dirt road that my bike just gets buried up to the axles in, I push the fucker for four tortuous hours, I finally hit pavement and make it to the Tetonia rodeo grounds, evasive now, I find a camping spot down low, in thickets where I shan't be detected. I am happy. I am content. I am comfortable. This is working!

The next day, I begin the bike ride out of the valley. I make it to the Teton River on the North end of the valley. There is just one problem. Those damn ruts they put on the side of the road to wake you up if cross the line are limiting my asphalt lane to about eight inches. I repeatedly hit the bumps on my wobbly, overloaded bike and have two choices: steer into the highway to catch a fender in the teeth; or, steer right off the shoulder of the road, eat shit in the grass/rocks/gravel landing. Three times I opt for the grass/rocks/gravel landing before realizing that my mission by bike is completely unviable.

No big deal, time for plan B. I return to the boat ramp next to the Teton River. Guess I will have to hitchhike to Eugene. I am not giving up now. In a spirit of good karma, I abandon the bicycle at the river with a note pinned to it - "Free to a good home". With Plan B in full effect, I hitched back to Tetonia, went to the old railroad stockyards near city park. Ain't gonna find me here in this old maze of corrals and chutes. Better turn off my phone so that the battery doesn't go dead tonight.

My bike was found about 10 p.m. by the Sheriff's office, my note attached "Free to a good home." The connections to me and my bike are quickly drawn, an individual with four-time suicide attempts, with diagnosed mental illness for no apparent reason has left his only means of transportation by a river. The warning bells are sounded, Teton County Search and Rescue is called, friends and family would spend the night trying to find my corpse in the river. Across the country, people who know, care and love me are spending the worst night in fear and almost certainty that I was gone. It is a tragedy unfolding that rends my heart knowing the inexorable pain I have caused, a pain that will always be a lifetime stressor to my loved ones.

About 8 a.m. I awake, rested and refreshed, I roll over to the rising sun and turn on my phone, BING, messages and an incoming call from an obviously exhausted former wife, relieved that I am not dead, yet less than pleased with my performance again. The search is called off, calls are made that I am safe, one of my brother's call me absolutely displeased with the last fifteen hours he has been subjected to. (Most warranted I might add). I now feel like a total piece of shyte for the unintended consequences of my actions. This still has been a source of sadness to me for what I put my loved ones through, even though I was just trying to save myself and get a fresh start. Instead of ending my life, I was trying to save myself by starting over. Ain't got much pride left Old Tommy Boy. And yet, the narrative continues.

Much to my dismay, hitchhiking out of the valley is a bust as well. Can't catch a ride out of the Valley, the gods must be aligned against me. Still persistent and focused as hell, I am going to escape this valley that wants to hold me captive whatever it takes. I turn my focus to motorized travel, a Greyhound bus to Eugene. My friend agrees to pay for my ticket as I have about $500 in cash left to my name. Thus, from Rexburg, Idaho I am off to Butte, Montana then off to Spokane, Portland and several other blurred cities en route to Eugene. It would take thirty hours to get there, with two bus stop transfers where I would roll out my sleeping bag and guard my belongings while sleeping with one eye open. The buses were jammed, every seat full, lots of discontented, large travelers. A domestic dispute broke out about five rows in front of me and at about 5 a.m., the bus driver ended pulling up into a truck stop and the two combatants were dismissed from the bus. Peace once again reigns on the bus.

I arrive in Eugene at last. It is the Friday before Memorial Day, a three-day holiday in which I can get nothing done to start my life over. Thus, I head to a county park North of Eugene, $20 a night, bathrooms, clean place to hang my beads. So, I bunker in for three nights. During the day, I would hitchhike a few miles to Coburg, Oregon - a cool, quaint village that had a great vibe. Decent food to be had, beverages to be quaffed in the charming city park with other unique characters, certainly not "normal" folks but most interesting nonetheless.

Tuesday dawns, the pressure to find and secure my "next" is upon me. Rather than drag my belongings back to town, I get a $10 cab ride to the Eugene Library will serve as my office with bathrooms for all the necessities. A pallor of negative doom hangs over my destiny, this just all feels wrong. Online digging reveals a vast array of human services available in Eugene: homeless shelter, food banks, free meals, mental health services, medical services, etc. It all sounds like a good smorgasbord of a safety net, yet there is one fact that is omitted. The better the services offered, the more people who will show up to use them. Thus, I wasn't prepared for the delay to get services and the enormity of the homeless problem. Walking down streets there were tents aplenty, people living on sidewalks, raw humanity on full display.

Meanwhile as of today, I am officially homeless. Scared and apprehensive, I feel a dire need to nest. Thus, I walk several miles hauling my stuff to the Willamette River, several fellow hobos eying my bags every time I have to leave one behind. (I am shuttling two bags and a backpack). Exhausted, I arrive at the river and spend the next hour trying to find a discreet location to make camp. At last, I find an elevated platform, hidden beneath the deep embankment of trees above, a city park is above the trees. I roll out my bivy sack, my bed roll and bunker down. Officially destitute and homeless, 'how's that feel Tommy Boy?" At least I had beer, so I survived.

The next day dawns, I am undetected. That's good, but I don't feel well. I am clammy, wet, must be running a fever, tough shit, suck it up and move forward. I head back to Eugene to a 24/7 crisis shelter. It is in the beyond gnarly section of town, graffiti everywhere, challenged people everywhere. In short, the scariest place I have ever been. Although open, services are unavailable until 10 a.m., so I waited with more than twenty-five other people with issues. I start by sitting on the side of the house with a direct view across the alley to the 4-5 guys trying to relight last night's crack pipe. These are not healthy folks. To my left is an IV drop box being emptied by a guy in a hazmat suit. To top it all off, I realize that where I am sitting smells familiar, urine. With that, I was off to sit in the waiting room.

Out on the porch, about ten people are camped with all their worldly positions in portable mode, shopping carts, trolleys, etc. As I await to be seen, a woman on the porch ticks her needle and injects a clear fluid into her right arm. This is going from bad to worse. At last my name is called, and I am meet with a therapist and her intern. I regale them with my story, not leaving out the least of flourishes. The therapist makes a list of seven resources for me, many of which can't see me until next week. I will be flat broke in two days, not sure how that is going to work. Back on the street, a woman who never looks at me directly is screaming that I am her brother 'Tyler'. Up and down the block she goes, calling for Tyler and if she sees me, I am Tyler.

Meanwhile, I am sweating and feeling shittier by the second. I tell the crisis shelter that I have had skin cancer removed recently in my right ear, and that I need to get the stitches out. They call the free clinic two blocks away and get me an appointment.

Off I trot, feeling worse by the second. I wait my turn. The nurse calls me in, does my vitals and my blood pressure is a stunning 172 over 122. I am literally drenched in my own sweat, my t-shirt looks like a bucket of water was poured over it. The nurse tells me that I am technically in critical condition, that I had best start declining on those numbers. In comes the Doc, my stitches are removed. I hightail out with little gas in the tank. Back to my homeless camp I head. It is early afternoon, and I am done! Into my bedroll I go, the next twenty hours attempting to bust this fever, ague, whatever the hell this is. In the morning, my sleeping bag and clothes are soaked with my sweat but fortunately, I think the bastard fever broke. I have an appetite and at least some energy. Time to give one last full force effort to this failing enterprise.

That Friday I tried to get with the Oregon Department of Health and Human Services. They could see me next Friday.

Nope, ain't gonna do it!

Complete devastation sets in, I came here for a fresh start, instead I just ended up with in a hopeless situation. That afternoon, I call two people; my friend Jeff back in Teton Valley, and my brother Bob. I am balling. I am despondent. The idea of puncturing my temple with my Leatherman knife is most appealing. In short, I have gambled it all on a wild enterprise, and I have failed.

'What the hell am I supposed to do?'

Best go back to Teton Valley, Idaho and reboot, rebuild, and emerge ready for the next fight. My brother Bill kindly offers to buy me an Amtrak ticket back to Salt Lake. It will be a milk run just like the Greyhound with numerous hours spent encamped in the train station. Amtrak sure as hell beat the GreyDog for comfort and space, love them trains. Sunday morning arrives, and I am penniless in Salt Lake City. My daughter Gina ponies up the $56 to get me back to Idaho. My brother Bob and Halina helped with pocket money as well to keep me moving. That afternoon I am in Rexburg, Idaho where Gina and her husband Dan kindly pick me up. They chauffeur me to my new accommodations, John Riley's comfortable abode in Victor, Idaho, just South of Driggs. I am once again safe, penniless, with a compass seeking a direction. Such is the life of a vagabond sailor.

## Today (Summer 2019)

Well folks, there you have it, 54 years of the full gamut of being human. Popeye ends at a perfect breaking point in my life. Back in Idaho, I am homeless, but I camp, work, cook my sausages by the fire, rinse and repeat. This Fall, I will once again sail off to foreign ports, friends to be made and adventures to be had. My compass hopefully pointing at Nepal, Africa, or some other exotic port of call. I am alone now after decades of family life. Yes, it feels scary, yet also exciting. I am once again free to live unbounded, unfettered, to create my own destiny. As the sand in my hourglass continues to run down, it is imperative that I use my time allotted being fully alive each day. Yes, I will have to take better care of myself and perhaps I will mellow as I age. But for now, I still have the same sense of curiosity and wonder I have always had. So, I set sail for distant horizons with Popeye and the mayhem that may ensue as long as there is still wind in my sails.

# Epilogue

Thank you! My deepest appreciation to you for sailing along on my life's voyage, adventures and escapades. I imagine you sitting there, scratching your head and wondering "What the hell did I just read?!" - Excellent, then I got it right. This book was written with you in mind, I had to write for those who don't know me, who might be entertained by my stories and perhaps even benefit from my some of my experiences. There was one guiding principle in my writing from the outset: "Don't worry what the reader will think of me". In so doing, I was freed to write without regard as to how it would be received by those who do know me, leaving me with an audience of just over seven billion people. After all, I will be dead a long time so why not roll the dice and enjoy the donnybrook that follows.

Storytelling is the foundation upon which *Popeye* is built. As I mentioned at the outset, hopefully it should have felt as if I was sitting next to you on a bar stool and we were swapping yarns in a faraway pub. I have always loved good stories, and I have strived to perfect my storytelling with wit, emotion, honesty and the Irish love of a great unexpected plot twist. Since the dawn of time, storytelling has always been the cornerstone of humanity, especially in the oral tradition, people gathering around a fire, looking to the heavens and attempting to impart wisdom, meaning and significance as it relates to the listener. My most ardent hope is that my best efforts have been equal to the task to keep you engaged and entertained, if not at least I went down throwing my best punches.

In the end, the crux of *Popeye - Cultural Barbarian* is suicide. It is the pink elephant in the room, the plot twist we don't see coming. Suicide is the scariest word in most languages. People go silent, turn away, change the subject and most frequently they are deeply afraid. Please do not look to me for any definitive answers. Please expect more questions than answers and then it shall be your turn to seek your own answers. I was opposed to suicide for forty-six years, at varying times it seemed to me: selfish, short-sighted, wasteful, immoral, unforgivable, cruel in regard to loved ones… and then I found myself cutting my own wrists on the bathroom floor. All of the negatives I had thought about suicide were now moot. I had entered a new paradigm, and I had attempted the unthinkable. How could the guy in this book, who grew up in a happy, wholesome family in an affluent suburb, well educated, intelligent, end up with scarred wrists and memories of trying to die by overdose? There has to be a disconnect somewhere but there isn't, that is the Catch 22.

I have many challenges to cope with: zero thyroid function, addictions aplenty, mental illness - Bi-Polar, Depression, Sleep Apnea, and on… and on and on, BUT the important thing is I am still here. I don't know why that is the case but perhaps, just maybe it is so that I can help someone else who is battling all the shyte that I do. In "The Funnel", the single most important piece in this book and the best Goddamn thing I have ever written, I have told you exactly what attempting suicide was like for me. The orange layer of the Funnel IS as bad as it gets. IF you or I are ever lucky enough to intervene in a loved one's life to avert the Funnel, to intercede before an attempt is made, me baring myself for all to see will have been worth it.

*Popeye* came along in my lifetime when it was sorely needed. It became a massive focal point of my intellect, creativity and passions. I am grateful to all those who have voyaged with me and for *Popeye* distilling my existence down so aptly, "I yam what I yam!"

And now, I will take my leave. There are more tales to regale you with, but those are for tomorrow, not today.

Slainte'

Tom H

## Acknowledgments

**Departed Friends yet Still Alive within me** - Kevin Denslow, Art Klavins, Janet and Sabrina Dunn, Alex "Bubbs" Lowery, Kathryn Miller Hess, Mark Ames, Katherine Nix, Tyler Strandberg

**Mom and Dad** - Lou Ann Marie Rabun Hickey and William Anthony Hickey. You both worked so hard and sacrificed so much for us, on top of that you were people of integrity, honest, hardworking and full of Irish wit.

**Bob and Bill** - My two meathead brothers who have achieved so much success, it was your destiny, mine was to be the Irish Prodigal son. I think we all played our parts well.

**Mary LaLiberty and Aileen Deegan** - Such amazing friends, family members and counselors over my 52 year life span. You brought so much joy into my life, thank you!

**Artur and Basia Muras** - Two people who accepted me into their family without reservation. I truly was fortunate to get a second set of parents. Know you are loved by your American son.

**Dr. Pete Edwards** - My dog hours partner, globetrotter, drinking pal and bathtub fishing companion. I have no idea where you are today. I think that is fitting.

**John Clayton "Mississippi" Caden** - During the most tumultuous years of my life, we became fast friends. This text exists because of your encouragement when I was wavering - Go Reb's!

**Matthew "Archie" Kavaney Kapsner** - Our paths go back a long way with so many great memories, thank you. I learned and benefitted so much from you, without you I would be a much duller person.

**Dr. Paul Foley** - Foles, I have so much admiration and respect for you, your career and your family. Through all these years you have retained your humanity and gained so much wisdom. Thanks for "getting and supporting" your atypical friend.

**Deb Sprague** - Ms. Deb, you may be the nicest person I have ever met, a massive heart, a desire to help others, etc.etc.etc. If it wasn't for marrying Kirk, I'd say you're perfect.

**Lou Parri** - Wow, the man who has rode my waves in hurricane season. Thank you for always being there and trying to help me to pick up the pieces, you have gone above and beyond the call of duty. Don't worry, I'll get you fixed soon!

**Shirley and Ed Cheramy** - Fortune smiled on me the day you came into my life. Shirley, you have become my second Mom, adviser and example to emulate. I wish you nothing but happiness and joy in your new home.

**Dave Lucke** - Mr. Lucke, 16 years of school together, college roommates, idiots in arms and the most nonjudgmental friend I have ever had. Your head has always been on straight, mine is sideways, guess that's why we get along so well.

**David Martin "Marty"** - You are the most talented, brilliant and caring man I have ever known.

Here's to the ABADA, Bernie and pizza in chaise loungers watching a meteor shower.

**Jeff "Smedley" Naylor** - Never have I had a friend who cares about me as much as you do, thank you. When I've been at my best, you have been there. When I have been at my worst, you have been there. Love ya!

**John Riley** - When everyone else had enough of my act, you took me in, graciously and warmheartedly to make me feel safe. You truly exemplify compassion, understanding and wisdom - thank you!

**Luke and Gina** - Wow, what two amazing, wonderful, beautiful people you have grown into. You both are the greatest thing that ever happened to me and every moment of your lives is in my heart. Sorry if your Dad is such a child!

**Halina** - Twenty-nine years of putting up with my shyte.

**40 Press - Kelly, Joe and Nick** - you guys are nuts! You took on this project, never wavered in your support and now have it through to publication - Thank You! I realize I may have been a wee bit ofa pain in the arse to work with, that is just how Popeye is.

**The Chicago Cubs** - Finally, heartfelt thanks to the Cubs and Wrigley Field. Together we ride the same roller coaster, win or lose, the relationship is a cornerstone of my life. 2016 WORLD SERIES Champions!!!!!!!!!!!!

## Publisher's Note

I have known Tom Hickey for more than thirty years. Let me rephrase that. I knew Hickey back in high school in the early eighties. He was a year older, wildly popular, and a baseball player who played soccer. In college, Hick spent some quality time with my brother, and in the summer or at the holidays, I also circulated in my brother's circle of friends who were also close to Hickey. Even three thousand miles away in Europe, I hung out with a couple of my brother/Hickey's Tommie friends who hunted me down in France.

Anyway, I knew Tom Hickey in the eighties, but I did not "know" Tom. Even though our social circles overlapped, we never really hung out. That being said, I always admired his unabashed zeal for life.

Flash forward thirty years later, and Hick tracks me down. He heard I was an author, did some editing, and even published other writers for Forty Press. Hick has written a book. Great, what's it about? His life.

Okay.

Now, I always knew Tom as a colorful person, and I understood he was out West, but I am still thinking to myself that this has vanity press written all over it.

Send it to me. I will read it.

Obviously, I loved it. Although there are many remarkable adventures, this is hardly a vanity project. Assuming you have read it given this Note is at the back of the book, I will go straight to why we published *Popeye*. This book was published not out of friendship or that it is a wonderful read. We published *Popeye* because of the important message the author has for the world: it's okay to talk about suicide.

Given my Irish Catholic background, suicide was not a conversation piece unless one was listing ways to directly go to hell. Fortunately, we evolved. As Fr. James Martin SJ so succinctly tweeted, "Suicide is usually the result of depression, which is an illness. And God does not condemn the ill (John 9:3)".

The author does not pretend *Popeye* will change the world. Nor do we. But we share Tom's perspective that *Popeye* is an overwhelming success if it only inspires one person to intervene, intercede, interfere in a suicide or even motivates one who knows "The Funnel" to seek help. If you or someone you know is feeling hopeless or suicidal, contact: National Suicide Prevention Lifeline at 800-273-8255.